OPTIONS TRADING
2021

DAVID MATTHEWS

Table of contents

Introduction 16
   How Options Work 16

Chapter 1: The Right Mindset to Approach Trading 19
   Why am I Making this Trade? 20
   How much will I Risk on the Trade? 20
   How will I Manage my Trade? 21
   Consider the Emotions 22

Chapter 2: Basics of Trading 23
   Stocks vs. Other Investments 24
   The Big Advantage of Stock Investing – Leverage 25

Chapter 3: What is Options Trading? 28
   What Is an Option? 28
   Options on Stocks 30
   Put Options 31

Chapter 4: Why Trade Options? 32
   Hedge and Speculation 32
   Advantages and Drawbacks in Trading Options 33

Chapter 5: Options Contracts – The Basics (Part I) 35
   What is an Options Contract? 35
   What is an Options Contract on the Stock Market? 37
      Call Options 37
      The Call Seller 38
      Derivative Contracts 39
      Profits from the Call 39
      What Happens if the Strike Price isn't Reached? 39
      Why Purchase a Call Option 39
      The Flexibility of Options 40
      Put Options 40
      Why Buy a Put Option? 41
      Summary: Buyers of Options 41
      Summary: Sellers of Calls and Puts 41
      Number of Shares 42

Chapter 6: Variety of Options and Related Styles 43
   Call Options 43

Put Options 43

How to Make a Profit Using Call Options and Put Options 44

Option Styles 45

American Options 45

European Options 45

Exotic Options 45

Bermuda Options 46

Barrier Options 46

Chapter 7: Covered Calls 47

Covered Calls 47

    Covered Calls Involve a Long Position 47

    Covered Calls Are a Neutral Strategy 48

    An Example of a Covered Call 48

    How to Go about Creating a Covered Call 49

    Benefits of Covered Calls 50

    Risks of Covered Calls 50

Chapter 8: How Prices Are Determined 51

The Value of the Asset 51

The Intrinsic Value 51

The Time Value 52

Volatility 52

Interest Rates 53

Dividends 53

Option Pricing Models 54

    The Black Scholes Model 54

    Binomial Option Pricing Model 55

    Monte Carlo Simulations 56

A Final Word on Pricing 56

Chapter 9: How to Choose the Strike Price for Options Trading 57

Strike Price Considerations 57

Hazard Tolerance 57

Hazard Reward Payoff 58

Picking the Wrong Strike Price 58

Strike Price Points to Consider 58

Have a Backup Plan 58

Evaluate Different Payoff Scenarios 59

    The Bottom Line 59

Chapter 10: Credit and Debit Spreads Options 60
    Credit Spread 60

    Debit Spread 62

        Put Debit Spread 63

Chapter 11: Iron Condor Options 64
    Option Trader 64

    Buying Back to Close 67

Chapter 12: Leverage of Options 68
    Why is Leverage Riskier? 68

    The Advantages of Leverage in Options Trading 69

        Liquidity 69

        Gauging a Country's Economy 69

        Securities Pricing 69

        Safety of Transactions 70

        Providing Speculation Scope 70

        Promotes an Investment Culture 70

        The Continuous Market for Securities 70

        Capital Formation 70

        Control Companies 71

        Fiscal and Monetary Policies 71

        Proper Canalization of Wealth 71

        Education Purposes 71

    Disadvantages of Leverage in Options Trading 71

Chapter 13: Which Options Trading Platform to Use 73
    A Platform Takes Trading to the Holders 73

    Competition 74

    Types of Trading Platforms 74

        User Friendliness 75

        Tools to Learn 75

        Professional Level Platforms 76

        Mobile Trading 76

    What Are We Looking for in Platforms and Tools? 77

        Software Trading Platforms 77

        Cost Implication 77

Chapter 14: Basic Mistakes Beginners Make and how to Avoid them 79

Buying OTM Call Options 79

Using the Same Strategy in different Conditions 79

No Exit Plan before Expiration 80

Making Up for Previous Losses with Risk 80

Trading Non-Liquid Options 80

Failing to Dividend Date in Strategy 80

Failing If You Are Assigned Early 80

Not Using Index Options in Neutral Trades 81

Spread Trades 81

Averaging Down 81

Struggling to Get Even 81

Under or Overstaying Your Welcome 81

Gambling 82

Mishandling Early Assignment 82

Ignoring the Statistics behind Options Trading 82

Being Overzealous 82

Not Being Adaptable 83

Ignoring the Probability 83

Not Dealing with Short Options Properly 83

Not Considering Exotic Options 83

Buying Out of the Money Call Options 83

Giving in to Fear and Greed 84

Doing Poor Allocation 84

Having a Finite Approach 84

Not Having an Exit Plan 84

Ignoring Consistent Profits in Favor of Home Runs 84

Having a Strategy That Doesn't Match Your Outlook 85

Attempting to Recover Past Losses 85

Trading in Illiquid Options 85

Chapter 15: The Components of an Option Contract 86

The Role of the Underlying Stock 86

Understanding the Strike Price 87

Strategy for Selling Covered Calls 88

The Market Environment 89

Your Underlying Stock 89

The Premium 89

The Expiration Date 90

The Strike Price 90

Chapter 16: How to Start Trading in Options 91

Steps of Optional Trading for a Beginner 92

Chapter 17: The Supports and Resistances 94

Chapter 18: Risk and Reward 97

Delta 98

Rho 98

Gamma 98

Theta 99

Vega 99

Chapter 19: Basic Options Strategies Going Long 100

Play name: Married Put 100

Play name: Bull Call Spread 100

Play name: Bear Put Spread 101

Play name: Straddle 102

Play name: Strangle 102

Play name: Butterfly Spread 102

Play name: Iron Condor 103

Play name: Iron Butterfly 103

ROI or Return on Investment 103

R.O.I = (Profits - Costs) / Costs 103

A Brief Introduction to Technical Analysis 104

Two Different Approaches 104

Chapter 20: Choosing a Broker 105

Brokers and Trading Platforms 105

Buy and Sell Shares with Online Banks 105

Full-Service and Discount Brokers 107

Financial Security and Stability 109

Chapter 21: Strangles and Straddles 111

Implied Volatility Strategy 113

Estimating Price from Implied Volatility 114

What is a Long Straddle? 114

Chapter 22: How to Profit from Trading Options 116

Buy Low, Sell High 117

- Using Options for Speculative Purposes ... 118
- Writing Contracts ... 119

Chapter 23: Options Strategies ... 121
- The Long Call ... 121
- The Long Put ... 121
- The Short Put ... 121
- Covered Calls ... 122
- Married Put ... 122
- Bull Call Spread ... 123
- Bear Put Spread ... 123
- Protective Collar ... 123
- The Long Straddle ... 124
- The Long Strangle ... 124
- Long Call Butterfly Spread ... 124
- Iron Condor ... 125
- Iron Butterfly Strategy ... 125

Chapter 24: Successful Trading Tactics ... 126
- Which Trade is Profitable? ... 126
- How to Be a Thriving Option Investor ... 126
- Strategies That Are Successful in Options Trading ... 129

Chapter 25: Tips to Become a Successful Trader ... 131
- Start Thinking of Trading Like a Business ... 132
- Maintain a Trading Journal ... 133
- Make the Best Use of Technology ... 133
- Understand Yourself ... 134
- Make Peace with Losing a Trade ... 135
- Avoid Buying Options that Are Out-of-the-Money ... 135
- Be Patient ... 135

Conclusion ... 137

Introduction ... 141
- Main Concepts of Options Trading ... 141
- Advantages of Options Trading ... 141

Chapter 1. Fundamentals of Technical Analysis ... 143
- Understanding Technical Analysis ... 143
- How Technical Analysis Can Help Traders ... 144

- Utilizing Charts in Technical Analysis 144
- Technical Analysis Indicators 145

Chapter 2. What a Beginner Needs to Know 147
- Adaptability Is Key 147
- Options as a Mitigating Factor 147
- Control the Game 148
- Purposes of Even-Breaking 148
- Go Beyond the Option Chart 148
- Follow the Trend 149
- Leave Plan 149

Chapter 3. Determining the Option Price 150
- Time 151
- Unpredictability 152
  - Chronicled Volatility 152
  - Suggested Volatility 152

Chapter 4. Getting Started With Options Trading 154
- You Needed Thought of What Options Exchange Is 154
- You Must Understand that Options Exchange Includes High Risks 154
- Guarantee that You Know About Their Expenses and Motivators. 154
- You Can Get the Important Endorsement Application From Your Business Organization Before You Can Begin Purchasing Options. 155
- Acquaint Yourself With the Different Specialized Examination of Options. 155
- At the Point When You Get Into Genuine Trading, It Is Unseemly to Begin Trading Right Away. 155
- Guarantee That You Occasionally Reconsider Your Technique. 155

Chapter 5. Development of the Options 157
- The Purchase Warrant (Call) 157
- How Are Warrant Options Different? 158
- Options and Warrants—A Comparison 158
  - Warrant: 158
  - Option: 159
- Trading Based on the Acquisition of Rights 159
- The Exercise Right Then and Now 160
- Preferences and Disadvantages Compared to Warrants 160

Chapter 6. Options Trading: The Language 161
- Ex-Dividend Rate 161
- Lognormal Distribution 161

    Typical Distribution 161

    Short Stock 162

    Model of Option Pricing 162

    Spread 162

    Time Value 162

    Compose 163

    Edge Requirement 163

    Mean 163

Chapter 7. Basic Investment Strategies 164

Chapter 8. Options Greeks 167

    Delta 167

    Theta 167

    Gamma 167

    Vega 168

    Minor Greeks 168

    Benefits and Risk From Buying Call Options 168

    Benefits and Risk From Selling Call Options 168

    Benefits and Risks From Buying Put Options 169

    Benefits and Risks From Selling Put Options 169

    Geniuses 170

    Cons 170

    True Example of an Option 170

    Options Spreads 170

Chapter 9. Intermediate Options Trading Strategies 172

    Strategies and Their Uses: 172

Chapter 10. Iron Condor Strategy 175

    What Is an Iron Condor? 175

    Key Takeaways 175

    Iron Condor Losses and Profits 176

    The Example of an Iron Condor on a Stock 176

    Long Iron Condor 177

Chapter 11. Advanced Options Trading Strategies 179

    1. Covered Call 179

    2. Hitched Put 179

    3. Bull Call Spread 180

    4. Bear Put Spread 181

- 5. Defensive Collar 181
- 6. Long Straddle 182
- 7. Long Strangle 183
- 8. Long Call Butterfly Spread 183
- 9. Iron Condor 184
- 10. Iron Butterfly 185

Chapter 12. How to Behave on Lateral Movements 186
- Utilizing a Trading Plan 186
- Utilizing Option Spreads 186
- Utilizing Diversification 186
- Utilizing Automated Trading 187
- Utilizing Money Management 187
- Position Sizing 187
- Multiplying Down 188
- Utilize Technical Analysis 188
- You Can Weather the Storm 188
- You Don't Make Emotional Decisions 188
- Be a Little Bit Math-Oriented 189
- You Are Market-Focused 189
- Zero In On a Trading Style 189

Chapter 13. Options Trading Strategies Used by Hedge Fund Managers 190
- Sellers of Covered Calls 190
- Sellers of Puts 190
- Sellers of Bull Call Spreads 191
- Sellers of Iron Condors 191
- Sellers of Calendar Spreads 191
- Sellers of Straddles 191
- Sellers of Vertical Spreads 191
- Sellers of Strangles 192

Chapter 14. Financial Leverage in Options Trading 193
- Financial Leverage 193
- Amplify Profit 193

Chapter 15. Trading Levels 195
- Level 1 Trading 195
- Level 2 Trading 195
- Level 3 Trading 196

  Level 4 Trading 196

Chapter 16. Butterfly Options Trading Strategies 197
  Getting Butterflies 197
  Long Call Butterfly 197
  Short Call Butterfly 197
  Put Butterfly 197
  Short Put Butterfly 198
  Iron Butterfly 198
  Switch Iron Butterfly 198
  Illustration of a Long Call Butterfly 198

Chapter 17. Covered Call Strategy 200
  Note 200
  Understanding Covered Calls 200
  Most Extreme Profit and Loss 201
  Advantages and Risks of Covered Calls 201
  Aces 202
  Cons 203
  The Danger of Covered Calls 203

Chapter 18. Credit Spread Options 204
  Put Credit Spread 204
  Call Credit Spread 205

Chapter 19. Day Trading Options 207
  Key Takeaways 207
  What Makes Day Trading Difficult? 209
  Choosing What and When to Buy 210

Chapter 20. Day Trading Tips the Pros Don't Want You to Know 211
  1. Prepare for Your Trading Day 211
  2. Explore the Chief Trading Hour 211
  3. Check a Monetary Timetable 211
  4. Examine Huge Market News 212
  5. Find Oversold and Overbought Budgetary Instruments 212
  6. Take Exchanges at the Course of the Trend 212
  7. Counter-Trend Exchanges Can Be Perilous 213
  8. Have Extreme Danger on the Board Frameworks Set Up 213
  9. Persistently Hazard a Fixed Level of Your Trading Account on Any Exchange 213
  10. Separate the Prize To-Chance Extent of Potential Courses of Action 214

Chapter 21. Errors on the Application of Strategies and How to Avoid Them 215
Fundamental Options Trading Mistakes 215
Freezing and Exiting Early 215
Engaging in Many Trades at Once 216
Utilizing Too Many Strategies 216
Taking Too Much Risk 216
Set It and Forget It 217
Disregarding Time Decay 217
When Selling Options, Stop Looking at Probabilities 217
Not Paying Attention to Volatility 217
Not Having a Training Plan 217

Chapter 22. The Mindset of an Options Trader 219
Realize When to Go Off-Book 219
Keep Away From Exchanges That Are Out of the Cash 219
Try Not to Hold Tight to Your Starter Methodology 219
Never Begin Without an Unmistakable Arrangement for Entry and Exit 219
Never Twofold Down 220
Think About Nothing Literally 220
Not Paying Attention to Your Decision of Trader 220
Discover a Mentor 221
Information Is the Key 221

Chapter 23. Additional Information on Options Trading 223
In-the-Money Call Options 223
In-the-Money Put Options 223
Out of the Money (OTM) 224
Key Takeaways 224
Implied Volatility—IV 224
Key Takeaways 224
Understanding Implied Volatility 224
Implied Volatility and Options 225
Option Pricing Models and IV 225
Factors Affecting Implied Volatility 226
Pros and Cons of Using Implied Volatility 226

Chapter 24. Advantages and Disadvantages of Options Trading 228
What Are the Advantages of Options Trading? 228
What Are the Risks of Options Trading? 228

Chapter 25. Difference Between Binary Options Trading and Real Options Trading 229

Differences Between Binary Options Trading and Real Options Trading—Limited Profit vs. Unlimited Profit 229

Differences Between Binary Options Trading and Real Options Trading—85% Loss vs. 100% Loss 229

Differences Between Binary Options Trading and Real Options Trading—Cannot Be Traded vs. Can Be Traded 230

Differences Between Binary Options Trading and Real Options Trading—Unlisted Instrument vs. Listed Instrument 230

Differences Between Binary Options Trading And Real Options Trading—Trading Against Binary Options 231

Differences Between Real Options Trading and Binary Options Trading—Real Underlying Asset vs. No Real Underlying Asset 231

Differences Between Binary Options Trading and Real Options Trading—Unregulated Brokers vs. Regulated Brokers 231

Differences Between Binary Options Trading and Real Options Trading—Ease of Depositing Money Vs. Difficulty in Depositing Money 232

Differences Between Binary Options Trading and Real Options Trading—Hard to Withdraw Money vs. Ease in Withdraw Money 232

Chapter 26. The Final Step—Learning From the Pros 233

The Most Common Mistakes 233

Contingent Only Upon the Market Timing 233

Trading Options That Are Illiquid 234

Bending Over Trying to Make Up for the Losses 235

Purchasing OTM (Out-of-the-Money) Options 235

Utilizing Complex Trading Strategies 236

Chapter 27. Time Management in Trading 237

1. A Decent Rest 237

2. Have Objectives 237

3. Organize 237

4. Go on Breaks 238

5. Stay Away From Interruptions 238

6 Must-Know Time Management Tips for Traders 238

Chapter 28. Markets 242

Markets 242

Financial Markets 242

The Function of the Markets 243

Chapter 29. Currency Option 246

What Is a Currency Option? 246

 Basics of Currency Options 246
 Vanilla Options Basics 246
 SPOT Options 247
 Example of a Currency Option 247
Chapter 30. Trading With LEAPS 249
 LEAPS 249
Conclusion 251

OPTIONS TRADING FOR BEGINNERS 2021

David Matthews

Introduction

If this is the first time you've read about options trading, then sit back and relax. This is an introduction to the world of options trading. In particular, you will find that options trading is based on logic and common sense. By using these elements, you can be successful at making money right from the start.

But first, let's talk about what options are. In essence, options are contracts that two parties make to buy and sell an asset. Now, the term "asset" refers to the object that is traded. This is important to note as the asset in question could be anything. Of course, we're talking about "financial assets." As such, there is a specific number of items at play.

Specifically, stocks are at play in options trading. When you buy and sell stocks, you do so at their current market price. So, if you want to buy or sell a stock on March 15th, you will pay the price of that stock on March 15th.

But what if you could buy or sell the stock on June 10th at March 15th's price?

This is what options are all about.

Options contracts give you the flexibility to negotiate terms and conditions based on any number of parameters. These parameters will determine the nature of the contract. Consequently, you'll have the opportunity to make a profit by taking advantage of these conditions.

It is also worth noting that options contracts provide you with the opportunity to protect yourself against the risk that comes with trading in the stock market. Since the future is uncertain, options give you the chance to protect yourself from any scenario that might unfold. Therefore, options are known to "hedge" against risk. In other words, options help you protect your investments in case things take an unexpected turn.

How Options Work

The way options contracts work is quite straightforward. The two parties that engage in the negotiation agree on the price and timeframe in which stocks are bought or sold. Hence, one party agrees to sell while the other party agrees to purchase.

Now, the reason why they are "options" is because none of the parties are obligated to go through with the deal. Therefore, the buyer or seller has the "option" to go through with the contract. Otherwise, they can let the contract expire without it being used.

Based on this concept, we can infer there are two important parameters, time and price. The time parameter refers to the duration of the agreement. Options contracts can range from a few hours to months. There is no fixed timeframe for options. The time parameter can be set to any time the buyer of the contract sees fit.

The price parameter is the price at which both parties agree to conduct the deal. This is called the "strike price." As such, a strike price refers to the price point at which the buyer and seller agree to make the deal happen. As a result, if the deal is executed, the transaction will occur at the specified price. Moreover, fluctuations in market valuation are meaningless. This implies that whatever the agreed price is, that's what the contract will be based upon.

Also, please note that the buyer of the contract has the option to go through with it or not. When we say the "buyer" of the contract, we're talking about the person who holds the right to the contract. Whether the contract is to buy, or sell is irrelevant. What matters here is the individual who holds the right to the contact itself. This concept means that the contract holder can own the right to buy or sell the stock in question.

If the contract holder chooses to exercise it, the transaction will occur at the specified price point. If the contract holder chooses not to exercise it, they can let the contract expired unutilized. Therefore, the contract expires worthless, that is, with no monetary value attached to it.

Let's take a look at a practical example to highlight the concept of an options contract.

Two parties enter a negotiation. The item in question is a diamond ring. At present, the ring is worth $1,000. The ring's owner is interested in selling it. The other party is interested in buying it at a specified price point. In fact, the buyer would be willing to buy it at a cheaper price point, that is, under $1,000. So, the prospective buyer approaches the ring's owner with a proposition.

The potential buyer will purchase the ring at $900 in one month. To seal the deal, both parties enter an options contract. In this arrangement, the potential buyer purchases the contract. The buyer stipulates the conditions while the seller accepts. Under these terms, the ring's owner cannot sell it until after a month. Now, the seller could offer it around and even make deals, but they cannot sell it until the contract expires.

Let's assume that the ring's value shoots up to $1,500 after a couple of weeks. Thus, the buyer sees an opportunity and decides to execute the contract. The ring's owner cannot hike the price of the buyer. After all, that's why the contract was signed.

In this example, the buyer stands to profit as they bought the ring for a price lower than its current market valuation. The buyer could now turn around and sell the ring for a significant profit. By the same token, the seller loses out on the deal as they could have sold it at a higher price point. Yet, they could not do so unless the buyer chose to let the contract expire.

Now, let's assume that the ring's price falls to $850. At this price point, it doesn't make sense for the buyer to purchase the ring at a higher price point. So, the buyer could simply let the contract expire unused.

In this example, the buyer, as the contract holder, can choose to do let the contract go unexercised. The buyer doesn't lose anything except for the premium paid on the contract.

The premium on an options contract is charge by the writer of the contract. The writer is the person who drafts the contract, thereby becoming the counterparty to the contract holder. In this example, the ring's owner would be the writer as they are the one who has to deliver the asset in question. If the contract holder chooses to allow the contract to expire, the writer (seller in this example) makes money as they collected a fee for writing the contract. As such, the only money the buyer would lose is the premium. Please bear in mind that premiums don't have a set point. Premiums can be as low as a few pennies on the dollar value of an asset while climbing to several dollars. This is why the first thing that options traders need to become familiar with is the cost of premiums.

Chapter 1: The Right Mindset to Approach Trading

Now we need to spend some time looking at the right mindset that you need to have to trade-in options. If your mind is in the wrong place, where you don't fully understand the risks and opportunities you are taking, it will make it hard to see profits. You need to be ready to take on the market and understand what is going on because options trading can be harder to work with than others. If you can keep your mind in the game, avoid letting your emotions take over, and come up with a good strategy along the way, you will find that it is a lot easier to see results with your trading.

Trading is more of a mental game than anything else. The best tactic or the technical indicators is going to be useful to help you spot a good way into the market. But they will be worthless if you do not bring in the right mental approach to the game. It all starts before you ever place any of your trades.

Being mindful the whole time you are in the trades, and even before you enter the trades, will keep your mind clear of any emotions that may get in the way. If you are a bit worried about how this will work and whether you are smart enough to go through these trades, there are a few simple questions that you need to ask yourself before you ever consider working with options contracts. The three main questions that you should consider include:

Why am I Making this Trade?

When we get started with trading, no matter what kind of trading, there are a ton of strategies that you can use to make this successful. Things like price action and the fundamentals of the market can be enough to make anyone feel overwhelmed in no time. This is completely normal no matter who you are. No matter what tools we want to use, we have to make sure we remember why we got into the trade to start with, and then make sure you stick with these tools and only make trades that fit with your strategy.

Let's take a look at an example of how to make this happen. If you want to trade using the strategy known as moving average crossovers, you have to look at the charts and tools you have and see if any averages are crossing. If you want to trade options when there are periods with a lot more volatility, it is IV at a level that seems to make the most sense. There are a ton of strategies, and you can pick out the ones you like most. No matter which one you go with though, you have to make sure that you only place trades based on objective information. Never make a trade just to be in the market. Only be in the market and make a trade when it looks like it will make you money.

How much will I Risk on the Trade?

Risk management will be one of the most important things that you need to consider no matter what kind of investment you choose to work with.

Before choosing to place any trade, you need to figure out how much you are willing to risk on that trade. Knowing this risk from the beginning will make it easier to maintain objectivity during the trade, especially if it ends up not going the way you want. Never get into options or any kind of trade without really knowing about the risks.

Each trade should have a minimal amount of risk. The only way you can eliminate the risk is to make sure that you never enter the market. But the best way to lose all of your money is to take all that is in your account towards one trade without saving some back. Neither of these is good risk management strategies, so we need to find something that is a little bit better.

A good idea is to figure out what percentage of your account you are willing to risk each trade. It is best to stay under ten percent as a beginner. As your account starts to grow more, you may want to consider going with maybe three to five percent. You won't be able to put as much money towards the trades you do, but it can help you avoid risking too much and ending up with nothing to work with any longer.

When you keep your risk down to only ten percent, and sometimes less, of your account at a time, you will find that you aren't as emotional about the trades. Even if it goes south, your whole account is not lost. You can still enter into other trades, sometimes at the same time, without having to worry that your whole account will be wiped out with one wrong decision. Considering that even professional traders can have trouble with some of their trades occasionally, this is a good thing to remember.

How will I Manage my Trade?

During this process, we need to consider how we will manage our trades. If you find that a trade will move in your favor, think about how you plan to manage that trade. There are many theories of thought on this idea, and none are necessarily the best ones. Some work best for a few traders, others are preferred in some cases, and so on. You have to determine which one is best for you to help make sure you manage the trades well and get the profits you would like.

For example, many traders, new and professional, like to set up a profit target when they first enter a new trade.

Others will use trail stops to help them because it ensures they will capture some of the larger moves or larger trends that are potentially going to happen. Sometimes you may find yourself in a situation where you want to add to a winning position. This is more a personal preference, so you have to see what works best for you. But it is still critical to see how you would properly manage a winning strategy ahead of time. This ensures you make as much as possible without staying in the market so long you lose out.

The strategy you choose will make a big difference in how you manage your trade. A good strategy will help you know how to enter the market, and when it is time to exit. They can often help us learn how to read many of the charts out there, making it so much easier to pick the right time to get into the trade. If you pick a strategy, use the steps and tips it talks about to manage each trade you use it on. This helps to take the guesswork out and can help you get healthy profits.

While it may seem like these are really simple questions, and we shouldn't even need to ask them, remembering what they are and asking them during each trade will be the trick you need to make sure your options contracts are as successful as possible.

As a beginner, you may ask these questions of others and be surprised at how many never even think about them at all.

Consider the Emotions

As we go through all of this, we must make sure that we can accurately handle all of our emotions along the way. If our emotions start to come into the trade, we instantly lose all of that critical thinking and start making really poor decisions along the way. This is easy to do, which is why a good strategy and some strong stop-loss points can help.

We will talk more about these stop-loss points and strategies later on, but they allow you to make a good plan for your investment right from the beginning. You won't get caught up in emotions because you know exactly when to keep going and when to leave ahead of time. Before entering the trade, you have no skin in the game, so you aren't worried about things going well or things going poorly. You make sound and rational decisions, which will help you along the way. If you wait to make these decisions after you have entered, it is possible the emotions will sneak in and can ruin even the best trade.

Chapter 2: Basics of Trading

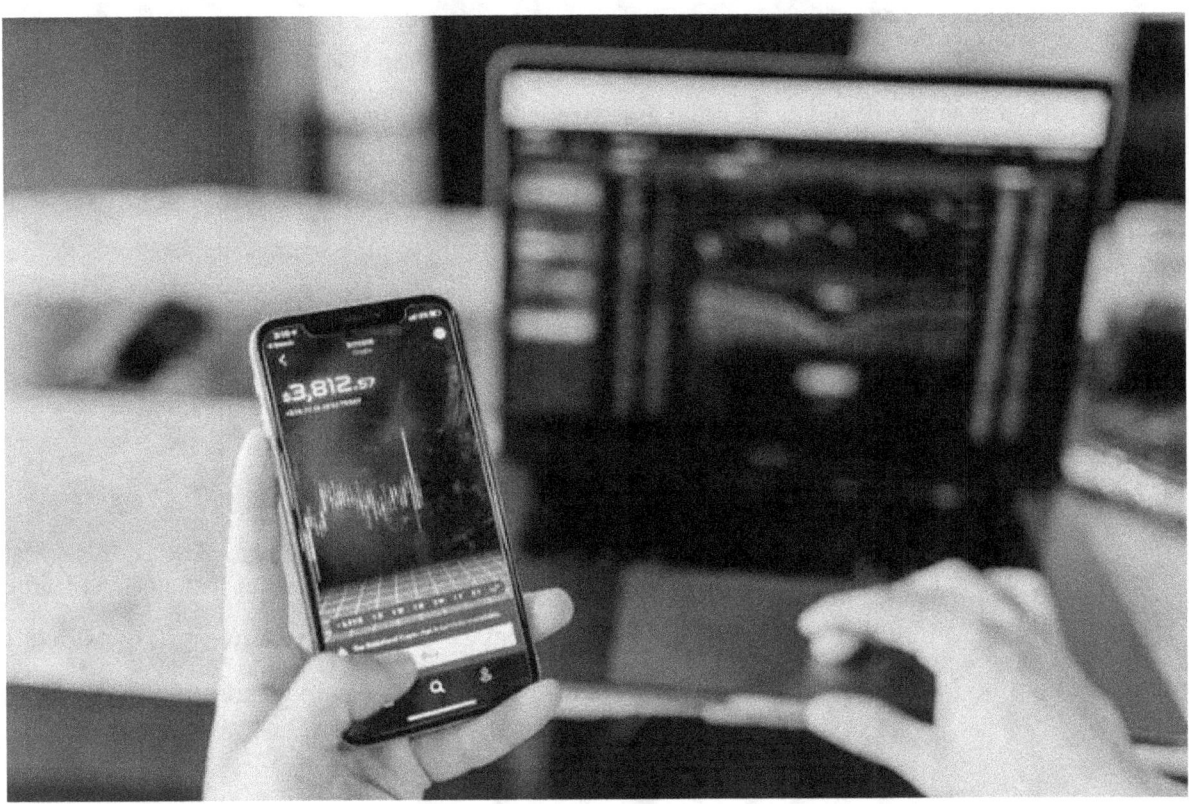

The main method for investing in the forex market, therefore, remains the classic forex market. When you operate on the forex market, you are buying and selling currencies.

However, other financial instruments have been introduced to invest in forex and currencies indices on the forex exchange over the years. We are talking about CFD (contract for difference) and binary options. The main feature of these two financial instruments is the following: when you use them to invest in forex, you will not own the lots you invest in.

That said, for those who do not intend to trade online, it could make little sense. Let's try to clarify. Both CFDs and binary options are contracts between investors and brokers. It's not like the classic forex market, where traders buy and sell among themselves. In CFDs and binary options, the asset movement (in this case the buying and selling of currencies) does not occur.

CFDs and binary options are used to speculate on the performance of the value of equity securities. If the trader's forecast is correct, the operation will lead to a profit; vice versa, if the trader's prediction is wrong, the operation will lead to a loss. So, the mode of operation is similar to the stock market: if I invest on the upside, whether I do it with CFDs or buy currencies, I only earn money if the value increases.

CFDs are also derivative instruments, so they are used to speculate on the performance of asset values. This means that you will never own the asset traded (as opposed to classic forex trading).

Moreover, as with binary options, with CFDs it is possible to trade on:

- Equity securities
- Equity indices
- Forex currencies pairs
- Commodities
- ETF

The online trading strategies are based on mathematical and graphic analysis that can suggest to the trader the best moment to buy and sell. As we have seen today, it is possible to invest in the stock market thanks to online trading, choosing between trading binary options and trading with the forex market.

It is evident right away that there is no suitable trading strategy for all traders, but there are different trading strategies, based on traders and their style of trading. Therefore, it is possible to customize different online trading strategies based on their trading objectives and their intellectual and psychological abilities.

We also recommend using 2 proven techniques not to turn winnings into losses:

Stop loss: it establishes a maximum loss that you are willing to suffer.

Take profit: you place a dynamic exit level that rises slowly.

Stocks vs. Other Investments

In this historical moment, the search for high returns has become almost spasmodic. Unfortunately, central banks' expansionary policy has caused the collapse of yields (now virtually 0). Anyone who wants to get a positive return must take risks.

In this context, many are deciding to invest in stocks. The answer? It certainly is worth it, but it all depends on the modality of the investment.

This is an investment that can still guarantee very high performance, provided, however, you follow some guidelines.

The first tip is to use only affordable platforms to invest in stocks. Among the best, we can remember Plus500 or Markets. These platforms are characterized by the fact that they are very easy to use, even for those who have never worked with the actions but, at the same time, guarantee advanced tools, suitable even for the most experienced traders and their needs. You receive a free bonus at the time of registration that amounts to 7,000 euros for Plus500 and 4,000 euros for Markets. This is additional capital that can operate on the stock markets but cannot be directly withdrawn. If you use the bonus and get profits, these profits can be taken without problems and constraints.

Both Plus500 and Markets are Trading Contracts for Difference (CFD) trading platforms: this is a particularly flexible and easy-to-understand derivative instrument that guarantees the possibility of obtaining high profits both when markets rise, and markets fall. This is the second condition that makes it worthwhile to invest in stocks: if you buy shares directly, you earn only when the markets go up. And in today's financial conditions, it's an immense gamble. It is not convenient to buy shares, the thing that must be done is to subscribe to derivatives (such as CFDs that are very simple) that have underlying actions. Plus500 and Markets are the ideal solutions for investing in stocks and, incidentally, they also allow investing in forex, indices, commodities, bitcoins, etc.

If you want to invest in shares and want to earn money, the advice is to open an account on Markets or Plus500.

The Big Advantage of Stock Investing – Leverage

Through the use of financial leverage (or simply "leverage"), a person can buy or sell financial assets for an amount higher than the capital held and, consequently, to benefit from a higher potential return than that deriving from a direct investment in the underlying and, conversely, to expose yourself to the risk of very significant losses.

Let's see how the concept of leverage works starting from a simple case. Let's assume you have $ 100 available to invest Leverage financial in a stock. Let's assume that the gain or loss expectations are equal to 30%: if things go well, we will have $ 130. Otherwise, we will have $ 70. This is a simple speculation in which we bet on a particular event.

In case we decide to risk more investing and our $ 100, with another $ 900 borrowed, then the investment would take a different articulation because we use a leverage of 10 to 1 (we invest

$ 1000 having a capital initial only of 100). If things go well and the stock goes up 30%, we will receive $ 1300; we return the 900 borrowed with a gain of $ 300 on initial capital of 100. So, we get a 300% profit with a stock that gave a 30% return. Obviously, on the $ 900 borrowed we will have to pay interest, but the general principle remains valid: the leverage allows to increase the possible gains.

Considering the case further of the investment in derivatives. Let's assume we buy a derivative that, within a month, gives the right to buy 100 grams of gold at a price set today at $ 5,000. We could physically buy the gold with an outlay of 5000 $ and keep it waiting for the price to rise and then sell it back. If we decide instead to use derivatives, we don't need to have $ 5,000, but only the capital needed to buy the derivative. Let's say that a bank sells for 100 $ the derivative that allows us to buy the same 100 grams of gold in a month at $ 5,000. If in a month the gold is worth 5,500, we can buy it and sell it immediately, realizing a gain of 500 $. With the 100 $ of the derivative price, we make a profit of $ 400, or 400%, at $ 100.

Without using derivatives and leverage, the same $500, I could have earned them only against an investment of $ 5,000, making a profit of 10%.

What are the potentials of its use?

The potential of leveraging is clear. For example, if we decide to invest $ 100 in our possession plus an additional sum of $ 900 borrowed, if the stock depreciated by 30%, we would be left with only $ 700 in hand; having to return the $ 900 borrowed plus interest and considering the $ 100 of our initial investment we would have a loss of over $ 300 on an initial capital of $ 100. Therefore, as a percentage, the loss would be 300% against a reduction in the value of the share of 30%.

Another element to keep in mind is that the different financial levers can be combined: speculation operations are carried out using a "squared lever" with clear reflections on potential potentials.

What may appear to be an interesting tool with positive potential for the investor, on the other hand, presents risks that must be considered. Suppose the financial system as a whole work with a very high leverage and financial institutions lend money to each other to multiply the possible profits.

In that case, the loss of an individual investor can trigger a domino effect by infecting the entire financial market.

Banks are typically entities that operate with a more or less high degree of leverage: against a certain net capital, the total assets in which the resources are invested is generally much higher. For example, a bank with equity of $ 100 and leverage of 20 manages assets for $ 2,000. A loss of 1% of the assets entails the loss of 20% of the equity capital.

The development of the market for the transfer of credit risk (from financial intermediaries to the market) has meant that the traditional bank model, called "originate-and-hold" ("create and hold": the loan remains in the balance sheet until maturity in the bank that provided the loan), has been substituted for many operators from the "originate-to-distribute" ("create and distribute": the intermediary selects the debtors, but then transfers the loan to others, recovering the liquidity and the regulatory capital previously committed or the pure credit risk (credit derivatives), with benefits only on capital requirements), with the effect of a further increase in leverage.

The spread of this second bank model is one factor that explains the crisis triggered on the sub-prime mortgage market.

Property price inflation has supported the issuance of securitized loans and the exponential growth of the related market, allowing banks to make huge profits and, at the same time, increase leverage. But "the money machine" could not last long. In the end, many banks found themselves without sufficient capital to absorb the losses deriving from the inversion of the real estate market trend, resulting in fact as failed companies.

Chapter 3: What is Options Trading?

The first step to consider when engaging in options trading is to have a clear and accurate understanding of an option. Most people barely understand what the stock market is and how it operates, and options are a level above even that. Then we will detail in the rest of the book to learn everything you need to be able to trade options with success. Remember that all forms of investing and trading carry financial risk, and not everyone who invests or trades on the markets will succeed.

What Is an Option?

Options are not restricted to the stock market. The name option gives us a clue as to what these financial instruments are, however. An options contract is one that enables the buyer to have the option to do something. Options contracts can exist in any context where you are interested in buying something. The proverbial example that is used is the option to buy a new home.

Let's say that Jane is moving to her new job in Houston, Texas. She is interested in buying a new home in a good neighborhood that is reasonably close to her job. She has two kids, so she's also interested in buying a home in an area with a low crime rate and good schools.

She finds out that there is a new housing development near her job. She also finds out that it will take about 4 months to have a home ready to move in. Because of the high demand in the area, home prices are changing rapidly. She'd like to lock in a price for a home but wants to look around in the meantime. How can she do that? The answer is she can enter into an options contract with the developer.

The type of homes that Jane is interested in are currently going for $350,000. Jane tells the developer she is willing to buy a house at this price, but she needs 120 days to decide. The developer knows that prices are rapidly increasing, but to make a deal he offers the possibility for Jane to lock in a lot and home for $360,000. She must buy the home on or before the date the contract expires 120 days from the date, she signs it. If she fails to close by that time, the contract expires, and the developer is free to sell the lot to someone else at market prices.

Jane is not taking too much risk because she is not forced to buy the home; she has the option. If prices end up dropping, she can simply let the option contract expire. If prices stay about the same or keep rising, and she doesn't find another home she is interested in, Jane can go ahead and exercise her rights under the contract and buy the house for $360,000. This is true even if the price of new homes in the area has jumped to $400,000 when the contract expires. So, by locking in a price, Jane may have put herself in a position where she could save a significant amount of money yet get the home (investment) that she wanted.

While laws may vary based upon the given specific contract type, generally speaking, the contracts themselves can be bought and sold. The contract itself becomes valuable because of the *underlying* asset (in this case, the home), and the ability to buy that asset at a fixed price. In an environment of rising prices, this can provide a big advantage to buyers. In many cases, the buyers won't go through with the contract. Executing the contract is called *exercising* the contract. Of course, if home prices in the area were to rise to $400,000, it would be worth exercising this option's contract.

Jane may not want to do so. Maybe she found a different home more to her liking. However, since the contract has obvious value, she could sell it to someone else. Ever since financial instruments were invented, secondary markets were created soon afterward, where people traded them. Options are no exception.

Since an option derives its value from an underlying asset that is not directly traded or even owned by the person who buys the option, it is called a *derivative*. The media often talks about derivatives as extremely exotic and complex, but it is nothing more than that. A derivative is a financial instrument or contract that derives its value from an underlying asset.

Options on Stocks

The basic concepts of options that we described above apply to options on stocks. Since we now understand those basic concepts, let's define the specifics of options contracts on stocks. It turns out that options contracts on stocks are slightly more complicated than what we've described so far, but it's not complicated if you take it step-by-step.

The first thing to note is underlying. As far as options on stocks are concerned, its corresponding asset is 10 shares of a specific stock. That stock is a stock of a publicly-traded company on a major stock exchange. Options on stocks also include index funds. So, you can trade options on Apple, Facebook, or Boeing. You can also trade options on SPY, DIA, and QQQ, which are exchange-traded funds for the most significant stock markets such as the Dow Jones Industrial Average, the Standard & Poors 500, and NASDAQ 100, respectively.

For example, using a home purchase, we only talked about the option for someone to buy the home – we never considered having the option to sell a home. But with stocks, both concepts are equally important. The most basic concept is imagining having an option that would give you the possibility of purchasing those 10 shares of a given stock at a pre-determined sale point on or before the contract's expiration date. This kind of deal is known as a *call option*.

You can see that in a market of rising prices, a call option favors the buyer. The potential buyer can lock in a price. If they choose to do so, if the price per share rises by a significant amount (and by significant we mean significant enough to earn a profit if you turned around and sold the shares on the market), the buyer can buy shares at a discount.

In an environment of rising prices, since the option contract would give buyers such an advantage, the contract itself becomes more valuable. With everything else remaining equal, the price of the said contract will be going up in a market of rising prices. People will be bidding up the price as more investors excitedly want to get their hands on the option.

There are going to be two types of buyers in the marketplace. Some buyers are interested in getting a hold of the stock at a discount price. Others are simply hoping or anticipating that prices will continue rising, so they anticipate that the price of the option will be higher in the future. In other words, they want to buy the option, and then turn around and sell it for a higher price a few days or weeks later at a higher price to make a profit *from the option contract itself.*

When we are talking about anticipating making a profit from future price changes, this is called speculating. The term speculating is associated with *trading*, which can be defined as short term purchase and sale of a financial asset with the sole intent of generating profits. It is important to keep this concept distinct from *investing*. The first difference between trading and investing in the time frame. Trading is generally done on short-term time frames of one year or less. In contrast, investing generally means five years or more. Investing is a long-term commitment to something you believe in.

Of course, investors hope that their assets are going to increase in value as well. Otherwise, they wouldn't invest. But they are in it for the long haul and will not be getting rid of their assets soon after they acquire them. The reasons for investing often go beyond simple profit. Investors may be passionate about the companies they invest in and the products they offer or believe that the companies they invest in represent the economy's future. They may also take a broad view, and invest in index funds, based on the idea that the economy will grow with time.

It is crucial to have a clear understanding of the difference between trading and investing, and understanding what "speculating" is, as an options trader. As we'll see later, you might have to express that you understand the difference as an options trader to satisfy regulators.

Put Options

Now let's turn our attention to the other major type of option on the equities market. The option we are going to be discussing is known as a "put option." This kind of contract entitles the buyer to acquire a set quantity of stock at a pre-determined sale point. That might appear to you as somewhat bizarre at first, so why would anyone want to do that? The answer is that put options are valuable to buyers in a market of declining prices. If the stock is dropping significantly below the fixed price agreed upon in the options contract, it makes sense to either do one. If you already own the shares, maybe you purchased them at a much higher price, and you want to limit your losses. In that case, a put option allows you to cut your losses at a given price point that may be significantly above the market valuation. You don't have to worry if the market price keeps dropping, you can sell your shares at a price agreed to in the contract at any time before it expires. So, in this case, a put option can be a form of insurance for a buyer who has invested in many shares.

It's also possible for speculators to profit. The first case is where you want to sell the stock. To do this, you wait until the stock price drops low enough to make a move on the option that would be profitable. So, you buy the 100 shares and then sell them to exercise your rights under the option. Of course, the way this would work is to sell them to the originator of the options contract, who is obligated to honor the contract and buy the shares.

Chapter 4: Why Trade Options?

This is a common question people are asking. Why do you want to exchange options?

Well, the first reason for this is to protect and control your risk. If you take a big risk, trading options is the way to protect yourself so that you don't lose all your money. It gives you full control of how and where your money is going.

But one thing you should know is that trading options should not be done with your eyes closed. You're going to have to keep an eye on the market. And if you don't, it's going to shoot you back.

Let's get started now.

Hedge and Speculation

Hedging and Speculation are the first two things you should learn before you spend a single penny on trading options. This is what's going to get you going and how you're expected to handle trading options.

Hedging is when you fear something could go wrong. It doesn't mean that anything is going to go wrong, it's just a way to protect yourself (I mean your money) if things start to go wrong.

Hedging is the way to ensure your investment if rates start to fall. In other words, hiding is your defense against losing a lot of money. Hedging is used by large companies and institutional investors to cover themselves.

On the other hand, if you have no knowledge of the underlying asset (stock, bond, or commodity) when using options as a hedging strategy, then according to experts, you will certainly lose money. This is because you're trying to hedge too much to buy premiums on something you don't know about. This means that instead of taking a gamble and growing your income, you're going to lose your insurance money.

However, if done properly, hedging is a perfect way to shield yourself from failure.

Next is speculation. But this is very dangerous.

There are three ways that any investor makes a profit – when the price goes up, when the price goes down, and when the price moves sideways (meaning, the price stays or goes up and down within the range).

A lot of money can be made from speculation. Speculation may be rendered by researching and analyzing the market. This includes assessing and forecasting patterns and finding out where the market is heading from the present point of view. This can be a big advantage if you're familiar with the market and have good knowledge of the underlying asset.

But as I said before, speculation is very risky. An investor who wants to make a profit as a speculator must be able to correctly predict the trajectory of the asset price (whether it will rise or fall), the timing of that direction, and the magnitude (the price will change by how much).

Advantages and Drawbacks in Trading Options

We do accept that selling options are difficult. But once you grasp it, it's going to be an ability that you know like the back of your hand. The best part of options trading is that you can make a profit from the price change of the underlying asset without directly investing in the asset.

And as I mentioned earlier, investing in options is actually cheaper than investing in the actual asset. Plus, if you invest directly in the asset, you will have less leverage. In short, by selling options, you now have access to more money than you would have initially had.

And if you add it up, leverage, capital, and so on, you can find that an investor will potentially make more money per actual dollar invested compared to investing directly in the asset. Often with options, an investor can only lose a fixed sum of money, which is effectively the premium he/she has paid.

This means that if you don't place anything in the premium, you're not going to lose everything. This is the safest thing to do if you're just trying to test the water, and you're not ready to go all in.

Another great benefit of Options Trading is that you can use hedging as an insurance strategy to shield yourself from losses that are getting too large. This ensures that you can also shield yourself from extreme swings in the stock market. I would strongly recommend that you begin with as much hedging as possible to reduce your losses.

Another advantage is that you can make money even if the stock doesn't make money. It's because of the ability to trade up, down, or sideways to maximize your power and income. You'll see the stock price dropping several times, and you can still make a profit at the end of it.

Plus, commissions are much less active in trading options (now you know why stockbrokers are advising you about it). And if you want to go through an online broker, those commissions are even smaller because they want to beat their competition.

Besides, trading options are flexible. It helps you to respond based on where the price is going. It gives you the freedom to participate in more than one business as well. This means you can invest in everything from agriculture to foreign currency. Plus, you don't have to spend a lot of money like large companies. All you need is a minimum sum, and you can start making money.

Last but not least, and this one is a biggie, the pace of having your profit in hand. Yeah, as soon as the stock increases, you'll get your benefit so that you can start investing in other markets or stocks. The pace of the market helps you to invest in more markets at the same time and make more money out of it. And unlike other forms of day trading, options trading is just a short-term bet. This means that even if you make an inaccurate prediction, you'll lose money within a few months instead of waiting for years to lose money because of that error.

Taxes are a detriment when it comes to trading options. Yeah, you're going to have to pay taxes on everything you do, except in those exceptional situations. So, make sure you fill out your IRA form to make sure you keep tax tabs before you start investing.

Moreover, unlike shares, there is no certificate of deposit when it comes to options. It's all paying rights, so it doesn't give you evidence of possession. This means that you will not be able to justify to people the ownership of the stock unless it is a stock certificate.

And then there's a matter of ambiguity. It's a little frightening when you're investing in something you don't know about. That's why most investors make sure they have an in-depth, detailed knowledge of what they're investing in because it can quickly turn into a gamble that isn't worth the winnings.

It's important to know your plan. And be sure to start small and slow to prevent losing high.

It's almost like driving a car. It's all scary when you're driving for the first time. But as you spend more and more time behind the wheel, you know the tricks of the trade, and you instantly become the best driver.

Chapter 5: Options Contracts – The Basics (Part I)

In our introductory discussion, we will be focusing on the most basic way to get involved in options, which involves buying options contracts based on bets you make on whether future stock prices will rise or fall. Later we will see that you can also write or sell options contracts and that the contracts themselves are traded on the markets.

What is an Options Contract?

An options contract sounds fancy but it's a pretty simple concept.

- It's a contract. That means it's a legal agreement between a buyer and a seller.
- It allows the purchaser of the contract to purchase or dispose of an asset with a fixed amount.
- The purchase is optional – so the buyer of the contract does not have to buy or sell the asset.
- The contract has an expiration date, so the purchaser – if they choose to exercise their right – must make the trade on or before the expiration date.
- The purchaser of the contract pays a non-refundable fee for the contract.

While the focus of this book is on options contracts related to the stock market, some options contracts take place in all aspects of daily life including real estate and speculation. A simple example illustrates the concept of an options contract.

Suppose you are itching to buy a BMW and you've decided the model you want must be silver. You drop by a local dealer and it turns out they don't have a silver model in stock. The dealer claims he can get you one by the end of the month. You say you'll take the car if the dealer can get it by the last day of the month and he'll sell it to you for $67,500. He agrees and requires you to put a $3,000 deposit on the car.

If the last day of the month arrives and the dealer hasn't produced the car, then you're freed from the contract and get your money back. In the event he does produce the car at any date before the end of the month, you have the option to buy it or not. If you really wanted the car you can buy it, but of course, you can't be forced to buy the car, and maybe you've changed your mind in the interim.

The right is there but not the obligation to purchase, in short, no pressure if you decided not to push through with the purchase of the car. If you decide to let the opportunity pass, however, since the dealer met his end of the bargain and produced the car, you lose the $3,000 deposit.

In this case, the dealer, who plays the role of the writer of the contract, must follow through with the sale based upon the agreed-upon price.

Suppose that when the car arrives at the dealership, BMW announces it will no longer make silver cars. As a result, prices of new silver BMWs that were the last ones to roll off the assembly line, skyrocket. Other dealers are selling their silver BMWs for $100,000. However, since this dealer entered into an options contract with you, he must sell the car to you for the pre-agreed price of $67,500. You decide to get the car and drive away smiling, knowing that you saved $32,500 and that you could sell it at a profit if you wanted to.

The situation here is capturing the essence of options contracts, even if you've never thought of haggling with a car dealer in those terms.

An option is in a sense a kind of bet. In the example of the car, the bet is that the dealer can produce the exact car you want within the specified period and at the agreed-upon price. The dealer is betting too. He bets that the pre-agreed price is a good one for him. Of course, if BMW stops making silver cars, then he's made the wrong bet.

It can work the other way too. Let's say that instead of BMW deciding not to make silver cars anymore when your car is being driven onto the lot, another car crashes into it. Now your silver BMW has a small dent on the rear bumper with some scratches. As a result, the car has immediately declined in value. But if you want the car, since you've agreed to the options contract, you must pay $67,500, even though with the dent it's only really worth $55,000. You can walk away and lose your $3,000 or pay what is now a premium price on a damaged car.

Another example that is commonly used to explain options contracts is the purchase of a home to be built by a developer under the agreement that certain conditions are met. The buyer will be required to put a non-refundable down payment or deposit on the home. Let's say that the developer agrees to build them the home for $300,000 provided that a new school is built within 5 miles of the development within one year. So, the contract expires within a year. At any time during the year, the buyer has the option to go forward with the construction of the home for $300,000 if the school is built. The developer has agreed to the price no matter what. So if the housing market in general and the construction of the school, in particular, drive up demand for housing in the area, and the developer is selling new homes that are now priced at $500,000, he has to sell this home for $300,000 because that was the price agreed to when the contract was signed. The home buyer got what they wanted, being within 5 miles of the new school with the home price fixed at $300,000. The developer was assured of the sale but missed out on the unknown, which was the skyrocketing price that occurred as a result of increased demand. On the other hand, if the school isn't built and the buyers don't exercise their option to buy the house before the contract expires at one year, the developer can pocket the $20,000 cash.

What is an Options Contract on the Stock Market?

An options contract on the stock market is somewhat analogous to the fictitious situation we just described w/ the car. In the case of the car, we saw that unforeseen events can make the bet made by the buyer and the car dealer profitable or not. The same thing happens in the stock market. Of course, in the case of the car, the buyer is simply hoping to get the car they want at what they perceive to be a bargain price, although if BMW really stopped making silver cars, they might sell it to a third party and then get a white one from the dealer. However, in most cases, the buyer wants the car. That isn't the case when it comes to options with stocks.

On the stock market, we are betting on the future price itself, and the shares of stock will be bought or sold at a profit if things work out. The key point is the buyer of the options contract is not hoping to acquire the shares and hold them for a long period like a traditional investor. Instead, you're hoping to make a bet on the price of the stock, secure that price, and then be able to trade the shares on that price no matter what happens on the actual markets. We will illustrate this with an example.

Call Options

A call is a type of options contract that provides the option to purchase an asset at the agreed-upon amount at the designated time or deadline. The reason you would do this is if you felt that the price of a given stock would increase in price over the specified period. Let's illustrate with an example.

Suppose that Acme Communications makes cutting edge smartphones. The rumors are that they will announce a new smartphone in the next three weeks that is going to take the market by storm, with customers lined out the door to make preorders.

The current price that Acme Communications is trading at is $44.25 a share. The current pricing of an asset is termed as the *spot price*. Put another way, the spot price is the actual amount that you would be paying for the shares as you would buy them from the stock market right now.

Nobody really knows if the stock price will go up when the announcement is made, or if the announcement will even be made. But you've done your research and are reasonably confident these events will take place. You also have to estimate how much the shares will go up and based on your research you think it's going to shoot up to $65 a share by the end of the month.

You enter into an options contract for 100 shares at $1 per share. You pay this fee to the brokerage that is writing the options contract. In total, for 100 shares you pay $100.

The price that is paid for an options contract is $100. This price is called the *premium.*

You don't get the premium back. It's a fee that you pay no matter what. If you make a profit, then it's all good. But if your bet is wrong, then you'll lose the premium. For the buyer of an options contract, the premium is their risk.

You'll want to set a price that you think is going to be lower than the level to which the price per share will rise. The price that you agree to is called the *strike price.* For this contract, you set your strike price at $50.

Remember, exercising your right to buy the shares is optional. You'll only buy the shares if the price goes high enough that you'll make a profit on the trade. If the shares never go above $50, say they reach $48, you are not obligated to buy them. And why would you? As part of the contract deal, you'd be required to buy them at $50.

We'll say that the contract is entered on the 1st of August, and the deadline is the third Friday in August. If the price goes higher than your strike price during that time, you can exercise your option.

Let's say that as the deadline approaches, things go basically as you planned. Acme Communications announces its new phone, and the stock starts climbing. The stock price on the actual market (the spot price) goes up to $60.

Now the seller is required to sell you the shares at $50 a share. You buy the shares, and then you can immediately dispose of these at a quality or optimal amount, or $60 a share. You make a profit of $10 a share, not taking into account any commissions or fees.

The Call Seller

The call seller who enters into the options contract with the buyer is obligated to sell the shares to the buyer of the options contract at the strike price. If the contract sets the strike price at $50 a share for 100 shares, the seller must sell the stock at that price even if the market price goes up to any higher price, such as $70 a share. The call seller keeps the premium. So, if the buyer doesn't exercise their option, the call seller still gets the money from the premium.

Derivative Contracts

You probably heard about derivatives or derivative contracts during the 2008 financial crisis. While they can be designed in complex ways, the concept of a derivative contract is pretty simple. What this means is that the contract is based on some underlying asset. For an options contract, the asset is the stock that you agree to buy or sell. The contracts themselves can and are bought and sold. That is why you may have heard about people trading in derivatives. The stock that is the subject of an options contract is called the underlying.

So, if you buy an options contract using the Apple stock price as a basis, the term "underlying" would apply to the stock from Apple.

Profits from the Call

Keep in mind the brokerage may have some additional fees. However, using our numbers remember that we paid a premium of $1 per share, and the strike price was $50. Computing for profit is one of the basics when it comes to trading. It is where profits are determined and forecasted for future options to buy or sell.

The profit per share was:

Profit = $60 – ($50 + $1) = $9 per share

The contract was for 100 shares, so the total profit would be $90.

What Happens if the Strike Price isn't Reached?

The strike price is the fundamental piece of information you need to keep in mind when trading options. If the strike price isn't reached, then the option will simply expire and be worthless. The difference between the current market price or spot price and the strike price is a measure of the profit per share that you will make.

For example, $100 is the price of the stock, and the strike price is $75, then the profit (disregarding fees) will be $25. If the strike price was $95, then the profit per share would only be $5. While the payoff from a strike price that is closer to the actual market price is smaller, it's more likely to pay off than a strike price that predicts a big move.

Why Purchase a Call Option

The reason that you purchase an options contract is to reduce your risk. When you buy an options contract, the only money you're putting at risk is the premium. In the case of our hypothetical example, that is $100. If the stock doesn't surpass the strike price, you can simply walk away from the deal and only lose the $100.

You could, of course, buy the stocks outright and hope to profit. To buy 100 shares, you'll have to invest substantially more money:

100 x $44.25 = $4,425.

If the stock goes up value, then you'll make some money. However, suppose that your hunch about the markets was wrong. Maybe Acme Communications, rather than announcing a new phone that will be in high demand, instead reveals that their next phone will be delayed for a year.

If you decide to unload the stocks you bought for $4,425, you will only get $4,000, and you'll have lost $425.

On the other hand, you can see how you reduced your risk by purchasing a call option. In that case, you won't exercise your right to buy the stock and only lose the premium. Your total loss would be $100.

The Flexibility of Options

In normal stock trading, you're betting in one direction, that the value of the stock will go up with time. And you're battling the opposite, hoping to avoid losses if the stock declines.

Options open the door to making a profit when stocks decline in value. Of course, it depends on being able to make the right call, but if you bet on a stock losing value and you're right, you can make substantial profits. Timing and the size of your trade will be important too, and you'll have to stay focused on the strike price and the current market price of the underlying.

Put Options

A call option is the choice to buy a stock if it reaches the strike price. Now let's look at the opposite situation. A put is an option contract where you get the right but not the obligation to sell a stock before the contract expires. You bet that it's going to decrease to at least $35 a share, so you buy a put option with a strike price of $35 a share. If your bet that the stock will decline in value and you're correct, let's say it drops to $30 a share, then you can make a $5 per share profit on the sale. If the stock meets the strike price, the seller of the put is obligated to purchase the stock at that price. In other words, even though the stock has dropped in value to $30 a share on the market, they must buy the shares from you at $35 a share.

Let's suppose that instead it only drops to $38 a share. In this case, you don't have to sell and simply walk away from the deal having paid the premium. So once again, as was the case with a call option, the premium is really the only money that you risk as to the buyer.

The seller of a put option must buy the stock from you at the strike price if you exercise your option. If the strike price is $35 but for some reason, the stock crashes to $1, the seller of the put must buy the shares from you at $35.

Why Buy a Put Option?

The answer is simple – when you buy stocks the usual way, you don't make any money from the declining values of stocks. You lose money. With a put option, it gives you the possibility of betting on the stock losing value.

Summary: Buyers of Options

The buyer of an options contract:

- Must pay the premium. This is non-refundable, so the premium is the minimum amount of capital you invest and is the amount you risk.
- You are not obligated to buy or sell any stock even when the deadline arrives.
- You have purchased the right to buy or sell the stock.
- If you buy a call, then you have the option to purchase the expiry of the agreement. If you buy a put, you have the option to sell the stock when the expiry arrives. The option to sell only falls in instances when there is a marked difference between the market price and your own strike price; with the market price being too low.

Summary: Sellers of Calls and Puts

Later we'll see that you may want to sell options and there are good reasons for doing so. Right now, we'll just summarize the general principles.

- The seller of an options contract will keep the premium no matter what. So, if the buyer doesn't exercise their option, you keep the premium as profit.
- If the buyer of a call option exercises their option to buy the stock, you must sell it to them at the strike price. So, if the strike price is $40 but the current market price is $65, you are missing out on a large profit per share. However, as we'll see later this can still be profitable.
- If the buyer exercises their right on a put contract, you must buy the stock from them at the deadline.

Number of Shares

The number of shares in one options contract is 100 shares. Typically, traders will trade multiple contracts. To you'll get the profit per share and then calculate total profit as (profit per share * 100 shares * # of contracts).

Now let's get familiar with the industry jargon so you can have a better understanding of what is going on when you start trading.

Chapter 6: Variety of Options and Related Styles

Call Options

These options provide you with the right to buy stock labeled as an underlying one. With Call Options, you can buy not only stocks but also commodities, bonds, or any other instrument that has a specified price, otherwise known as the strike price, within a specific timeframe. Call Options contract gives you the right to buy, but you don't have an obligation to do so. A person who is bullish on the stock is usually the investor who expects the value of the stock to increase shortly. This kind of investor buys call options and manages them in the specified time frame. Again, let's take an example.

Let's say that the investor we will name Mr. B thinks that next month CCC Company will have more significant earnings for the stock, and the stock will have a higher value. In this case, Mr. B buys a call option for the CCC Company's stock for 20 dollars, for example. The contract of the option has a term that Mr. B can buy up to 100 shares from CCC Company within the next two months. The strike price for these shares within this time frame is 100 dollars. So, if the value of the stock goes 100 dollars in the next period, Mr. B won't exercise his option, which means that he will lose his first 20 dollars of investment (remember, if the option is not exercised within the specific time frame, or two months in this particular case, the contract expires and becomes worthless).

On the other hand, if the value of the stock goes over 100 dollars, and the next price is 130 dollars, for example, Mr. B can exercise his option. He can now buy the stock for 100 dollars and sell it for 130 dollars on the market. The risk that Mr. B took paid off, and he earned a significant profit.

Put Options

These options have opposite traits from the Call Options. Put Options represent the contract in which the purchaser has the right to sell his or her stocks. These stocks, like all others, must be sold for the strike price (a price that's been specified for a specific time). Put Options, like Call Options, give the right to sell, but they are not obligatory. Now we can return to Mr. B and observe him as an investor who is bearish on a particular stock.

In this example, Mr. B thinks that the price of the stock he is interested in will decrease, and, in that case, he will purchase a put option. According to Mr. B, the stock that CCC Company has is overpriced, and its value will go lower in the next two months. Let's say that Mr. B buys a Put Option on this stock for 20 dollars again. Contract of the Put Option gives Mr. B a chance to sell the stock he bought from CCC Company for 120 dollars in the next 60 days. So if the stock value increases more than 120 dollars per share, Mr. B won't have to exercise his Put Option, the time frame will pass, and the option will become worthless, which means that he would lose only his initial capital of 20 dollars. However, if the value of the stock goes down and the price goes from 120 dollars to 90 dollars, for example, the Put Option will be exercised, and Mr. B can sell this stock for 120 dollars per share. Once again, he judged correctly, and he has made a considerable profit.

How to Make a Profit Using Call Options and Put Options

There are many ways for a trader to use Call Options and Put Options and be successful in the process. The best way to show some of the most efficient ways to use these options is by using real numbers. Imagine you want to buy shares from US Bank. Let's suppose that the bank currently sells them for the price of 200 dollars per share and that you conclude that this number is going to go up since the shares are underpriced. Let's also suppose that the predicted amount of time that the shares will need to increase their value is a few months from now. At the moment, you don't have enough capital to buy 100 shares from the US Bank. However, you still want to make some profit from the stock that will rise in value according to your estimation. If this is the case, you can use Call Option and buy it for the stock. This way, you reduce the cost, and you pay only a fraction of the original stock price. Once that you purchased the Call Option, you gained the right to buy 100 shares of US Bank stock for 200 dollars per share in the next two months. One of your doubts might immediately be how you are supposed to buy that stock for 200 dollars per share in the next 60 days when you don't have the initial amount of money for that in the first place? Well, the thing is that you are not under obligation actually to buy the stock if you want to make money. If your estimation is correct, and in the next period, the value of the stock goes over 200 dollars per share, the Call Option that you bought would increase in value too. In other words, your option contract value rises with the value of the stock price. Keeping this in mind, you get the opportunity to sell your Call Options contract to make money, not the shares. That is the real connection because once when the stock price rises, your contract is worth a lot more than the money you invested in buying it.

A similar thing happens if you purchase the Put Options contract. The only difference is that your estimation has to be decreased in the stock value rather than prices going higher. Once when the underlying security price goes down, the price of your Put Option will go up. The more that the stock price falls, the more expensive your contract becomes. Using options in both cases means that you can make a profit regardless of the rise or fall of the stock prices.

Option Styles

There are various styles of options used in the trader's market, and it is essential to understand them. However, most of the options that are used in everyday trading belong to one of the main styles—American style or European style. These two categories are often called vanilla options, and their main difference is the time of execration for both types of options.

American Options

The first style of options that we will introduce is also one of the two that are used most often. These options are called American Options, and their main characteristic is that they can be exercised at any point as long as the option hasn't reached its expiration date. American Options are also considered to be the most frequent type of contract traded on the market when it comes to future exchanges.

European Options

On the other hand, have a different excretion policy. The expiration date of the option has to be defined in the contract, which means that the option can be exercised only during that specific period. The type of market called 'over the counter' or OTC for short is the market in which European Options are traded the most.

However, the value of American and European Options is calculated differently. Additionally, the expiration date is also different for each of these styles. For American Options, the expiration date is pre-determined before the investor purchases the contract. The American Option always expires on the third Saturday of the following month. Contrarily, the European Option becomes worthless on Friday—a day before the third Saturday of the specified month. There are a few similarities between these so-called vanilla options too. They both have the rule of buying and selling at the strike price, and they both include pay-off. Furthermore, whether you calculate pay off for the Call or Put Options, the process is the same, and it usually means that the strike price for these options is the same most of the time.

Exotic Options

As we already mentioned, vanilla options are the two main styles that investors use while trading. However, many other option styles should be aware of. These other styles that are not that frequent are called Exotic Options.

Bermuda Options

In this case, are a style of option that qualifies as something in between American and European versions? The critical difference is that Bermuda Options can be exercised on more than a few dates as long as the contract is valid.

Barrier Options

On the other hand, there are Barrier Options. These options are the most different ones so far, and the reason is that there is a border that needs to be passed to get the payoff for the underlying security price. This is the case for both Call and Put Options. Barrier Options are divided into four categories:

- "Down and Out" Barrier Options – the purchaser of this option has the right (but like in every other case, no obligation) to buy or sell shares, depending on the type of option that he chooses. The condition is that whether these underlying assets are bought or sold, it has to be done using an already determined strike price. The strike price, however, mustn't go lower than a barrier that is pre-determined with the option contract until the expiration date. If by any chance, the price of the owner's shares goes below this barrier, the option loses every value, and that is why it was named "down and out."
- "Down and In" Barrier Options – this option is the total opposite of the "down and out" category. An investor who has this option should know that the only time when the "down and in barrier" has value is when the price of all assets that are underlying and allowed to be purchased by the contract goes below the barrier that was pre-determined for that particular option until it expires. The purchaser has the right to sell or buy shares (again, depending on the type of purchased option) if the barrier was crossed. This trade also has to be done before the expiration date is due and at the strike price.
- "Up and Out" Barrier Options – this category of Barrier Options is similar to "down and out." The main distinction is the fact that the barrier itself is placed differently. In this case, "up and out" means that if the price of any underlying asset being purchased increases above the barrier predetermined by the contract, the option will lose its value.
- "Up and In" Barrier Options – unlike "up and out," this category has similarities with "down and in" options rather than "down and out." The barrier, in this case, is set above the current value of any underlying asset purchased by the investor. The only time that this kind of option carries value is when the price of the stock reaches the placed barrier before the contract expires.

Chapter 7: Covered Calls

Covered Calls

This strategy is called covered calls. By covered, we mean that you've got an asset that you own that covers the potential sale of the underlying stocks. In other words, you already own the shares of stocks. Now, why would you want to write a call option on stocks you already own? The basis of this strategy is that you don't expect the stock price to move very much during the lifetime of the options contract, but you want to generate money over the short term in the form of premiums that you can collect. This can help you generate a short-term income stream; you must structure your calls carefully.

Setting up covered calls is relatively low risk and will help you get familiar with many of the aspects of options trading. While it's probably not going to make you rich overnight, it's a good way to learn the tools of the trade.

Covered Calls Involve a Long Position

To create a covered call, you need to own at least 100 shares of stock in one underlying equity. When you create a call, you're going to be offering potential buyers a chance to buy these shares from you. Of course, the strategy is that you're only going to sell high, but your real goal is to get the income stream from the premium.

The premium is a one-time non-refundable fee. If a buyer purchases your call option and pays you the premium, that money is yours. No matter what happens after that, you've got that cash to keep. If the stock doesn't reach the strike price, the contract will expire, and you can create a new call option on the same underlying shares. Of course, if the stock price does pass the strike price, the buyer of the contract will probably exercise their right to buy the shares. You will still earn money on the trade, but the risk is you're giving up the potential to earn as much money that could have been earned on the trade.

You write a covered call option that has a strike price of $67. Suppose that for some unforeseen reason the shares skyrocket to $90 a share. The buyer of your call option will be able to purchase the shares from you at $67. So, you've gained $2 a share. However, you've missed out on the chance to sell the shares at a profit of $35 a share. Instead, the investor who purchased the call option from you will turn around and sell the shares on the markets for the actual spot price and they will reap the benefits.

However, you really haven't lost anything. You have earned the premium plus sold your shares of stock for a modest profit.

That risk – that the stocks will rise to a price that is much higher than the strike price - always exists, but if you do your homework, you're going to be offering stocks that you don't expect to change much in price over the lifetime of your call. So, suppose instead that the price only rose to $68. The price exceeded the strike price so the buyer may exercise their option. In that case, you are still missing out on some profit that you could have had otherwise, but it's a small amount and we're not taking into account the premium.

If the stock price doesn't exceed the strike price over the length of the contract, then you get to keep the premium and you get to keep the shares. The premium is yours to keep no matter what.

In reality, in most situations, a covered call is going to be a win-win situation for you.

Covered Calls Are a Neutral Strategy

A covered call is known as a "neutral" strategy. Investors create covered calls for stocks in their portfolio where they only expect small moves over the lifetime of the contract. Moreover, investors will use covered calls on stocks that they expect to hold for the long term. It's a way to earn money on the stocks during a period in which the investor expects that the stock won't move much at price and so have no earning potential from selling.

An Example of a Covered Call

Let's say that you own 100 shares of Acme Communications. It's currently trading at $40 a share. Over the next several months, nobody is expecting the stock to move very much, but as an investor, you feel Acme Communications has solid long-term growth potential. To make a little bit of money, you sell a call option on Acme Communications with a strike price of $43. Suppose that the premium is $0.78 and that the call option lasts 3 months.

For 100 shares, you'll earn a total premium payment of $0.78 x 100 = $78. No matter what happens, you pocket the $78.

Now let's say that over the next three months the stock drops a bit in price so that it never comes close to the strike price, and at the end of the three months, it's trading at $39 a share.

The options contract will expire, and it's worthless. The buyer of the options contract ends up empty-handed. You have a win-win situation. You've earned the extra $78 per 100 shares, and you still own your shares at the end of the contract.

Now let's say that the stock does increase a bit in value. Over time, it jumps up to $42, and then to $42.75, but then drops down to $41.80 by the time the options contract expires. In this scenario, you're finding yourself in a much better position. In this case, the strike price of $43 was never reached, so the buyer of the call option is again left out in the cold. You, on the other hand, keep the premium of $78, and you still get to keep the shares of stock. This time since the shares have increased in value, you're a lot better off than you were before, so it's really a win-win situation for YOU, even though it's a losing situation for the poor soul who purchased your call.

Sadly, there is another possibility, that the stock price exceeds the strike price before the contract expires. In that case, you're required to sell the stock. You still end up in a position that isn't all that bad, however. You didn't lose any actual money, but you lost a potential profit. You still get the premium of $78, plus the earnings from the sale of the 100 shares at the strike price of $43.

A covered call is almost a zero-risk situation because you never actually lose money even though if the stock price soars, you obviously missed out on an opportunity. You can minimize that risk by choosing stocks you use for a covered call option carefully. For example, if you hold shares in a pharmaceutical company that is rumored to be announcing a cure for cancer in two months, you probably don't want to use those shares for a covered call. A company that has more long-term prospects but probably isn't going anywhere in the next few months is a better bet.

How to Go about Creating a Covered Call

To create a covered call, you'll need to own 100 shares of stock. While you don't want to risk a stock that is likely to take off shortly, you don't want to pick a total dud either. There is always someone willing to buy something – at the right price. But you want to go with a decent stock so that you can earn a decent premium.

You start by getting online at your brokerage and looking up the stock online. When you look up stocks online, you'll be able to look at their "option chain" which will give you information from a table on premiums that are available for calls on this stock. You can see these listed under the bid price. The bid price is given on a per-share basis, but a call contract has 100 shares. If your bid price is $1.75, then the actual premium you're going to get is $1.75 x 100 = $175.

An important note is that the further out the expiration date, the higher the premium. A good rule of thumb is to pick an expiry that is between two and three months from the present date. Remember that the longer you go, the higher the risk because that increases the odds that the stock price will exceed the strike price and you'll end up having to sell the shares.

You have an option (no pun intended) with the premium you want to charge. Theoretically, you can set any price you want. Of course, that requires a buyer willing to pay that price for you to actually make the money. A more reasonable strategy is to look at prices people are currently requesting for call options on this stock. You can do this by checking the asking price for the call options on the stock. You can also see prices that buyers are currently offering by looking at the bid prices. For an instant sale, you can simply set your price to a bid price that is already out there. If you want to go a little bit higher, you can submit the order and then wait until someone comes along to buy your call option at the bid price.

To sell a covered call, you select "sell to open."

Benefits of Covered Calls

- A covered call is a relatively low-risk option. The worst-case scenario is that you'll be out of your shares but earn a small profit, a smaller profit than you could have made if you had not created the call contract and simply sold your shares. However, you also get the premium.
- A covered call allows you to generate income from your portfolio in the form of premiums.
- If you don't expect any price moves on the stock in the near term and you plan on holding it long term, it's a reasonable strategy to generate income without taking much risk.

Risks of Covered Calls

- Covered calls can be a risk if you're bullish on the stock, and your expectations are realized, and there is a price spike. In that case, you've traded the small amount of income of the premium with a voluntary cap of the strike price for the potential upside you could have had if you had simply held the stock and sold it at the high price.

If the stock price plummets, while you still get the premium, the stocks will be worthless unless they rebound over the long term. You shouldn't use a call option on stocks that you expect to be on the path to a major drop in the coming months. In that case, rather than writing a covered call, you should simply sell the stocks and take your losses. Alternatively, you can continue holding the stocks to see if they rebound over the long term.

Chapter 8: How Prices Are Determined

Pricing is a complex subject when it comes to options trading. Not only is the price of an option based on the value of the asset, but other external factors have influence.

As an options trader, you want to make sure that you maximize your efforts to make a profit. Learning how to determine the prices you should pay for options is one of the basic ways that you can ensure that your yield is as high as it can be. You do not want to be stiffed by paying higher premiums than you should.

The pricing of options is determined by several factors.

The Value of the Asset

The effect this has on options prices is straightforward. If the value of this asset goes down then exercising the option to sell becomes more valuable while the right to buy becomes less valuable.

On the other hand, if the value increases, the right to sell it becomes less valuable while the right to buy it becomes more appealing due to this increase.

The Intrinsic Value

When an options trader pays a premium, this sum represents two values. The premium is made up of the intrinsic value, which is the current value of the option and the potential increase in value that this option can obtain over time. This potential increase over time is known as the time value.

The intrinsic value is how much money the option is currently worth. It represents what the buyer would receive if he or she decided to exercise the option at the current time.

Intrinsic value is calculated by determining the difference in the current price of an asset and the strike price of the option.

For an option to have an intrinsic value of zero, the option must be out of money. Therefore, the buyer would not exercise the option because this would result in a loss. The common strategy here is allowing the option to expire so that no payoff is made. As a result, the intrinsic value results in nothing to the buyer.

For a buyer to be in the money, the intrinsic value has to be greater than the premium to increase the value of the option. This places the buyer in a position to make a profit. The intrinsic value of for in the money for call options and put options are calculated slightly differently. The formulas are as follows:

In the money call options:

Price of Asset - Strike Price = Intrinsic Value

In the money put option:

Strike Price - Price of Asset = Intrinsic Value

The Time Value

This value is the additional amount an investor is willing to contribute to the premium of an option in addition to the intrinsic value. This willingness stems from the belief that an option will increase in value before the expiration date reaches. Typically, an investor is only willing to put forth this extra amount if the option expires months away. There would be little to no change in the value of an option in a few days.

The time value is calculated by finding the difference between the intrinsic value of an option and the premium. The formula looks like this:

Option Premium - Intrinsic Value = Time Value

Therefore, the total price of an option premium follows this formula:

Intrinsic Value + Time Value = Option Premium

Both time value and intrinsic value help traders understand the value of what they are paying for if they decide to purchase an option. While the intrinsic value represents the worth of the option if the buyer were to exercise it at the current time, the time value represents the possible future value before or on the expiration date. These two values are important because they help traders understand the risk versus the reward of considering an option.

Volatility

This describes how likely a price change will occur during a specified amount of time on the financial market. If a financial market is nonvolatile then the prices change very slowly or remain unaffected over a specific amount of time. Volatile markets, on the other hand, have fast-changing prices over short periods.

Options traders can make use of a financial market's volatility to get a higher yield for their investment in the future. Options traders normally avoid slow-changing financial markets because these non-volatile markets often mean that no potential profit is available to the trader. Therefore, options traders thrive on volatility even though volatility increases the risk of option trading. As a result, an options trader needs to know how to read the financial market correctly to know which options are likely to yield the highest returns. This ability comes with experience, continuous learning, and keeping up to date on the happenings of the financial markets.

Many factors affect the volatility of the financial market. These factors include politics, national economics, and news reports. Options traders typically use one of two options strategies to gain the best yield from volatile markets. They are called the straddle strategy and the strangle strategy.

Interest Rates

Most people are familiar with the term interest rates. Interest rates apply to mortgages bank accounts and more. Interest rates as it applies to option trading is slightly different from the common variations.

The interest rate is defined as the percentage of a particular rate for the use of money lent over a period. This interest rate of an option has different effects on the call option and put option. The premiums for call options rise when interest rates rise and fall when interest rates fall. The effect is the opposite of put options. The premiums for put options fall when interest rates rise and rise when interest rates fall.

Interest rates affect the time value of options no matter what category they fall in.

You will come across the term risk-free interest rate many times in your study of options trading. This is described as the return made on an investment with no loss of capital. This is a misleading term because all investments carry some level of risk, no matter how minute. This more serves as a parameter in options pricing models such as the Black-Scholes model to determine the premium that should be paid.

Dividends

Dividends are distributions of portions of a company's profit at a specified period. This distribution must be decided and managed by the board of directors of a company. It is paid to a particular class of shareholders. Dividends can be distributed in the form of cash, shares of stock, and other types of property. Exchange-traded funds and mutual funds also pay out dividends.

As it relates to options trading, options do not actually pay dividends. However, the associated assets attached to that option can have them and thus, an options trader can receive those dividends if he or she exercises that option and takes ownership of those particular assets. While both call and put options can be affected by the presence of dividends of the associated asset, this effect on the types of options is widely varied. While the presence of dividends makes call options less expensive due to the anticipation of a price drop, it makes put options more expensive because the price will be decreased by the amount of the dividend.

Option Pricing Models

Option pricing theory uses all of the variables mentioned above to theoretically calculate the value of an option. It is a tool that allows trainers to get an estimate of an option's fair value as they incorporate different strategies to maximize profitability. Luckily, there are models that traders can use to implement option pricing strategies to their advantage. Three commonly used pricing models for option values are:

- The Black-Scholes Model
- Binomial Option Pricing Model
- Monte-Carlo Simulations

The Black Scholes Model

Also known as the Black-Scholes-Merton (BSM) model, this pricing model won a Nobel Prize in economics because of its effectiveness. It was designed by the three economists, Fischer Black, Robert Merton, and Myron Scholes in 1973. Originally used to price European options (meaning the option can only be exercised on the expiration date), this is a mathematical system that has a huge influence on modern option pricing. The pricing model helps differentiate options from gambling by determining the option premium to be paid logically. It calculates the return on the income the investor is likely to earn less than the amount paid.

As this is primarily used to determine a European call option, the formula used to calculate it looks like this:

$$SN(d1) - Xe - rt\, N(d2) = \text{Call Option Premium}$$

The letter representations in this equation stand for:

S – Current asset price

N – A normal distribution

X – Strike price

r – risk-free interest rate

t – Time of maturity

While this pricing system is great, it does have limitations. One of these limitations is that it assumes that factors like volatility and risk-free interest will remain constant, which is not the case in actuality. It also does not factor in other costs in setting up the option.

Binomial Option Pricing Model

More commonly used to develop pricing for American options, this pricing system was developed in 1979. Even as popular as the Black Scholes Model is, this model is even more frequently used in practice because it is more intuitive. This pricing system allows the assumption that there are two possible outcomes—one where the outcome moves up and one where the outcome moves down.

This system differs from the Black Scholes Model in that it allows calculations for multiple periods whereas the Black Scholes Model does not. This advantage gives a multi-period view, which is very advantageous to options traders.

This model makes use of binomial trees to figure out options pricing. These are diagrams with the main formula branching off into two different directions. This branching is what gives the multi-period view that this pricing system is famous for.

For this pricing system to work, the following assumptions are made:

- There are 2 possible prices for the associated asset, hence the name of the pricing system. Bi means 2.
- The 2 possibilities involve the price of the asset moving up or down.
- No dividends are being paid on the asset.
- The rate of interest does not change through the life of the option
- There are no risks attached to the transaction.
- There are no other costs associated with the option.

Clearly, just like with the Black Scholes Model, there is some limitation with those assumptions. Still, the pricing system is highly valuable in the valuing of American options since such options can be exercised at any time until the expiration date.

Monte Carlo Simulations

Used in multiple fields across the board like science, engineering, and finance, this model allows the options trader to consider multiple outcomes due to the involvement of random factors. It allows for the consideration of risk and unpredictability, unlike the first two pricing models. This is why it is also sometimes called multiple probability simulation.

A Final Word on Pricing

The reason I went into such depth on pricing options is that I want you to realize that everything related to options requires careful consideration right down to the premiums paid. This needs to be a fair trade for all the parties involved and premium pricing needs to reflect that fairness. When considering the options premium, remember to search deeper than the surface level to ensure that fairness and to ensure that you are gaining the profit that you need out of the transaction.

Chapter 9: How to Choose the Strike Price for Options Trading

The strike price of an option is the price at which a put or call option can be exercised. It is otherwise called the exercise price. Picking the strike price is one of two key choices (the other being time to expiration) a financial specialist or trader must make while choosing a specific option. The strike price has a tremendous bearing on how your options trading will play out.

Strike Price Considerations

Accept that you have identified the stock on which you need to make an options exchange. Your subsequent stage is to pick an options strategy, for example, purchasing a call or composing a put. Then, the two most significant considerations in deciding the strike price are your hazard resistance and your ideal hazard reward result.

Hazard Tolerance

Suppose you are thinking about purchasing a call choice. Your hazard resilience ought to decide if you picked an in-the-money (ITM) call option, an at-the-money (ATM) call, or an out-of-the-money (OTM) call. An ITM choice has a higher affectability—otherwise called the option delta—to the price of the fundamental stock. If the stock price increments by a given sum, the ITM call would acquire than an ATM or OTM call. Be that as it may, if the stock value decays, the higher delta of the ITM option additionally implies, it would diminish over an ATM or OTM call if the price of the fundamental stock falls.

Hazard Reward Payoff

Your ideal hazard reward result uses methods that measure the capital you need to chance on the exchange and your anticipated benefit target. An ITM call might be less dangerous than an OTM call; however, it costs more. If you just need to bet a modest quantity of capital on your call exchange thought, the OTM call might be the best, pardon the joke, option.

An OTM call can have a lot bigger increase in rate terms than an ITM call if the stock's floods past the strike price; however, it has a significantly less possibility of achievement than an ITM call. That implies, even though you plunk down a little measure of money to purchase an OTM call, the chances you may lose everything of your venture are higher than with an ITM call.

Given these considerations, a relatively conservative financial specialist may choose an ITM or ATM call. Then again, a dealer with high resilience for hazard may incline toward an OTM call. The models in the accompanying area illustrate a portion of these ideas.

Picking the Wrong Strike Price

If you are a call or a put purchaser, picking an inappropriate strike price may bring about the loss of the full premium paid. These hazard increments when the strike price is set further out of the money. On account of a call essayist, an inappropriate strike price for the shrouded call may bring about the fundamental stock being called away. A few speculators want to compose somewhat OTM calls. That gives them a better yield if the stock is called away, even though it implies sacrificing some top-notch gains.

For a put trader, an inappropriate strike price would bring about the hidden stock being relegated at prices well over the present market price. That may happen if the stock dives unexpectedly, or if there is an abrupt market auction, sending most offer prices forcefully lower.

Strike Price Points to Consider

The strike price is an essential segment of making productive options play. There are numerous interesting points as you calculate this value level.

Have a Backup Plan

Options trading necessitates a considerably more active methodology than commonplace purchase and-hold contributing. Have a management plan prepared for your options trading, on the off chance that there is an abrupt swing in sentiment for a specific stock or in the wide market.

Time rot can quickly disintegrate the value of your long choice positions. Think about cutting your misfortunes and moderating venture capital if things are not going in your direction.

Evaluate Different Payoff Scenarios

You ought to have an approach for different situations if you plan to exchange options effectively. For instance, if you consistently compose secured calls, what are the reasonable adjustments if the stocks are called away, as opposed to not called? Assume that you are bullish on a stock.

Would it be progressively beneficial to purchase short-dated options at a lower strike price, or longer-dated options at a higher strike price?

The Bottom Line

Picking the strike price is a key decision for an option's financial specialist or trader since it has a significant effect on the gainfulness of an option. Getting your work done to choose the ideal strike price is an essential advance to improve your odds of success in options trading.

Chapter 10: Credit and Debit Spreads Options

Credit Spread

Most options traders that make money doing options trading for income do it by selling put options. The goal is basically to pick a strike price that is low enough, so the probability of the put option going in the money is remote. For level three traders, using a put credit spread is the method of selling put options. It involves buying and selling a put option simultaneously. But in this case, we are going to set up the trade so that the higher strike put option is the one that we sell.

Then you are going to choose a lower-priced put option to buy. This is going to mitigate the risk, but the type of risk we are mitigating when selling a credit spread is different than the kind of risk we have thought about mitigating to this point.

First off, let's clarify when you would enter into a put credit spread. This is a trade that you will enter when you think that the price of the stock will stay the same, or it will rise. We can add to this and say that it's even OK if the stock price drops, but you want it to avoid dropping too much. This can all be encapsulated by saying that we only hope that the share price will stay higher than the put option's strike price that you sell. Otherwise, you don't care a whit what the stock price does.

As a part of the trade, the put option is bought at the same time with a lower strike price. Since the strike price is lower, it will cost less than the amount that you received from selling the high priced put option. Therefore, there is a net credit for the transaction, which is the gained premium for selling the put option with the high price of the strike, minus the premium payment for buying the put option with the low strike price. This transaction is carried out in a single trade. Many brokers will have some put credit spreads already set up for you, so you don't have to do anything but enter into the trade.

Let's get a clear understanding of how this works. Furthermore, we need to note that you are not going to have to buy any stocks; the stocks are bought and sold on your behalf automatically by the broker if this occurs.

The lower strike price put option is going to cap the possible losses incurred by having to buy the shares of stock. The way this is going to work out is if the stock drops by a large amount, you are going to have shares put to you at the higher strike price, meaning that you are going to have to buy the shares at that high price. But then you will be able to turn around and put the shares to the seller of the lower strike price put option so that you don't have to pay full price.

Let's look at a specific example to see how it would work. Also, remember that you have to factor in the breakeven price of the put options. So, if the price of the share falls lower than the price of the strike of the higher put, it has to drop below the price strike less the paid premium for that option. Otherwise, the option is not going to be exercised because the other party to the trade would lose money.

Now, let's create a hypothetical example that illustrates the concepts.

We will use Apple to see how this works. We can sell a $230 put (with the share price at $236) for $410. That is $4.10 a share. Therefore, the breakeven price would be $230 - $4.10 = $225.90. The share price is going to have to drop below $225.90 before any trader would consider exercising this option. Since it's a put option, exercising means that, as the seller of the option, you would be forced to buy 100 shares of stock. For a hypothetical example, suppose that the share price had dropped to $224 a share. This would be done at the strike price. So, the total cost would be 100 x $230 = $23,000. In this case, you could sell the shares on the open market for $22,400. So, your total loss would be $600.

If you didn't buy a put option to offset the risk, this means you would be open, at least in theory, for much larger losses. Say the stock price dropped to $190. In that case, you could still sell the shares after being forced to buy them when the put option was exercised, but you would have to sell them for $19,000. So, your loss, in this case, would be $4,000.

The way a put credit spread works is you buy a put option to prevent this kind of loss. For example, you can buy a put option with a strike price of $225 for $253, or $2.35 a share. So the way that things work out, in this case, is that if the share price drops below $225 to $190, to use as our example, since you bought the second put option, you would be able to sell the 100 shares you were forced to buy at $230 a share for $225 a share. Your total loss would be $5 a share, the difference between the two strike prices, for a total loss of $500. But we have to subtract the net credit for that, which is $4.10 - $2.53 = $1.57. So, the risk mitigation would limit the total loss to $500 - $157 = $343.

You can earn substantial income selling put credit spreads. You can increase your income by selling multiple put credit spreads simultaneously, or you can aim for high priced stocks. For example, consider GOOG (Google, which has a share price of $1,243). Choosing strike prices of $1242.50 and $1227.50, you can earn $545 as long as the options expire with the share price higher than the higher strike price. The maximum possible loss, in this case, would be $955.

The longer the expiration date, the more money that can be earned. Considering Amazon, which has a share price of $1,769, with a six-month time to expiration, you can earn $3,765, provided that the share price stays above $1,685.

Debit Spread

The key to long-term options trading is to get level three trading status. Once you have done this, many new strategies will become available that will significantly increase your odds of making profits.

A call debit spread involves two options in the same trade. You are going to buy one call option, and then you are going to sell a call option. The trade is entered into using one step, so you are not going to be focused on selling a call option. You simply pick the two options you want to use, and then you tell the broker which one to buy and which one to sell, and they take care of everything for you.

Then an option should be sold with the price of the strike that is higher. The strike price option that is higher is used to put a cap on your potential losses. Let's see how this works.

For the sake of example, say you trade a stock per share that costs $200. Let's say that you buy a call option with a $195 strike price for $500. If you only did this, your potential loss is $500.

But you can reduce the loss by selling a second call option in the same trade, creating a call debit spread. You pick a second call option that has a $202 price of the strike. For example, we will say that you can sell this for $250 (prices are for illustration only). Now, you have capped the possible loss to $250, cutting it in half.

The premium you receive for selling the $202 strike is yours to keep, so no matter what happens, that mitigates the losses. Potential profit occurs when the share price stays above the strike price of the lower strike used in the trade, which is $195 for our hypothetical example. The higher it goes above this value, the more profit you earn until you get to the higher strike of $202. From this point onward, the amount of profit earned is capped.

For a call debit spread, you calculate the net debit for the transaction. That will be the price paid per share of the call option you buy, less the price received per share of the option you sell. Then the breakeven price is the option's strike price you buy, plus the net debit for the transaction. So, if you have a net debit of $6.82 for a call debit spread with a $240 lower price of a strike, the price of the breakeven is $246.82.

Max gain is reached when the share price reaches the price of the strike of the option that has a higher price in the pair that you sold, and it is fixed for any share price that goes above that value. Call debit spreads work like calls but allows you to earn limited, fixed profits.

Put Debit Spread

The same type of strategy can be used with put options. In this case, we obtain a put debit spread. The numbers are simply reverse. The first part of a put debit spread is buying a put option with a higher strike price. This is where you hope to make your profits. Then, you will sell a put option that has a lower strike price to help mitigate your risk. The premium received from selling the put option, although it will be smaller than the premium paid to buy the put option with the higher strike price, will help you to reduce the potential losses if the trade does not work out.

The price paid for the higher strike price put less the price received for selling; the lower strike price put will give you the net debit for the trade. The breakeven price, in this case, is found by taking the higher strike price and then subtracting the net debit. Profits are obtained when the price of the stock falls to or less than the breakeven price. When the price of the stock reaches the lower price of the strike, then the maximum profit happens. It is constant from there, despite how little the price of the stock drops.

A put debit spread helps you to mitigate your overall risk, at the expense of limiting your possible profits. If you had one put option, the potential earnings are obtained if the stock were to drop to zero. For example, if we bought an Apple put option with a price of a strike of $225, you could earn 100 x $225 = $22,500, if Apple stock was completely wiped out. Of course, that is a very unlikely scenario, but we describe it to give you an idea of what is theoretically possible for earnings when you invest in a put option. However, if we were to sell a put option as a part of the same trade with a strike price of $205, our gains would be capped at $1,415. That is a substantial profit, but even if the stock drops to $100 a share, $50 a share, or even $0 a share, we would only make $1,415. That is a good example that shows you how debit spreads work.

Chapter 11: Iron Condor Options

Do you know that iron condor is something you want to apply when the highs and lows of stock prices seem to be bounded? It is as if the stock price is trapped. It never breaks above a certain pricing level, called resistance. But it never drops below a given price level, which is called support. Sometimes a stock can be trapped in this pattern for a long period.

To have support and resistance, you want to see the price touch the line of support at least two times, and the line of resistance at least two times. The difference in prices might be relatively small. Of course, there are some possibilities for trading calls and puts; when the price drops down to the support level, you can buy call options and take profit as the price goes back up toward the resistance price level. Then you can buy put options and sell them when the price drops back down to support.

Option Trader

This type of options trader seeks to minimize risk and set up trades so that they can earn a regular income from the markets. There are many different ways to do this, and most of them involve selling rather than buying options. When you are a regular options trader, you buy to open your positions. So, you are going to be running your business buying low and selling high to make profits.

Income traders sell to open their positions. They seek to make money selling options, and while you have been concerned about things like theta and time decay so far. As an income trader, your value time decays, and can't wait for options to expire.

An iron condor is the first type of strategy that we are going to consider that works in this fashion. When you trade an iron condor, you are going to sell it to open your position. Then you are going to make money from the time decay. As long as the stock stays within the range that you use to define the iron condor, you will earn a profit. If it moves outside the range of the iron condor, then you are going to lose money.

A single iron condor isn't going to make you a huge amount of money. The basic philosophy behind it is that this is a limited risk—limited profit type of trade. It eliminates having to guess which direction the stock is going to move, and instead, we are only going to estimate the bounds of stock price movement over the lifetime of the option. Under normal conditions, this type of bet is going to work in most cases. Of course, if there is unexpected news, such as bad news coming out about the company that can cause prices to move outside the bounds of the iron condor and turn the trade into a loser. The unexpectedly bad news about the economy or political situation can have the same effect.

To create an iron condor, we are going to trade four options at once. We are going to sell two options and buy two options. First, let's look at the high price range for the trade. We want to sell a call option with a lower strike price. The strike price used for the call option sets the upper boundary of the iron condor. So, you are setting this up with the belief that the stock price is not going to exceed the strike price of the call option that you select.

Second, we are going to buy a call option that has a higher strike price than the first call option. This is done because we are going to use it to hedge our risks a little bit. Let's see how that would work. For our example, we will assume that the stock price is $200.

We could sell a call option with a strike price of $205. This means we are setting up our iron condor with the belief that from now until the expiration date of the option, the price of the stock is not going to rise above $205. If there are 30 days to expiration, and volatility is a relatively low 15%, the price of a call option with a $205 strike price is going to be $1.55.

The breakeven price is found by adding the cost of the call option to the strike price, which would give $206.55. As long as the share price stays at $206.55 or below, it's not worth it for the option to be exercised. However, if the share price goes above that value, the option can be exercised. In the case of a call option, as the options seller, this means that you have to sell 100 shares of stock at the strike price of $205 a share.

So how would that work in practice? The way it works is your broker buys the shares at the market price, sells the shares to the counterparty to the option contract to close the transaction at the lower strike price, and then they stick you with the losses. So, if the share price was $208, you would have a $3 loss per share or a total loss of $300 for each contract that would cover 100 shares of stock.

Of course, stock prices can rise to any value, at least in theory. So, you could be getting into real trouble if the stock price rose much higher. The iron condor caps maximum losses by including a second call option, with a higher strike price. You buy this call option, which means you cap possible profits because you have this added expense. But besides limiting possible profits, it will also cap possible losses.

Since you are buying a call option, you can exercise your rights on that option and buy shares of stock at that strike price that you can sell at the higher market price to make up for some of the loss.

Using our price setup, we could choose $210 as the second-strike price. Suppose that the stock price rises to $212. In this situation, the first option with the $205 strike price is going to be exercised. So, we have to buy shares at $212 and then sell them to the counterparty of the $205 option at $205 a share, giving us a net loss of $7 a share.

But now we can exercise the second call option that we have purchased. In this case, we buy shares of stock at $210, but then we sell them on the market for $212, giving us a net of $2 a share. This helps mitigate the total losses, reducing the total loss to $5 a share, or a total loss of $500. The loss is capped. It's going to be the difference between the two strike prices chosen for our options.

The options that you sell are the ones that set the boundaries for the iron condor. In this case, we have the call option with a strike price of $205 and a put option with a strike price of $195. That means as long as the stock price stays between $195 and $205 among the time, we sell to open this position, and when the options expire, we will earn a profit.

In addition to selling a put option, we will attempt to mitigate risk in the same way that we did with our setup of the call options. This means that we are going to buy a put option with a lower strike price to set the final lower boundary for the iron condor. Again, it can be any value, but for the sake of clarity, we will put it at the same $5 distance.

Now let's take a look at what would happen if the stock price went outside the range we have set up to the downside. We have sold a put option with a strike price of $195 and purchased a put option with a strike price of $190. If the share price of the stock falls below $195 but remains above $190, the put option that we sold can be exercised. When a put option is exercised, that means that we will be forced to buy shares of stock at the strike price. So, we have to buy shares at $195 a share even though the price on the market is between $190 and $195, let's say for the sake of example, it's $192. We then have to sell the shares at the market price. So, if we sell the shares for $192, we are out $3 a share for a total loss of $3 a share.

If the stock price kept dropping, we would find ourselves with ever-increasing losses. But that is why we buy the second put option; it serves the same purpose as the second call option in mitigating our losses. So, if the share price drops to say $170, our losses will be capped at the difference between the strike prices of the two put options. Instead of being forced to sell the shares at the market price of $170 a share, we would be able to exercise the second put option and sell the shares at $190 a share. So, we had to buy them at $195 a share even though the market price was $170 a share, but then we can sell them to someone else for $190 a share.

Let's see what the prices are for each of the options in this case:

$210 Call Option (BUY): $0.57

$205 Call Option (SELL): $1.55

$195 Put Option (SELL): $1.45

$190 Put Option (BUY): $0.47

The cost of buying the two options is $0.57 + $0.47 = $1.04. But we receive a credit from selling the other two options of $1.55 + $1.45 = $3. Our net credit is $3 - $1.04 = $1.96.

We start ahead by $1.96. So, if we end up losing on the trade because the stock breaks one way or another, our losses, which were already capped at $5, are reduced by this amount, and so our total possible loss in any situation is $5 - $1.96 = $3.04. That means the maximum possible loss is $304 (for a total of 100 shares), and the maximum profit, which is fixed, is $196.

In the example we've deliberated so far, the losses seem to outstrip the gains. However, that is a deceiving way to look at the trade. With an iron condor, the probability of winning on the trade—provided that you've done your homework and picked stock in a low volatility situation—is high. The key to succeeding with an iron condor is carefully studying and choosing your trades. Don't just randomly pick a stock and then enter an iron condor.

Buying Back to Close

One strategy people use is they buy back the iron condor to close the position. You can choose to do this or not. The reason you would do it would be if there is a possibility of the stock breaking one way or the other, and then you would be put in a position of having the options that you sold exercised.

You can trade iron condors on different time frames. The longer you select for your time frame, the longer you are going to have to wait for either time decay to work well enough for you to buy it back and still make a profit, or for you to let it expire and make the maximum profit.

Chapter 12: Leverage of Options

The process of using borrowed capital (debt) to increase the shareholder's return on their investments or equity in capital structure is called financial leverage or Trading on equity. The financial leverage analyzed by the firm is intended to earn more return on the fixed charge funds rather than their costs. The surplus will increase the return on the owner's equity, whereas the deficit will decrease the return on the owner's equity. Financial leverage affects the EPS (Earnings per share). When the EBIT increases, then EPS increases.

For example, if the firm borrows a debt from creditors for $1000 at 7% interest per annum, i.e., $70, and invests this debt to earn a 12% return on this, i.e., $120 per annum. Then the difference of surplus, i.e., $50, which is after interest payment made to the creditors of the firm, will belong to the shareholders or owners of the firm, and it is referred to as profit from financial leverage. Conversely, if the firm would earn a 5% return, then the firm has a loss of $20 (i.e., $70 - $50) to the shareholders.

Highly leveraged companies may be at risk of bankruptcy if they are unable to make a payment on their debt, but it can increase shareholder's return on their investment, and there are tax advantages associated with leverage.

Financial leverage ratio = EBIT / EBT

The financial leverage ratio is used to analyze the Capital structure and financial risk of the company. It explains how the fixed interest-bearing loan capital affects the operating profit of the firm. If EBIT is more than EBT, this ratio becomes more than 1. A slightly higher ratio is favorable, i.e., if this ratio is marginally more than 1 that is nearer to 1, it indicates moderate use of debt capital, low financial risk, and good financial judgment.

Why is Leverage Riskier?

Another significant risk to be aware of is that of leverage. Because Options don't cost much as stock as they are simply a contract, this means that they experience disproportionately larger percentage price gains in reaction to the far more expensive underlying stock's very small price movements. The huge benefit of this is that it results in large percentage gains when the underlying stock moves in the anticipated direction by even a small amount. The downside, though, is that it also results in a 100% wipe-out of the investment if the stock moves by even the smallest amount in the wrong direction. This is not necessarily an issue with beginners, or at least it shouldn't be as the risk manifests itself mainly through trading too large a position size. However, you need to be aware that as beneficial as leverage is, it can also be a double-edged sword, so be aware that leverage is a risk that needs to be addressed. One simple way to nullify or minimize this level of risk is to keep your position size small.

Lastly, Options, as we know, possesses a time value (extrinsic value) in addition to their inherent intrinsic value (in the money value), which is also another double-edged sword. For option buyers, time-decay acts as a headwind because it is continually decreasing the value of the option. By doing so, increases the dependency on greater stock price movement to break even on the trade. For option writers, it acts as a tailwind because it allows a profit to be generated through steady premium incomes regardless of whether the stock moves or not.

The Advantages of Leverage in Options Trading

The options exchanges play a critical role in ensuring that there are enough securities to base options contracts on. Following are some of the significant functions of an options exchange.

Liquidity

Perhaps the biggest function of options exchanges is to ensure ready markets for options contracts. The markets ensure that holders of options can exercise their options and that there are enough buyers to purchase the options. Traders are looking for avenues to increase their earning potential, and liquidity helps them achieve that. Options contracts have a time limit, unlike other securities such as shares, which necessitates liquidity. The existence of market makers is particularly responsible for liquidity.

Gauging a Country's Economy

The state of an options market can reliably inform us what the country's economic situation is like. The most common underlying assets that traders base their options on our shares. The prevailing economic conditions are always reflected in the share prices of various companies. If the country is experiencing prosperity, the share prices will be up, and if the country is experiencing market crashes, the share prices will go down. Thus, the options exchanges play a critical role in ensuring that traders have a sense of how their country is performing economy-wise. Stocks are the pulse of an economy, and they are accurate predictors of a country's economic state.

Securities Pricing

Options traders have a wide pool to choose from when it comes to underlying assets. However, the value of an underlying asset is determined by the options exchange according to the forces of demand and supply. The financial securities of prosperous companies are worth more than the securities of moderately successful companies. The valuation of securities is important not only for traders but also for governments. Governments levy taxes on earnings drawn from options trading, so they first have to get the value of the securities.

Safety of Transactions

Traders want to be sure that they can trust all the parties that they are getting into business with. Therefore, it is the work of an options exchange to ensure the players are trustworthy. For one, most options contracts are based on financial securities of publicly listed companies, and these companies must operate within stringent rules and regulations. Thus, the trader is assured of security when dealing with other parties. The options markets should provide all relevant information about options contracts and securities to discourage the trader from making a move out of ignorance.

Providing Speculation Scope

Speculation of securities is critical to ensure a healthy balance of demand and supply of securities. Many traders earn their profits from purely speculative risk. They have developed a skill of determining the movement of prices. The options exchanges provide traders with the resources and tools of speculating on the securities performance, thus allowing traders to earn profits.

Promotes an Investment Culture

Options exchanges are critical in promoting the culture of investing in valuable securities like the stock as opposed to unproductive assets such as precious metals. Traders have a wide selection of underlying securities to base their options contracts on; thus, they are not limited in the range of their strategies. A strong saving and investment culture is critical for the economic advancement of a country.

The Continuous Market for Securities

Options exchanges allow traders to base their options on a wide range of underlying securities, and in case of any risks, traders are at liberty to switch from one security to the subsequent. This is different from purchasing stocks wherein you are stuck with the consequences of poor decisions.

Capital Formation

Options exchanges promote the pooling together and redistribution of resources. The exchanges create a win-win situation for both sides. Companies raise capital when their stocks are publicly listed, and their securities act as the underlying. On the other hand, traders stand to benefit from the high earning potential and low-capital requirements for options contracts. So, options exchanges play a critical role in ensuring that the parties are in a position to generate capital.

Control Companies

The significance of transparency within the derivatives market cannot be overstated. If a trader has the misfortune of working with shady companies, they could easily lose their earnings. Options exchanges make it hard for shady companies to spoil the market. For instance, publicly-traded companies have to submit relevant documents and adhere to certain performance standards, as doing so will boost investor confidence. Companies that refuse to cooperate with exchanges are blacklisted from the market.

Fiscal and Monetary Policies

The fiscal policy and the monetary policy of the government must not hurt the players in the financial industry. Options exchanges facilitate the creation and execution of key policies that will govern the financial markets.

Proper Canalization of Wealth

Options are a great way of putting capital into greater use, as opposed to having the capital just sitting around. Thus, the economy benefits from an injection of capital, which would otherwise have been inactive. The injection of capital into the economy promotes wealth distribution and fights off economic disgraces like unemployment.

Education Purposes

Options trading features complex processes. Even people who claim to understand options trading might be low-key deluded. Thus, the importance of education cannot be overstated. Many traders just get the hang of things and set about purchasing and selling options contracts, forgetting that it is critical first to educate one's self. Options exchanges provide a wealth of resources and information that are meant to enlighten traders. Empowered traders improve trading activity.

Disadvantages of Leverage in Options Trading

Again, I won't bore you with elaborate explanations of the disadvantages of options trading. Instead, here's another helpful list that clearly outlines why traders might choose to shy away from potential options trading opportunities:

- Options are time-sensitive investments. Yes, you can pick and choose options based on expiration dates, but you'll always be confined to a certain expiration date where you must choose to act or choose to exit.

- Successful options trading requires your attention and time. Without it, you risk losing out on potential profit-generating opportunities that come from buying or selling your call or put option at the right, most profitable time.
- Options are without a paper-trail. With stocks and bonds, for example, you'll receive some sort of paper certification regarding your investment. Options are "book-entry" investments, meaning you receive no paper certification that shows your claim to an option or your ownership of an option.
- You're working in the stock market, a highly volatile place where changes occur suddenly and dramatically. You'll need to be on constant alert, or at least hire a broker who will.
- You'll need to be in a somewhat stable financial situation before you can successfully trade. Establishing and frequently adding to some sort of "trading fund" before you begin your options, trading endeavors will somewhat remedy an unstable financial situation, however.

Chapter 13: Which Options Trading Platform to Use

A vital aspect of options trading is the platform that one uses to trade. This is because options trading requires monitoring and requires a continuous analysis of trends. Performance is also monitored, and since the trade is impacted upon by a complex of factors, one must choose a suitable platform for trading.

A good platform should offer a lot of opportunities for traders. These are opportunities to orient beginners into trading, development for the existing ones, and actualization for those with a record on the platform. Such a platform should also prescribe the available products and any resources that subscribers on the platform can benefit from to push themselves to profitability.

With the technology developing at high speed, platforms continue to improve by the day. This is both complicating the trading itself as well as providing avenues of spreading awareness about the business. A platform should have the ability to offer the best possible experience for the traders to do trade and grow both in experience and returns without meeting a lot of platform limitations and frustrations.

A Platform Takes Trading to the Holders

Trading involves a lot of complexities that may sometimes be scary. It makes people lose interest as soon as they develop it. They perceive it as too complicated. The impression is that it is a venture meant for the people who have higher comprehension of concepts in the economics specialty and that those who do not a background in this area will have difficulty getting on board.

A trading platform needs to present options trading as a venture that is possible and in which anyone with interest can succeed. The days when options trading and any other forms of trading were presented as a show of sophistication are long gone. In this era, every sector of investment is portrayed as conceivable, and businesses are now being made easier to create a better chance for people to dare. A platform that limits investment so much and is exclusive in terms of how it carries out its trading activities is irrelevant to modern economic patterns.

Platforms, thus, have to be interactive and user-friendly. They should have the ability to encourage users to feel like they can handle the trade. It should also have the capability to gauge the level of use and give feedback about how well they can use it. If it's a website, for instance, it should report the numbers as people visit it and how many eventually end up creating accounts and trading.

Counting traffic is essential for feedback that can lead to the creation of a better experience for the users.

Competition

In choosing a platform sometimes, one would want to take advantage of the advantages of different platforms. This is looking at one's style of trading and how they wish to monitor their business and see if a platform is more transparent in handling the tares or whether it offers a clear lens of controlling purchases and sales of options. This is the reason why the various platforms must be assessed in terms of their potential. Usually, platforms are related to the tools of trading. Some of the tools of trading can be found right on the platform of trading.

When a platform of trading also has various tools of aiding trading, it ensures that one can gain a lot of benefits in one place. This makes the platform a utility where a person can visit for more purposes than just trading. It also makes it better. For instance, if a platform has videos that offer trading tutorials. This can make it resourceful in imparting competency in participating in the very sector that the platform operates.

To best benefit from competition, one should understand the type of trade they want to do. This is by naming their price and gauging which platform can serve better in ensuring returns and value generation. This is to avoid going into trading in desperation, and one has to be patient to see if the platform can also come out and meet a trader at their point of ability and also help in trading in comfort where risk is at a minimum.

Types of Trading Platforms

There are various platforms in options trading that one could consider. There is web-based trading that utilizes the power of the search engines. This platform has many operators since the building of websites in the modern age is easy. This is responsible for the growth in the popularity of options trading. People can trade with anyone, open brokerage accounts, make deposits, and participate in the buying and selling of assets in the comfort of their homes.

With the presence of a lot of technological gadgets such as smartphones, tablets, and computers, web-based trading has been easy and within reach. Websites can be built with additional resources for learning and tools that can be an advantage for both novice and seasoned traders. On the websites, regular updates on the market can be posted to keep traders informed about trends, patterns, and even help in analyzing price movements for the subscribers.

The web is also a good platform when it comes to filtering opportunities and options based on suitability and preferences given the various abilities of users. They can be designed to be customizable even when the options markets are standardized.

User Friendliness

Friendliness is also in terms of the efforts that are made to create peer assistance. This is through creating groups of traders that influence each other and can learn from the vast experiences in the trading of the options. This can be a positive influence on the journey to gaining competence and help support an environment where people can relate and interact as they pursue their various financial goals.

Tools to Learn

Upon mastering the various basics of trading and making the initial moves to start trading, one will use various tools that help indicate the advancers and decliners on the market. Greeks are metrics that those involved in options trading capital to ensure maximization of returns. These "Greeks" include the delta matrix that measures the correlation between price movements of the underlying asset relative to the price of the option. The tools for monitoring the movements for these parameters of trading are vital as everyone trades with a focus on minimizing losses while geared towards profit maximization.

Some salient features of options are measured in terms called the Greeks and labeled with Greek letters. It's really essential to understand the Greeks if you're going to get serious about trading options.

- Beta: Beta, β, is a characteristic of the underlying stock and measures the historical volatility of that stock. It gives equal weight to volatility on the upside as well as on the downside. When you're evaluating a stock, you can get a sense of how variable the stock's price is by looking at the β. A stable stock that moves with the market will have a beta value of about 1. If beta is less than 1, it tends to lag the market that is a $1 movement in the market a stock with a beta less than 1 means it will increase or decrease less than $1. Conversely, a stock with a beta greater than 1 means the stock price will move more than the market, up or down. Stocks with low betas are more stable than those with a higher beta. Examples of low beta are utilities. Stocks with a high beta include industries like biotechnology.
- Vega: Vega is a measure of the volatility of the option price. The option price is related to the underlying stock price, but the option price is also variable. Vega is a measure of that

volatility, but it's an implied volatility, not a historical volatility as is beta. Vega is the only Greek trading term without a Greek letter symbol.

- Delta: Delta, δ, measures the change in the price of an option in response to a change in the price of the underlying stock. For example, if an option has a Delta of 0.45, when the underlying stock changes by $1, the option will change by $0.45.
- Gamma: Gamma, γ, measures the rate of change in the underlying stock, not the change itself. Gamma expresses how fast the option responds to changes in Delta. Gamma is expressed as a positive or negative number. A positive gamma indicates that changes in the delta will be correlated with positive movements in the underlying stock. A negative gamma has the opposite indication.
- Theta: Theta, θ, measures how much value the option will lose as days pass until expiration comes. The loss is due primarily to the time value of money. As a wasting asset, an option's value will decline because of the concept behind time value. A dollar today is worth more than a dollar next week. This time decay is difficult to calculate and most economic models are complex and often not particularly accurate.

Professional Level Platforms

There is a level in trading where one attains sophistication and attains the intuition to thrive in options trading regardless of the ways market forces seem to behave. At this level, someone needs tools that enable them to edge into the horizon of complexity in trading. The platforms for this professional level exist, and they have to offer tools that are an edge above the basic level. These tools have to offer strategies of competing to control the stocks and rise above the market forces. At this level, one becomes daring, and the possibilities that the platform offers should only be dared by those who have mastered trading and are sure of beating odds as they speculate about squeezing out value-form trades that otherwise be perceived as highly risky.

Mobile Trading

Mobile trading also comes to keep people abreast. This is because opportunities sometimes appear and disappear on people because they aren't using a device that enables them to be precise and timely in decision making and action.

With mobile trading, apps have been developed, some with notification capability. One can customize the apps to ensure that no opportunity comes that is not taken advantage of. Opportunities in trading must be seized and relying on a platform that is less reliable and useful means that opportunities for trading are lost.

What Are We Looking for in Platforms and Tools?

First is the opportunity to learn. There is no worse platform of trading than that which targets only to admit traders who do not understand what they are getting into. The education that a platform has to offer should be free as trading is itself risky enough to prohibit any extra expenses in the process. Platform operators should understand that anyone to visit their platform is a potential subscriber, and they should freely offer support to educate them for the acquisition of requisite knowledge on options trading.

Excellent broker services try to suit customer needs. They ask options traders on their platform what their preferred means of communication is. Whether a live chat or phone call suits the customer or not. They also dedicate a desk for trading communications and queries and have the discipline to listen to customers and their issues with patience. They, in fact, have feedback on the quality of customer service that those who reach out get.

Software Trading Platforms

These are more complex than web-based ones. This is because they are run on the trader's computer, and the trader is required to understand what the software does and interpret it. Even when the brokerage can assist, software-based platforms require the trader to have enough technical know-how to read charts, graphs, and understand patterns that represent various components of options trading.

For beginners, a complex platform is to be avoided by all means. This is because one is bound to engage in aspects of trading that they do not understand. A trading platform needs to be clear and simple. The interface should not be too busy as to scare away those traders who aren't accustomed. This is the reason why operators usually separate the platforms that as designed for basic use, which is suitable for novices, and advanced trading for the seasoned ones.

Then a broker has to offer a tutorial that guides the user on how to navigate their platform. Everything should be explained, even those that one would deem to be obvious. Screenshots can even be available to be categorical and emphatic. This ensures that a broker has offered all possible assists for the trader to benefit from the offers and products on the platform successfully.

Cost Implication

The trader needs to know that some brokers may have charges attached to some of the services, resources, and tools that they provide on their platform. These must be assessed in terms of their worth and whether the costs are necessary. Making some tolls premium may be an indicator of quality but not always. This is particularly the case when other platforms provide similar services toll-free.

Screening tools are particularly the ones that are bound to attract charges because they have abilities to analyze and assess market trends. They can think about the trader and help him in decision-making. One should read about the specifications of the tools and ascertain what they or cannot do. This is so they know if they are customizable according to the needs and conveniences of traders.

Some charges can even be attached to the quotes update feed. Usually, the quotes can be accessed in real-time for those who want to see them in real-time. The quotes are useful in influencing idea generation and sometimes can tip people of opportunities in the market. There is usually a delay for those who access the quotes updates for free.

Chapter 14: Basic Mistakes Beginners Make and how to Avoid them

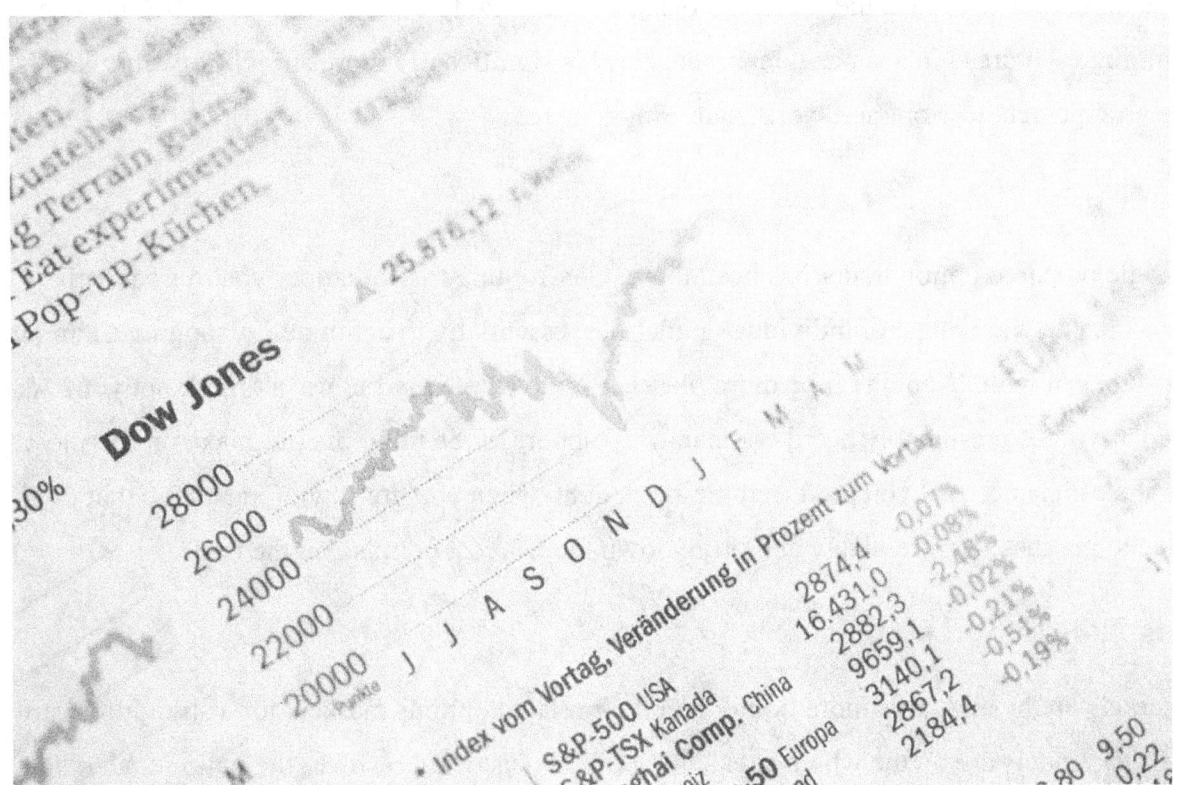

Buying OTM Call Options

As anyone might expect, these options are shabby which is as they should be. When you purchase an OTM shabby option, they don't consequently increment because the stock moves the correct way. If the move is near termination and it's insufficient to achieve the strike, the likelihood of the stock proceeding with the move in the now abbreviated period is low. Consequently, the cost of the option will mirror that likelihood.

Using the Same Strategy in different Conditions

Option exchanging is strikingly adaptable. It can empower you to trade adequately in a wide range of economic situations. Be that as it may, you can just exploit this adaptability on the off chance that you remain open to adopting new systems.

When you purchase a spread, it is otherwise called a long spread position. Every new options trader ought to acclimate themselves with the potential outcomes of spreads, so you can start to perceive the correct conditions to utilize them.

No Exit Plan before Expiration

. In exchanging options, much the same as stocks, it's essential to control your feelings. This doesn't mean gulping each dread in a super-human manner. It's significantly more straightforward than that: have the arrangement to work and work your arrangement.

Making Up for Previous Losses with Risk

Every single prepared option trader has been there. Confronting this situation, you're frequently enticed to break a wide range of individual guidelines, essentially to continue exchanging a similar option you began with. Wouldn't it be more pleasant if the whole market wasn't right, not you? As a stock trader, you've presumably heard comparative support for bending over to make up for a lost time: on the off chance that you preferred the stock at 80 when you got it, you must love it at 50. It can entice to purchase progressively and bring down the net cost premise on the trade.

Trading Non-Liquid Options

Stock markets are by and large more liquid than their related options markets for a straightforward reason: Stock traders are on the whole exchanging only one stock, however, the option traders may have many options contracts to browse. Stock traders will run to only one type of IBM stock, for instance, yet options traders for IBM have maybe six distinct lapses and plenty of strike costs to look over. More decisions by definition imply the options market will likely not be as liquid as the stock market.

Failing to Dividend Date in Strategy

It pays to monitor profit and profit dates for your hidden stock. For instance, on the off chance that you've sold calls and there's a profit drawing closer, it builds the likelihood you might be allotted early. This is particularly valid if the profit is relied upon to be expansive. That is because option proprietors have no right to a profit. To gather it, the options trader needs to practice the option and purchase the fundamental stock.

Failing If You Are Assigned Early

For instance, imagine a scenario where you're running a long call spread, and the higher-strike short option is doled out. Starting traders may frenzy and exercise the lower-strike long option with a specific end goal to convey the stock. However, that is presumably not the best choice. It's generally better to offer the long option on the open market, catch the rest of the time premium alongside the option's inborn esteem, and utilize the returns toward buying the stock. At that point, you can convey the stock to the option holder at the higher strike cost.

Not Using Index Options in Neutral Trades

Singular stocks can be very unstable. For instance, if there is major unanticipated news in one specific organization, it may well shake the stock for a couple of days. Then again, even genuine turmoil in a noteworthy organization that is a piece of the S&P 500 presumably wouldn't make that list vary in particular.

Spread Trades

Most starting options traders attempt to leg into a spread by purchasing the option first and offering the second option at a later date. They're endeavoring to bring down the cost by a couple of pennies and it isn't justified regardless of the hazard.

Averaging Down

Most traders tend to wander across averaging down. It isn't what they had in mind when they first start to trade but end up doing so anyway. Several problems can arise when averaging down. The main thing is that they can lose a position that they are holding on to. This is sacrificing money and time. This money and time could be placed elsewhere that could prove itself to be better.

Struggling to Get Even

If you ever hope to be an expert trader, you need to get used to the idea of being wrong regularly and then work it into your business plan. Letting emotion come into play when you make the wrong bet will only lead you to make additional mistakes down the line. The goal should always be to focus on the cold logic behind the numbers, not a hunt for a way to improve your image or self-esteem. Always focus on price action, leave the worry about magic numbers, and breaking even for when trading is done for the day. The final win/loss ratio can't be tallied until the last trade is made.

Under or Overstaying Your Welcome

Many traders find that they have a good entry plan but a poor exit strategy. This, in turn, leads them to choose a less than ideal time to exit a given trade which leaves them stuck with an investment when they were only looking for a trade. If you find yourself in this scenario you must add detailed technical specifications that will determine when you will exit the trade in question. The specifics of this maneuver will likely change over time and it is common for the strategy to evolve over years, not weeks or months.

Gambling

While there is an inherent level of risk in every trade, there is a wide disparity between that and actual gambling. When trading your goal should always be to capitalize on predictive directional signals you have gleaned from checking the statistic, never to bet your money on a hunch. Your goal should be to ensure you remain as disciplined when it comes to making trades as possible. If you are interested in gambling with the stock market, you will likely find better odds for a return on investment in Las Vegas.

Mishandling Early Assignment

An early assignment occurs when a holder exercises an option that you are the writer upon much earlier than you had anticipated, and at terms that are much less favorable than you had initially hoped. If this happens, it can be easy to become flustered and simply sell as requested, taking a loss in the process. Instead, you must consider all the possible options, including purchasing another option for the express purpose of selling it, to ensure that you mitigate the extra costs as completely as possible.

Ignoring the Statistics behind Options Trading

One of the biggest mistakes that most newbie options traders make is that they forget that probability is a real thing. When you check a potential stock before purchasing an option, it's important to understand that the history of an option is important when deciding whether or not you should be investing in it, but so are the odds and probability surrounding whether or not a particular event will occur.

Being Overzealous

Oftentimes when new options traders finally get their initial plan just right, they become overzealous and start committing to larger trades than they can realistically afford to recover from if things go poorly. You must take it slow when it comes to building your rate of return and never bet more than you can afford to lose. Regardless of how promising a specific trade might seem, there is no risk/reward level at which it is worth considering a loss that will take you out of the game completely for an extended period. Trade reasonably and trade regularly and you will see greater results in the long term guaranteed.

Not Being Adaptable

Successful options traders know when to follow their plans, but they also know that no plan will be the right choice, even if early indicators say otherwise. There is a difference between making a point of sticking to a plan and following it blindly and knowing which is which one of the more important indicators of the separation is between options trading success and abject failure. This means you must be aware of when and where experimentation and new ideas are appropriate and when it is best to toe the line and gather more data to make a well-reasoned decision.

Ignoring the Probability

Always remember that the historical data will not apply to the current trends in the market at all times which means you will always want to consider the probability as well as the odds that the market behaves the way it typically does. The odds are how likely the market is to behave as expected and the probability is the ratio of the likelihood of a given outcome.

Not Dealing with Short Options Properly

While, in theory, it might seem like buying back short options at the last moment is the best choice, this practice is sure to hurt you more than helping you in the long run. It may be tempting to hold onto profitable options to squeeze the maximum return out of each investment, but you need to be aware that the potential for a reversal is always lurking in the shadows. Instead, a good rule of thumb is to buy back options that are currently at 80 percent of your ideal return or higher and let the extra take care of itself. While it may hurt to leave some potential profit on the table, it will improve your overall reliability, netting you a profit in the long run.

Not Considering Exotic Options

An exotic option is one that has a basic structure that differs from either European or American options when it comes to the how and when of how the payout will be provided or how the option relates to the underlying asset in question. Additionally, the number of potential underlying assets is much more varied and can include things like what the weather is like or how much rainfall a given area has experienced. Due to the customization options and the complexity of exotic options, they are only traded over the counter.

Buying Out of the Money Call Options

Most options traders adhere to the strategy of buying low and selling high. However, when you buy out of the money calls, you hurt your chances of making a profit, and when the losing streak becomes prolonged, it could render your trading strategy unproductive. Those highly susceptible to this mistake are the traders who operate on a small budget.

Giving in to Fear and Greed

Options trading requires a trader to be very forward-thinking and in charge of their emotions. But traders don't always exercise their emotional intelligence. For instance, when a trade is winning, an investor might get greedy and resist closing their position, simply because they want to allow the trade more time to go even further up. Greed can also manifest when an options trader is adamant although they are losing consistently. When losses become your constant companion, it's time to pull out and reevaluate your strategies. If you're executing appropriate trading strategies, there's no reason you should struggle to make a profit. Traders who are driven by fear tend to overreact to every small thing that goes wrong. For instance, they bail out at the first sign of incurring a loss.

Doing Poor Allocation

Never commit more than 5% of your portfolio to one options trade. As much as options have leverage and high earning potential, you cannot ignore the high level of risk exposure. Thus, you have to allocate prudently.

Having a Finite Approach

Options are flexible and can work with almost any securities market. But a single trading strategy doesn't achieve the same results across all securities markets. If an underlying asset is hardly moving, an out of the money call or put option is likely to expire worthlessly. However, taking covered options can be profitable in this scenario. Iron Condor, a trading strategy that involves taking many positions, would generate a profit if the underlying moves slowly.

Not Having an Exit Plan

Before you start trading, you should fully understand what you're trying to get into. How much money do you intend to make? What are your risk-reduction measures? Once you have answered the critical questions, you will be in a position to make appropriate strategies and learn how to exit with the least possible scars when you're losing money.

Ignoring Consistent Profits in Favor of Home Runs

Options traders tend to forgo the chance of making small yet consistent amounts of profits and focus their energies on nailing the elusive home run. If you have a trading strategy that seems to net you small but consistent earnings, you should stick to that.

Having a Strategy That Doesn't Match Your Outlook

An options trader is supposed to have an outlook of what they expect to happen. Technical analysis and fundamental analysis play a part in developing your outlook. Technical analysis promotes the interpretation of the market's volume and price on a chart, whereas fundamental analysis is mostly about reviewing a company's performance data. Thus, a trader must always take the trading strategy that marries their outlook.

Attempting to Recover Past Losses

A trade can move against you and make you lose money. Most traders have been there. Sometimes you may put your capital on options, and the outcome is not exactly what you expected. In such a scenario, most traders tend to double up their options strategy to see if they can recover the loss. Doubling may lower your potential for loss in a given trade, but it is surrounded by a lot of risks.

Trading in Illiquid Options

Liquidity in options trading refers to having active sellers and buyers on the market all the time. This is what drives competition. It also affects ask and bid prices for options and stocks. The stock market is often more liquid than the options market because stock traders focus on one commodity, while options traders often have several contracts to select from. An option quote always has the bid price and the asking price indicated on it. These prices do not indicate the actual value of the option. Illiquidity in options trading may result from illiquid stock. It is therefore important to trade options that are derived from a highly liquid stock.

Chapter 15: The Components of an Option Contract

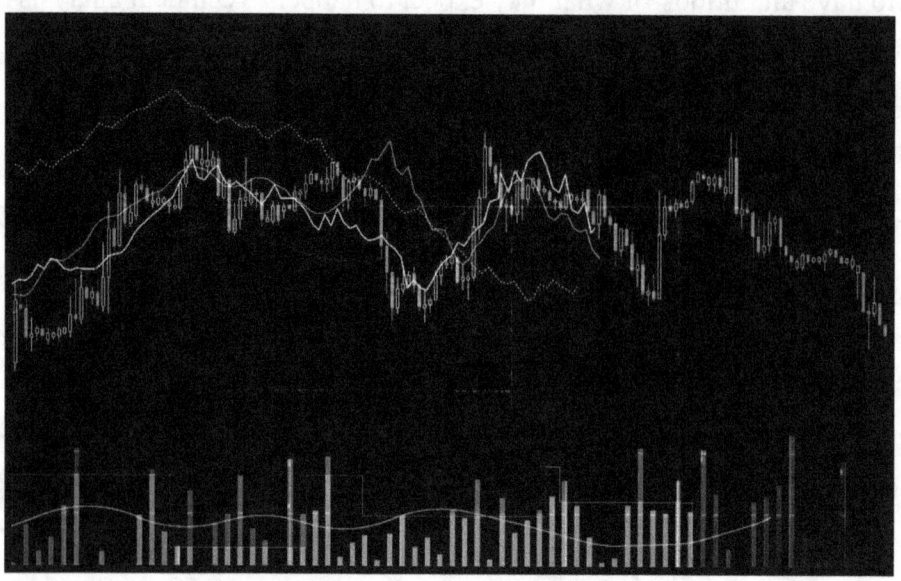

The Role of the Underlying Stock

It's vital to understand that stocks do play a fundamental role in options trading, even though they are not what you are buying and selling. Bear in mind that an option is only a piece of paper that gives you the right to buy or sell that stock–without the stock, you would have nothing to buy or sell.

You might say that the stock is Oz behind the curtain, changing and moving while your attention is fixed elsewhere. Letting Oz get up to his tricks without you is a bad idea–you need to be keeping an eye on your stocks just as much as you do the options themselves.

Not every stock is allowed its options to be traded on an options exchange. In total, you'll find somewhere in the region 3600 stocks spread across 12 different exchanges, though this number changes all the time.

What does this mean? Well, the exchanges have in place some very solid rules that dictate which stocks may and may not participate in options trading. You'll find some of the biggest business names on the planet there, and you'll also find what are known as "penny stocks," which buy and sell for less than $3.

In general, the latter won't do you much good for options trading. There simply isn't enough liquidity in such a small number for you to bother with the effort required to trade on them.

Instead, I would recommend sticking with the big names–the recognizable companies, such as Microsoft, Apple, Google, and McDonald's.

Another point to bear in mind is that there is a fixed relationship between options trading and its underlying stock. One option contract will always equal a hundred stock shares.

In other words, a single contract will give you the right to buy or sell 100 shares (or one stock). Multiply the number of contracts involved in a trade by 100 and you'll know how many shares are also involved.

The third factor of that relationship between an option and its underlying stock: whenever the stock goes up or down, in most cases, so too will the option contract.

Because the two are so inextricably linked, you will need to study the stock market in detail to be whizzing at options trading. You will need to be able to predict which stocks are going to head in which direction and when–only if you get this right will your trading be truly successful.

For that reason, a lot of options traders started with the stock market itself, giving themselves the experience of its whims before taking a step up to the next level. If you haven't done this, it will be worth spending a month or three tradings on the stock market, even a theoretical portfolio that you manage in a folder rather than on your own desktop and never pay a penny to invest in is a helpful step.

Doing this will allow you to get a sense of how the market functions overall and will familiarize you with some of the stocks you might be interested in trading on with options. The best options traders have almost a sixth sense of how an underlying stock is going to perform. The only way to develop that uncanny ability is through exposure, research, and experience.

Understanding the Strike Price

The strike price is the fixed price at which the underlying stock can be either sold or bought. When you purchase a call option, what you are purchasing is the right to buy that stock at this price, while selling a call option means that you are selling the right for your buyer to purchase the stock at that price.

The strike price is an aspect of every options trade that you will want to hone in on every time–it's that important. Never forget that, if the underlying stock never reaches that strike price, the trade is worthless because the option will simply expire on the deadline.

The difference between the current market price of the stock and the strike price of the option also represents the profit-per-share you can expect to make.

Let's say, for example, that you find two trades on a stock that is currently worth $150. One has a strike price of $125 and the other has a strike price of $100.

In the first trade, the stock price will need to drop to $125 before you have the right to buy or sell it (depending on whether the option is a call or a buy). In the second, it will need to drop to $100 before you get that right.

The value of the option is simple to calculate: it's the difference between the strike price and the current worth of the stock. In the first of these examples, the trade has a potential worth of $25; in the second, the potential worth is $50.

At first glance, it would seem to mean that the second option is the one to go for because its value is so much higher. However, you also need to bear in mind that you cannot dictate what the market does.

This is where the risk comes in. How confident are you, in this example, that the stock will plummet $50 before the expiration date of the option? If you're as certain as it's possible to be, it's a great investment. If you're not, you stand to lose the premium you paid for the option, because it will never reach the price at which you have the right to realize the trade.

The trade that has a strike price of $25 is, therefore, a sure bet–it's always going to be more likely that a stock will rise or fall by the smaller amount than the larger one. The trade-off, as you can see, is that you won't make nearly the profit you would on the riskier option, so you have to ask yourself whether the premium you'd be paying is worthwhile.

Strategy for Selling Covered Calls

We've covered the process, but what about the strategy behind it? We looked at the absolute basics of that strategy, but an experienced trader knows there's always going to be more to an option than meets the eye.

There's a whole list of considerations that you will eventually want to bear in mind as you expand your knowledge and develop your own personal strategy. Every trader has a different attitude towards what works and what doesn't–there are plenty of ways to make selling a covered call work, but you'll probably find yourself preferring one or two strategies.

We'll take a look now at those considerations in more detail to guide you as you delve into the covered call more deeply:

The Market Environment

You are no doubt aware that traders of stocks and shares are happy in a bull market and disgruntled in a bear market. You may also know that such traders hate a flat market most of all because very little is happening and there aren't many big profits to be made. For you, as a seller of covered calls, the opposite is true. I highly recommend waiting for the market to temporarily flatten before embarking on a spate of covered call sales. This is because you're only really interested in small changes to your share prices–if they are skyrocketing, you're losing more money on your contract. There also isn't as much danger of the bottom falling out of the market and your stock prices plummeting at the same time, which would be problematic.

Your Underlying Stock

There is nothing more important to your success than choosing the right stocks to invest in the first place. I cannot stress strongly enough that your success will be heightened if you pick stocks that move up very slowly. You don't want stocks that rise and fall very quickly, especially as a beginner, because they have a habit of making surprising moves that ruin your strategy. If they drop too far, you stand to lose a lot of money in the sale; if they rise too high, you lose the money you could have made if you'd sold them at that price. Traders who deal at risk often enjoy these stocks because they have higher premiums and a chance for huge profits, but that goes against the idea of selling covered calls: you're looking for a steady income that will underpin your riskier strategies elsewhere. By all means, go for the riskier stock elsewhere in your strategy, but avoid it like the plague for this particular function.

The Premium

Always remember that the premium is your guaranteed profit. Whatever else happens, you're going to walk away with that cash. When you factor in the cost to list the option and any commission you will lose to your broker, you'll be able to calculate the actual profit you'll make on that premium. Set yourself a minimum premium–a number that you consider to be enough to provide a profit you'll be happy with, on the assumption that it's the only profit you make. When you move ahead on setting the strike price, you'll likely adjust this base figure up or down based on what you think the underlying stock is going to do before the expiration date. Remember that the premium is only one component of the overall profit you will make–if you then set a strike price that means you lose the same amount of cash on selling the shares as you made through the premium, the trade wasn't worth doing in the first place.

The Expiration Date

There's a reason that the premiums on covered calls get higher the further out the expiration date. It's because, much like the weather forecasts we all deride daily, it gets harder and harder to predict what's going to happen to a share price the further out you go. Also bear in mind that your money is going to be tied up until the expiration date, so the premium will increase as a nod to that sacrifice. Most investors believe that a period between a month and three months works best.

The Strike Price

You might think that the strike price you set should be based on what you, as the seller, are comfortable with, but actually, it's the opposite. You're looking for a strike price that your buyer will feel comfortable with because otherwise, they aren't going to buy. That, in turn, is going to be dictated by the expiration date you set, as well as the premium you're asking for and how stable or volatile the underlying stock is. Your best bet is to put yourself in the shoes of your buyer: would you purchase that contract? How much would you stand to gain? Set your strike price accordingly and then take a look at it from your own point of view. Would this be an acceptable profit for you? If so, you've hit the nail on the head.

Chapter 16: How to Start Trading in Options

Would you agree that optional trading is exceptional? Some of you may not agree with this because you are fond of trading in the shares or the currencies which you consider less risky and volatile. How would you feel playing around with a figure which future-oriented? Like a game of chess where you fill a puzzle of uncertainties, it is the same deal with optional trading where you do not know the future. Most of you discredit this trading because you think it is filled with uncertainties. However, with useful speculation of the trade, it will not earn you much of the risk. There are certain things you as a beginner you ought to follow. The following strategies to come up with the right option.

First is that you have to think of your investment objective. You do not go there in the trading aimlessly because you will lose a lot of money. Remember that options require that intelligent speculation because you are dealing with future gains. You have to establish realistic and measurable values that you expect. Such goals will give you a way to go and the route to follow. You may plan which type of optional trading you want. That is where you want the put off option or the call option. Moreover, do you want to speculate on the performance of the underlying asset or hedge out their risks?

You have to examine the risks and the returns that the assets may bring you. Your biggest aim is always to harness sizeable gains while reducing the risks. You think that there are risks in the present and decide to buy them in the future. Or you with the put-up option you predict that the shares will fall in the price and you award others right for protecting their expected depreciation. You have to be tolerant, optimistic, and persistent in your tasks. If you are a risk-taker, this is the right avenue for you. If you sense a volatile market exploit that opportunity to gain much.

Identify the different events of the market of the sector you are trading. Those events will institute the volatility of the occurrence. You can either experience a drift or a rise in the market. Those events can be grouped in two ways, where one is the market-wide, and the other is the stock specif. The market-wide are like those government jurisdictions that affect the economy of the whole sector. For example, the government banning or subsidizing some products. In the stock-specific one, they include issues like product launches and many others.

You have to derive the right strategies after knowing the stocks to trade and the returns you desire. These are distinctive tactics that you will apply to harness many gains. You must be that intelligent speculator who will read the patterns and try to realize the peak points and the volatility of the market. Moreover, device some strategies like selling a call option against the stock. That is a tactic where you exercise a covered call approach on the security that you already own. You must sell the cover calls against your shares to identify the profitable spot. The other strategy is using the bullish or bearish strategy for the call option and the put option, respectively. Always buy puts options on significant stock platforms where you anticipate a substantial fallout of the top players in the industry.

Decide on the right parameter to facilitate your marketing. These are like the variables you will use to make a successful trading. Remember that for this trade, it requires one to know the trend, price analysis, and many other types.

Steps of Optional Trading for a Beginner

The first thing is to identify the right brokerage account. You can do that by researching those that pay well and with the right features. You can still seek recommendations from expert dealers. Check on their websites and create an account by keying in your correct details. Therefore, try to log in where you should remember your password vividly.

When you log in to that platform, you will be asked to select the right trade options you want. By now you should know the firm you want to buy from which you choose. It depends on the brokerage account because you should click on the odder or trade platform after identifying the shares to buy. This page should be clearly labeled, where click on to go to the next phase.

Search for the specific stock you want to buy. If you cannot find it in the list of the many securities, search for it in the search box. There will be multiple displays of the live quotes of shares that are being traded, hence select the one you want to buy. Still, you can navigate on the quote table to identify the primary and the options. Chose those alternatives because they are the reasons you are doing the trading.

Then there is the maturation month option where you must identify the peak times. That expiry period is the point where your contract ends; thus, you should set it according to your potential. The month should be realized when you have studied how the market behaves. You may have discovered that in a particular month the selling of shares is relatively high while in another period they are low. Choose that month that looks productive on your strike index.

Selecting your strike is the second last step. That is the amount of an asset in the predetermined period. It should level up to what you can afford and oversee if it generates good revenue. You should not set the illogical or unrealistic figure just because you want to earn more. Know your potential and the size of your wallet.

Select the put or call options that are found in different columns of the table. Usually, calls are grouped on the left and the puts on the right. Recognize the side you want to venture.

There is a platform for the quantity too. That is where you should fill the number of contracts you want to trade. Moreover, set the price to pay for the option. Check and recheck the orders, when everything is clear now is right for you to confirm and send.

Chapter 17: The Supports and Resistances

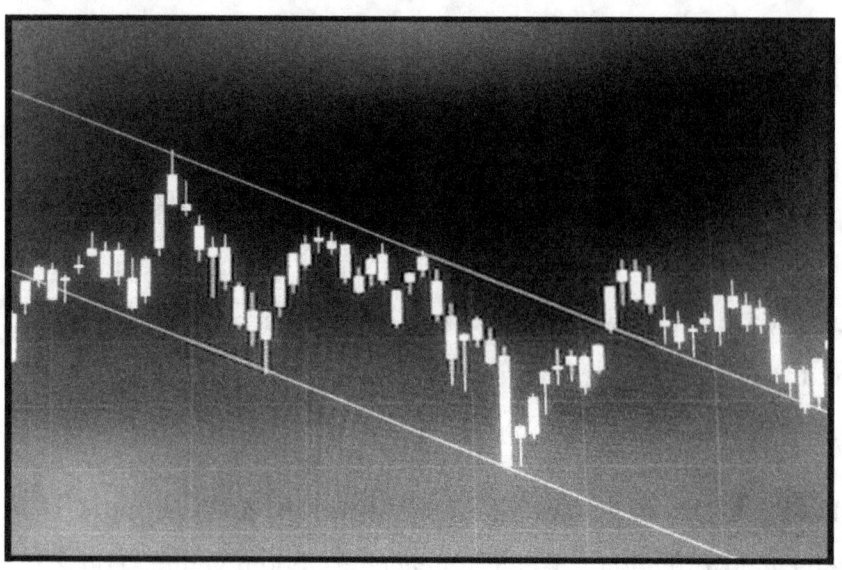

The chart patterns in any kind of trade calls for support and resistance. Whether you are dealing with fired trading, commodities, stocks, futures, or options. In any world of trading, it is the basis of the chart patterns. To understand better what support and resistance mean in the options trade, you can relate to the most common type of trade that is easily accessed by almost everyone because everyone is involved in at least one type of trade in the market.

Let's take an example of a situation where you go to the market to purchase a commodity that you've been using frequently. In this case, you are the bull. This is a product that you like so much and to encourage the seller to restock this product, there's that price that you will support so hard that you don't want it to fall. This is what we refer to as 'Support.' The buyer takes control of the prices and protects it so that it doesn't go down. The reason why the buyer would want to prevent the price from going down to the extreme is because of the fear that the seller would stop bringing the commodity on the market because they won't see its value. This is the concept of support that can be easily understood by anyone.

For resistance, it's the other way round. Here the seller now takes control of the price and prevents it from rising higher. For trading to carry on successfully, the buyer and the seller must agree on a specific price. Raising the price too high may make the bull reconsider an alternative commodity with a lower price depending on the amount of money they would want to spend. On the other hand, the seller would not consider trading at an extremely lower price than what they expect. This is because no one easily accepts a loss. Selling at weird spoils the motive that someone had for participating in the market.

Investors trade depending on the price levels. For instance, someone would prefer to purchase a good when the price of commodities is at a level where it is more likely to shoot after some time. When it happens as per their expectations, then it's a favor on their side because they are going to record again when they resell the commodity. This level where a large number of investors tend to believe that the prices will rise higher is what is known as the support level. It is what determines the decisions made by the majority of investors. When a support level is broken, it changes its worth and becomes the new resistance level.

At the resistance level, the investors always assume that the prices will fall lower. This makes the major investors think otherwise. Those who purchase commodities in bulk when the price is lower and is expected to move higher would not want to proceed to purchase the same commodity when they know that the price is more likely to drop so low that if they go ahead and sell it at that price, they will record a huge loss. Also, when the resistance level is broken, it changes and becomes the new support level.

On many occasions in the market, you will realize what is referred to as 'Noise'. This is when there are errors in pricing making them go beyond limits. The tops and bases of pricing are exceeded which may lead to misunderstanding between the bulls and the bears. However, this is a normal activity in the market and the traders always take care of it to ensure that trade moves on, even though it always brings some disagreements in most cases.

Beginner traders must always understand the concept of support and resistance to enable them to trade successfully without having diverted minds on what they are doing. When they get to understand how the market prices fluctuate with different seasons, they will be in a position to decide which commodity to trade with during what season. The errors associated with market pricing should be clearly understood by the beginner trades to prevent them from getting stranded when the price levels change from time to time.

Someone new to the trading market is sometimes made to believe that when the commodity prices are low, they are definitely meant to rise higher after some time, and this is where they normally get disappointed when the prices fall lower. Normally, the prices go extremely down, and this is always assumed to occur when new goods arrive in the market and replace the old ones.

Buyers and sellers must always agree upon the prices of every commodity. This is because the investors' plans are always different from the plans of any other normal trader. Understanding the level prices is not always easy for beginner traders but once they get used to it, trading becomes easy for them and they find it more comfortable dealing with different clients. Maintaining support levels and resistance levels helps both the bulls and bears to maintain a good trading relationship and remain positive about the results of the trade.

A good support level encourages the investors to invest more in the commodity with the belief that when they will be exchanging this particular commodity at a later date, the market prices will be fair on their side making them earn a reasonable profit. Everyone has a different preference when it comes to trading. Setting a higher resistance level can sometimes make it difficult for the seller to earn the expected profit. This normally happens when the buyers shift to a lower price commodity and let go of yours because it is not affordable to them. This only leads to you

Chapter 18: Risk and Reward

Risk is at the heart of all types of investment as without it there would be a need for reward. As such, options trading is risky at the best of times, even for those who might be considered experts and certainly for those who are still new to the field. Luckily, there are certainly ways to mitigate that risk as many of the major pitfalls of options trading have been well documented by those who have come before. What's more, they have also been distilled down and classified so that all you need to do is memorize the following and ensure that you do your best not to let it intrude on your trading success.

It doesn't matter what type of trade you are working with, the first thing you are going to want to do is to consider three main things. First, you will want to be aware of how much a specific price is likely going to change before the expiration of the option in question. From there, you will want to determine how volatile the underlying asset is as well as how much time the option has to turn you a profit before its expiration. When you are purchasing options, it is important also to identify the direction you expect the underlying stock to move in as well as how long you expect it to continue to move in the specified direction. In these instances, the amount of time that is still available won't be as important when it comes to ensuring the overall maximum value.

To ensure that you minimize risk, it is important to keep in mind that the best strategies are those that focus on either high positive risk value or high negative risk value; there is little value in betting on the middle ground. Remember, some option types are always going to end up being more profitable than others in specific scenarios, you just need to have the patience and the foresight to know what's coming before it gets here. With that being said, however, it is important to always keep in mind that statistical projections cannot actually tell the future which means that any analysis that is done is strictly hypothetical. Never invest more money into a particular trade, no matter how reliable it seems, than you can ultimately afford to lose.

When it comes to making trades in groups, or combining them in other ways, it is important to consider the net risk of the entire trade instead of focusing on the specific risk likelihoods of parts of the whole. This will make it easier for you to determine the most profitable way to move forward at any juncture because it makes the risk/reward split much easier to analyze. Remember, there are multiple different types of risk which means that understanding what each means for your specific trade is crucial to covering all your bases and making successful options trades on a reliable basis.

Delta

Delta can be thought of as the amount of overall risk that you take on depending on how likely the underlying asset in question is going to move before the point where the option expires. If the asset is at the money at the moment, then the delta is going to be .5. What you can take from this is the fact that when the underlying asset moves a single point in either direction then the option will move .5 points. Puts are always going to have a delta of somewhere between -1 and 0 and calls will always have a delta that is somewhere between 1 and 0.

Delta should always be the first type of risk that you consider as it will do the most to help you immediately determine if a specific trade is going to be in your best interest or not. You will find that it is the most helpful when it can be used to make decisions related to puts you are interested in making as it will help make it clear the direction the underlying asset is going to be likely to move in. To determine the delta, you are going to want to start by considering historical data related to the underlying assets by looking at previous strike prices in comparison to their comparable puts. When it comes to measuring delta, it is important to keep in mind that cheaper options are naturally going to have a lower delta. This occurs naturally as delta measures the chance an option will be profitable at expiration. This is why you are going always to want to avoid options with a delta that is either .4 or -.4 because it is rather unlikely that they are going to end up being favorable trades by the time everything is said and done.

Rho

Rho is the name given to the quantity of risk that surrounds the interest rates relating to an underlying asset and the probable that changes in this area will result in changes to the underlying asset price and thus negatively affect the price of the option as well. As a general rule, you can expect interest rates to increase along with call prices, causing a decrease in put values. The reverse of this statement will also be true, causing an increase in put prices and a decrease in interest rates. Rho is going to be the most influential when the price of the underlying asset is greater than or equal to the option price. Calls will always have a positive Rho and puts will always have a negative rho. Rho is going to be relevant primarily to those who are interested in options trading as a form of long-term investment.

Gamma

If delta measures the amount of change that occurs between the underlying asset and the option in question, then gamma measures the likelihood that the delta is going to remain the same as long as the option remains active. The larger the gamma grows, the closer the underlying asset and the related option are likely to be to one another and a smaller gamma means that the variation between them is quite large because the stock has fallen beneath the strike point. Big gammas mean big profits but also larger degrees of risk. Additionally, you will want to keep in mind that the gamma will increase naturally as it gets closer to the point at which the option is going to expire. If you need to know just how much the gamma is likely to increase during this period you can certainly find out, all you need to do is consider the gamma of the gamma.

Theta

Theta is a representation of the rate at which the time the option has left is currently expiring in comparted to how much time it has as a whole. Theta starts as a positive amount that starts to tick down the instant that an option comes into existence. Theta decreases at a steady rate compared to the price of the related option as it is guaranteed to lose value each second it ticks closer to expiration. A trade will remain profitable for the holder as long as the delta remains greater than theta and will make money for the writer once this balance reverses itself.

As an options trader, it is important always to be aware of the fact that theta will constantly be changing, and that this change will increase in frequency the closer the option it is measuring gets to its expiration point. Theta is going to be the most important variable to consider if you are planning to make a trade based on the assumption that the market is not going to change before the options expiration. If this is not the case, then theta will be the least relevant element of risk to your trades as long as you work around it as needed.

Vega

Vega is the type of risk that measures how volatile the underlying asset is compared to the market as a whole. Vega can be difficult to accurately determine at points, simply because it is possible to change although the price of the asset it points to remain neutral during the same period. As such, making a successful options trade doesn't mean being able to avoid Vega completely, it means understanding how to take advantage of it regardless of the level of volatility that is in play.

Different options are going to respond in different ways to increasing Vega; those that respond positively are known as long volatility options and those that respond negatively are called short volatility options. Options that have long volatility will have a positive amount of Vega and short volatility options are going to have a mega Vega. If you find an option with a neutral Vega, then it will have a neutral level of volatility to go along with it.

Chapter 19: Basic Options Strategies Going Long

While it can be easy to feel as though there is too much information out there regarding options trading to ever hope to keep it straight, there are several key strategies you will regularly use that you can focus on at the start to make the entire process far more manageable. As long as you take the time to utilize them correctly, you will find that each of the strategies outlined below will dramatically improve your success rate while decreasing your overall risk at the same time.

Keep in mind that the strategies that you use aren't nearly as important as the fact that you choose strategies that suit your trading style and compliments the trading plan you are focused on using for the time being. Keep in mind that just because a strategy seems useful, doesn't mean it is going to be useful in your hands.

Play name: Married Put

Details: A married put is a great strategy if you have reason to take a bullish attitude towards the price of a given underlying asset while at the same time aiming to shore up any potential losses you might come across. To use this strategy properly, the first thing you will need to do is to purchase any amount of the underlying asset in question while at the same time purchasing a put that covers the same amount. This will act as the price floor that will help you to prevent serious, unexpected losses in the case of a sudden price drop.

While the married put will not be the best choice in any situation, if used in the right way, and with plenty of caution, it can be a reliable way to improve your successful trading percentage successfully. To ensure this always works out in your favor, you will never want to begin a new transaction without having a clear understanding of the risk you are working with beforehand. You will then be able to factor in additional costs more easily and compare the total cost to the amount of risk you are going to mitigate as a result.

After that, all that's left is going to be doing the math and choosing the option that makes the most fiscal sense at the moment. What's more, married puts also help to reduce the risk potential when it comes to early options to exercise as it ensures you always have available shares waiting in the wings.

Play name: Bull Call Spread

Details: To utilize the bull call spread successfully, you will want to start with a call option that is purchased at a strike price that is worth returning to in the future. You will also need to sell an equal number of calls at a strike price that is above the initial strike price yet still within a reasonable distance. Both of these calls will also need to include the same timeframe as well as the same underlying asset. This is an excellent strategy to use if you feel bullish on the strength of the asset in question or you have research that shows the price is likely to increase during your chosen timeframe.

This strategy also goes by the name vertical credit spread thanks to its mismatched legs. Those that sell close to the money result in a credit spread that includes a positive time value and a net credit. Debit spreads are created if a short option ends further away from the money than the point it started from. Regardless, you can consider this strategy a net buy.

Play name: Bear Put Spread

Details: Similar in practice to the bull call spread, the bear put spread is useful under opposite circumstances. To use it effectively, you will need to purchase a pair of put options that have different strike prices, own lower and one higher. You will then need to purchase an equal number with the same timeframe and the same underlying asset. This can be an especially useful strategy if you have a bearish opinion of the underlying asset in question as it will help to limit your losses if you judge the market incorrectly. It is still important to be cautious; however, as the profits that it will bring, you are always going to be limited to the difference between the two puts you initially purchased, minus any relevant fees.

The most profitable time to utilize this strategy is if you are already planning on short selling a specific underlying asset and a traditional put option won't provide you with the protection you need. You will likely find them especially useful if you plan on speculating and also feel that prices are going to decrease. This will allow you to avoid employing additional capital while only waiting for the worst to happen. As such, you will be able to hope for the best and plan for the worst at the same time.

Details: The protective collar strategy can be executed by buying into a put option that is already out of the money. From there, you will then want to write a secondary call option that is based on the same underlying asset and is also out of the money. After that, you will then be able to create one already. Thus, this strategy is useful if you are already committed to a long position on an underlying asset that has a history of strong gains. Using a protective collar properly then allows you to ensure that you can anticipate a steady level of profit while also retaining control of the underlying asset if the positive trend does continue.

Play name: Straddle

Details: The straddle can be used to either go long or short. The long straddle can be extremely effective if you feel as though the price of a given underlying asset is going to move significantly in one direction, you just don't know what direction that will ultimately be. To utilize this strategy, you will need to purchase a put and a call, both using the same underlying asset, strike price, and timeframe, after the long straddle has been created successfully you will be guaranteed to generate a profit if the price in question moves in either direction before it expires.

Play name: Strangle

Details: Functionally, strangle is similar to a straddle except that it is often cheaper to execute on as you are buying into options that are already out of the money. As such, you can typically pay as much as 50 percent of the cost of a straddle for strangling which makes it even easier to play both sides of the fence. Typically, a long strangle is more useful than a short straddle because it offers up twice the premium for the same amount of risk.

To use the long strangle correctly, you will want to purchase a call along with a put that is both based on the same underlying asset with the same timeframe and different strike prices. The strike price for the call will need to be above the strike price for the put and both should be out of the money. This strategy can be especially useful if you plan on the underlying asset moving a great deal without having a clear idea as to the direction. When used properly, this will virtually ensure you turn a profit once you have taken any fees out of the equation.

Play name: Butterfly Spread

Details: A butterfly spread is a combination of a bear spread and a traditional bull strategy that uses a total of three strike points. To begin with, you will need to purchase a call option at the lowest point you can manage before selling a pair of calls at a higher price and then a third call that has an ever-higher price. Your end goal with these purchases is to make sure that you have a range of prices you can profit from when everything is said and done.

This strategy can prove particularly effective when you have a completely neutral opinion on the current market. What's more, you should also expect the underlying asset to move in the direction you favor, even if you don't have all the details locked down just yet. This then means that you will want to strive to keep the market volatility as low as possible. The greater the overall level of volatility, the greater the cost of this strategy will be. Furthermore, it is extremely important to keep in mind that if you choose incorrectly when it comes to the direction the underlying asset is going to move, then the amount you stand to lose can be significant.

Play name: Iron Condor

Details: To utilize the iron condor strategy, you will need to begin by taking a short position as well as a long position via a pair of strangles that is situated so they will take full advantage of a market that is staunchly low volatility. The pair of strangles should include both a long and a short, with both sets to the outer strike price. You can accomplish the same general effect with a pair of credit spreads if you are so inclined. In this scenario, the call spread would be placed above the market price and the put would be placed beneath the current market price.

Play name: Iron Butterfly

Details: The iron butterfly strategy can be anchored by either a short straddle or a long straddle, depending on your needs. Regardless, you will want to then orchestrate strangle based on the straddle you needed to use. The iron butterfly utilizes a mixture of puts and calls to limit the potential for loss (but also profits) around the strike price you formerly determined. This strategy is best used with options that are out of the money as they allow you to minimize both risk and cost.

ROI or Return on Investment

The Term ROI stands for Return on Investment. ROI is a measure of performance and is used by both investors and traders to measure the effectiveness and efficiency of an investment. This includes your trading capital. ROI deliberately endeavors to measure directly the total return derived from a particular investment.

One of the most important aspects of your investment portfolio is its profitability. You need to regularly monitor your investments, which are best achieved using the ROI or return on investment. It is advisable to work out what each dollar invested has generated. There is a formula for working out this figure.

R.O.I = (Profits - Costs) / Costs

Even then, investors need to understand that the ROI depends on numerous other factors such as the kind of investment security preferred and so on. Also, note that a high ROI implies a higher risk, while a lower figure means reduced risk. For this reason, appropriate risk management must be undertaken.

A Brief Introduction to Technical Analysis

What is technical analysis? It is simply a method used by traders, investors, and other market players to examine and predict price movements in the markets. Technical analysis makes use of market statistics as well as historic chart prices. The idea behind this type of analysis is that identifying past market performance can help to accurately predict future performance.

As a trader, you want to be able to identify the shares to trade, the best entry points, volumes, price, and the best exit points. The best way to find out information about all these is through technical analysis.

Two Different Approaches

According to finance experts, there are two basic approaches to technical analysis. These are the top-down approach and the bottom-up approach. In most cases, short-term traders will opt for the top-down approach, while long-term investors prefer the bottom-up approach.

Chapter 20: Choosing a Broker

Brokers and Trading Platforms

The use of shares, whether it is to collect dividends or to speculate on their listing, is an increasingly widespread and interesting practice. The risk of loss is always present but depending on the way you buy and sell your shares; this risk can be reduced. If you are wondering how to buy and sell the shares of large, listed companies online, here are some explanations that may interest you.

Buy shares to become shareholders

A large part of private individuals and institutions that buy stocks do so to become shareholders.

It is the simplest use of actions and their main purpose.

In fact, when a company issues its shares, it is possible to buy them directly online.

However, for the already listed shares to do so, it is necessary to go through an intermediary, which can be an online broker or an online bank.

Buy and Sell Shares with Online Banks

The easiest way to buy and sell shares is to go through one of the placement products offered by banks and, in particular, by online banks. Thanks to the 100% online operation of these banks, you can easily pass your purchase and sale orders directly via the internet without moving.

The advantages of this system are numerous because it is your bank that will take care of executing your orders and then buying and selling your shares. To take advantage of stock market shares through these systems, you must underwrite an Investment Plan in Shares, a securities account, or life insurance, which are the main banking products on the stock market. The only drawback of this method concerns the expenses that may be higher than those that you would have to pay if you bought and sold the shares yourself.

However, bank commissions rarely exceed 4%.

One of the main advantages of bank placement products is that market intermediaries supervise your purchases and sales of shares and you can benefit from advice.

Buy and sell shares with online brokers

Another method is to contact an online mediator. Their operation is almost identical to that of online banks, with the difference that you do not enjoy assistance and advice, but at the same time, the costs are lower because you decide for yourself what actions to buy or sell.

These online brokers also allow trading through stock market shares, without actually having to buy them. To do this, you just need to speculate on the evolution of their value. The tools that allow you to proceed in this way are CFDs.

Ultimately there are several methods to buy and sell shares on the internet. Before deciding on one or other of these solutions, take care to correctly evaluate the commissions involved as well as your level of knowledge on the stock exchange. Depending on these criteria, each of these two methods has different advantages. It is also good to understand the quotation system of an action to be able to speculate on this type of asset.

Choosing and using a financially sound and responsive brokerage should be a high priority for every trader. And that brokerage should provide access to every trading venue: equities, options, futures, or forex. Many brokerages are running slick TV ads that do not qualify. When you examine the list of financial products served by brokerages, you may be disappointed. Some well-known brokerages support stocks and options. But they do not offer futures or foreign exchange. So, walk away and keep looking.

Many who are new to trading select a brokerage because they know someone who has an account with that particular brokerage. But this is not how you should choose your brokerage, particularly if you are an entry-level trader. Conduct some research before you make a final decision. You want to choose a brokerage that fits your investment and trading style. This may not be the same as your friend's.

Fortunately, you can use the Internet to evaluate brokerages. A website provided by the Financial Industry Regulatory Authority (FINRA) provides a substantial amount of information about the conduct of both individuals and firms. Of course, it essentially lists regulatory citations, and never makes recommendations or posts complimentary comments. The listed regulatory citations are mostly for failures in oversight or careless trading practices. Corresponding fines are also listed. You can read these to find FINRA citations similar to the following:

This permits you to see a list of former employers, the time a counselor has been working with financial securities, and any past FINRA citations that may exist.

Charts like these never tell the entire story. And like so much Internet content, they are often misleading. The range of securities supported in addition to the sophistication of the trading platforms was ignored. The Kiplinger rankings are far from accurate when you consider the breadth of services, platform technologies, number of branch offices, availability and quality of customer support, and more.

In the author's opinion, TD Ameritrade's thinkorswim platform would rank #1 for trading options and stocks. It has the most extensive feature set. And Trade Station, which is superior to many of those listed, wasn't even included. Furthermore, a trade that costs $0.0050/share looks good at first glance. But a 4,000-share trade costs $20 in commissions. Most experienced investors know brokerages will likely reduce their commissions and exchange fees to meet competition. This is especially true for high-net-worth clients and/or high-volume active traders.

Full-Service and Discount Brokers

Full-service brokers typically provide financial investment counselors. The counselors may suggest financial securities products, managed funds, or recommend investment management companies with which they maintain business relationships. These full-service brokerages also provide research and education to their clients. The fees charged by full-service brokers are usually higher than those charged by discount brokers. Required minimum account deposits may also be higher than those required at discount brokerages. Besides, the maintenance of a minimum account balance may be required.

Discount brokerages also require a minimum account deposit and the maintenance of a minimum account balance. This can range from $500 to $1,000. And experienced active traders who manage their own trading activity have little interest in receiving trading advice from an investment counselor, who may not have as much trading experience or knowledge as their clients.

Many old-timers have clear recollections of their dealings with the traditional brick and mortar brokerage houses and the so-called "stockbrokers" in their employ. They'd look at the lists of stocks in the daily news or the Wall Street Journal. When they spotted a trade opportunity, they'd phone their broker to put on a trade, and pay a $70 commission. They also remember receiving phone calls from their broker who had been advised by the "boys in New York" to solicit their clients to buy shares of stock that were part of an issue that their brokerage house was promoting. Some clients wised up and referred to these stocks as the "stock de jour."

This was an unscrupulous "pump and dump" practice used by brokerages to increase the sales of an underlying stock held within the brokerage's own portfolio. Once the solicitations drove the price up as a result of the sudden influx of buy orders, the brokerage dumped the stock for a profit, leaving their clients "holding the bag." Obviously, they couldn't do this every day, and it didn't take long for regulatory agencies and clients alike to catch on. But according to many, this actually happened. Today, the regulatory agencies watch for these kinds of practices and levy heavy fines when detected.

But stories like these often drive traders to the discount brokerages. All an experienced trader wants or needs for that matter is access to the market through a full-featured, reliable trading platform, reasonable commissions and exchange fees, and fast execution times.

Develop a checklist that evaluates prospective brokerages. Look for the following, arranged in no particular order:

- Account types (Brokerage, IRA Rollovers, checking, bill pay, savings, money market, etc.)
- Minimum balance requirement.
- Transaction fees.
- Margin interest rate.
- Supported trading venues (equities, options, futures, and/or forex)
- Execution speed.
- Access to different trading venues.
- Trading platforms (online for PCs and/or Macintosh Computers)
- Trade scanning engine(s).
- Market research (either web-based or trading platform-based)
- Account access via brokerage website.
- Trading via brokerage website.
- Earnings and dividend releases.
- Mobile trading apps (iPhone, Android, iPad, Android Tablets, Windows Mobile)
- Paper (simulated) trading for practice.
- Back trades (testing strategies with historical pricing data)
- Support (online chat, telephone, e-mail, and text messaging)
- Training (live and/or online)
- Complete financial reporting (monthly, year-to-date, prior years, 1099s, IRA minimum required distribution calculations, commissions paid, margin fees, etc.)

- Nearby branch offices.

Financial Security and Stability

When opening an account, you may want to know who is underwriting the security of your account in addition to the maximum amount protected. Congressional action in 1970 requires all brokerages to register with the Securities Investor Protection Corporation (SIPC). The SIPC is to brokerages what the FDIC is to banks. The SIPC protects the brokerage accounts of each customer. If the brokerage firm is closed due to bankruptcy or fraud, the SIPC protects customer assets up to $500,000 in securities and $100,000 in cash. If your accounts exceed these insured values, you may want to consider distributing your funds across more than one brokerage, although very few investors actually do this.

Although the SIPC protects against bankruptcy and fraud, it doesn't protect against market losses caused by a decline in security values. If a brokerage firm does fail, the SIPC works to merge the failed brokerage into a successful one. Failing this, the SIPC will transfer a client's securities to another firm. If stocks or bonds are missing from an investor's portfolio, the SIPC will rebuild portfolios by replacing every missing share of stock or bond, penny for penny, up to the insured limits.

Many investors never consider what can happen to their account holdings in the event of a run on the financial markets or an institution. What effect can this have on the stability of your broker, also called broker-dealer?

It's somewhat reassuring to know that during such condition's insurance is extended and liquidity facilities are created to back depositor accounts. The Securities and Exchange Commission (SEC) has instituted several reforms on liquidity. These liquidity reforms ensure that each broker-dealer maintains a suitable reserve to cope with inordinate levels of client withdrawals.

Despite these regulations, short-term unstable funding can prevent broker-dealers from order fulfillment. This can be due to a short-term lack of funds required to carry temporary imbalances in the volume of buy and sell orders. This impairs the ability of traders to buy and sell a wide variety of stocks and bonds. It can also have the effect of bringing trading to an abrupt halt.

Many investor-traders remember the failures of broker-dealers Lehman Brothers and Bear-Sterns during the housing mortgage fiasco of 2008. As a result of the lessons learned then, many broker-dealers have increased their capital holdings, increased liquidity, and reduced their holdings in risky assets. All of these policies are attempts to protect themselves against the reoccurrence of events like those that brought down these huge brokerage houses.

As the holder of a brokerage account, you should know that the potential for broker-dealer failures still exists. Both broker-dealers and banks have been encouraged to form either asset-rich bank holding companies or intermediate holding companies to help spread capital risk.

Broker-dealers typically find short-term security by negotiating repurchase agreements with underwriters, such as money market funds. This provides the financing needed by broker-dealers to fund their transactions. In exchange, the underwriters receive reasonably low financing fees. The money market funds, among a few others, avoid long-term, risky securities. They happily settle for shorter-term, low-risk securities with less vulnerability to a potential market run.

Chapter 21: Strangles and Straddles

Options allow you to create strategies that simply are not possible when investing in stocks. There are two ways that you can do this, they are known as strangles and straddles. This is a more complex strategy than simply buying a long call option or a long put. But it's not really that complicated, you just have to understand some basics on how to set them up to make a profit.

The strategy that is used in this case is dependent on a large move by the stock. There are many situations where this might be appropriate. But mainly, this is something you will consider using when you are looking to profit from an earnings call.

Earnings calls cause major price shifts in the big stocks. The price shift is largely determined by what the analyst's "expectations" are for earnings, and so this is not always a rational process. If the company beats the analyst expectations when it comes to earnings per share, this creates a positive "surprise" that will usually send the stock soaring. The amount of "surprise" is given by the percentage difference between the actual value and the expected value. So, in this case, if you had bought a call option, you could make amazing levels of profit from the option by selling it in the next day or two, as long as the new higher price level is maintained.

But the problem is, you have no idea beforehand whether the earnings are going to exceed or fail to meet the analyst expectations. The silly thing about this (from a common-sense perspective) is that even if the company is profitable if they fail to meet analyst expectations, these results in massive disappointment. So, you might see share prices drop from a sell-off even if the company is profitable. This is "surprise" in a negative way.

The impact of failing to meet expectations can be magnified if the company also has some bad news to share. This news hit Netflix stock hard, it dropped by a walloping $42. If you had purchased a put option, that could have meant a $4000 profit.

The problem is that you don't know ahead of time which way the stock is going to go. It's one thing to look back and say well you could have had a put option and made $4k in a day, but often companies reveal information in earnings calls that have been under wraps. Nobody had any inkling that Netflix was going to be losing subscribers until the earnings call.

Second, analyst expectations are somewhat arbitrary. Defining success or failure in terms of them is actually pretty silly, but that is the way things work right now. But the point is it's really impossible to know whether or not these arbitrary expectations are met before the earnings call. It's also impossible to gauge the level of reaction that is going to be seen from exceeding or failing to meet expectations.

Since we don't know which way the stock is going to move, it would seem that a good strategy to use is to buy a call and a put at the same time. That is precisely the idea behind a straddle and strangle.

That way, you profit no matter what happens, as long as the price on the market changes fairly strongly in one direction or another. When you set up a straddle or strangle, there is a middle "red zone" that bounds the current share price over which you are going to lose money. But if the share price either goes above the boundaries of this zone or below it, you will make profits.

If the stock shoots upward, this means that the put option is going to drop massively in value. So, it's basically a write off for you. But if the stock makes a strong move, as they often do after positive earnings calls, you stand to make enough profits from the call option that was a part of your trade to more than make up for the loss of the put. The potential upside gain is in theory unlimited. Of course, in practice, share prices don't rise without limit, but they might rise, $10, $20, or $40, and that could potentially earn profits of roughly $1,000-$4,000, more than covering any loss from the now worthless put option.

The opposite situation applies as well. If the stock drops by a large amount, you make profits. Profits to the downside are capped because a stock price cannot decline below zero. That said, if the stock drops by a significant amount, you can still make hundreds to thousands of dollars per contract virtually overnight.

Doing this requires some attention on your part. You are going to have to think ahead to implement this strategy and profit from it. Remember that you can use a straddle or strangle any time that you think the stock is going to make a major shift one way or the other. An example of a non-earning season situation, where this could be a useful strategy, would be a new product announcement. Think Apple. If Apple is having one of their big presentations, if the new phone that comes out disappoints the analysts, share prices are probably going to drop by a large amount. On the other hand, if it ends up surprising viewers with a lot of new features that make it the must-have phone again, this will send Apple stock soaring.

The problem here is you really don't know which way it's going to go. There are going to be leaks and rumors but basing your trading decisions on that is probably not a good approach, often, the rumors are wrong. A strangle or straddle allows you to avoid that kind of situation and make money either way.

Other situations that could make this useful include changes in management or any political interaction. We mentioned the government recently made a privacy settlement with Facebook. If you knew when the settlement was going to occur but wasn't sure what it was going to be, using strangle or straddle might be a good way to earn money from the large price moves that were sure to follow.

The same events that might warrant buying a long call such as a GDP number or jobs report, for options on index funds, are also appropriate for strangles and straddles.

Implied Volatility Strategy

Implied volatility is very important when a big event like an earnings report is coming. This gives you a way to make profits. In fact, we are going to call this the implied volatility strategy.

Remember, implied volatility is a projection of what the volatility of the stock is going to be in the near future. When there is an earnings call, the volatility is going to be extreme on the day after the call. Therefore, you are going to see the implied volatility growing as earnings day approaches.

At the time I am writing this, it is 24 hours before Facebook's earnings call. The implied volatility is 74%, which is very high. In contrast, for Apple, which is more than a week away from its next earnings call, the implied volatility is only 34%. This is for a $207.50 strike put, with a share price of $207.9.

The strategy is to profit from the implied volatility. You want to enter your position one to two weeks before the earnings call or big announcement. As implied volatility increases, this is going to swamp out time decay and cause a big rise in the option price.

Using that Apple put option if we assumed that there were only 4 days to expiration, but the implied volatility had risen to about where Facebook is and there were no other changes (so we will leave the share price where it was), the price of the put option would increase by about $330.

So if nothing else, you could profit from the change of implied volatility. It will probably go highest the day before the earnings call.

This is going to be magnified if you trade a strangle or straddle. Before the earnings call, both the put and the call option are going to increase a great deal in value because of implied volatility. So you could sell the strangle the day before the earnings call and book some profits then. Since a strangle or straddle can earn big profits if there is a large move in the share price, you won't find any problems locating a buyer.

Estimating Price from Implied Volatility

If you know the implied volatility, you can estimate the price range of the stock. This can be done using a simple formula.

(Stock price x implied volatility)/SQRT (days in a year)

If you don't want to do the calculation, if we take the square root of 365, it is about 19.1. For example, we use Facebook with a share price of $202.50 and an implied volatility of 76%.

Facebook	
Stock Price	$202.50
Implied Vol.	0.76
Days in a year	19.1049732
Expected Change	$8.06
Upper Range	$210.56
Lower Range	$194.44

The implied volatility gives us an idea of what traders are thinking, about the upcoming earnings call, but of course, we can never be sure what is really going to happen until it does. But this gives us upper and lower bounds. Using the information that we have available, we can guess that Facebook might rise to $210.56 a share after the earnings call, or it might drop to $194.44 per share after the earnings call. You can use these boundaries to set up your strategy. However, remember that if there is a big surprise, it can go well past these boundary points in one direction or the other.

What is a Long Straddle?

To set up a straddle, you buy a put option and a call option simultaneously (buy = take a long position). The maximum loss that you can incur is the sum of the cost to buy the call option plus the sum of the cost to buy the put option. This loss is incurred when you enter the trade.

With a straddle, you buy a call option and a put option together. And they would be with the same strike price. By necessity, this means that one option is going to be in the money and one option is going to be out of the money. When approaching an earnings call, the prices can be kind of steep, because you want to price them close to the current share price. That way, it gives us some room to profit either way the stock price moves.

A maximum loss is only incurred if you hold the position to expiration. You can always choose to sell it early if it looks like it's not going to work out and take a loss that is less than the maximum.

Chapter 22: How to Profit from Trading Options

Making money from trading options is rather straightforward. However, it largely depends on your understanding of the market. Thus, it is paramount that you get the proper know-how. As you gain more knowledge and experience, you'll be able to make more and more consistent profits.

Now, it's important to note that options naturally lose value over time. This is called "time decay." Therefore, time decay is proportionally inverse to the expiration of the contract. So, options contracts are more valuable the more time have before they expire. The reasoning behind this is that a contract that is very close to expiration does not provide the holder enough time to maneuver. In contrast, a contract that has plenty of time left on it can provide the holder with room to maneuver.

Let's look at an example.

A put option is valued at $100. This option is for 100 shares of a corporation valued at $1 apiece. Please keep in mind that the standard for options contracts is 100-share lots. So, if you wanted to purchase 500 shares, you could take out five 100-share contracts. Since the stock in question is highly coveted, the writer agrees to the deal while charging a premium of $0.10 per share. Thus, the total premium paid would be $10. Additionally, the contract is a one-month expiration.

On day one, the contract is worth $10, that is, the full premium that was paid for it. So, if you wanted to turn around and sell your rights, you could easily collect the $10. But if you decided to sell your rights on day 15, the contract would be worth roughly half of what you paid for it.

How so?

The contract only has half of its term left on it. So, it makes sense for a third party to pay only half of the premium. Now, suppose you tried to sell on day 27 or 28, you could reasonably expect to collect only a fraction of the original premium's value.

This is where savvy options traders can make money.

Savvy options traders like to scour the market to find contracts that are close to expiration. Then, they bid for the rights of the contract at a fraction of the original cost. The angle here is to pick up a cheap contract that provides an opportunity to pick up stock at a price point that's better than its current market valuation.

In the case of a call option, investors might be looking to buy shares at a lower price. However, there are none to be found. So, scouring the market for cheap options are a good alternative. If the opportunity is present, then a deal can be made.

Conversely, an investor might be looking to sell their shares. However, the current market valuation does not seem appealing. Hence, a put option makes sense. The investor purchases the rights to a contract at a reduced price and then sells the stock.

Consequently, time decay opens up the door for options traders to make money in two ways. Let's take the time now to explore these alternatives.

Buy Low, Sell High

In this strategy, investors use options to find shares at the desired price point. This means either taking out the option themselves or finding other parties willing to sell their rights. In either case, investors are looking to pick stocks at a much more favorable price.

Investors approach this strategy in one of two ways. Firstly, they go searching for open contracts on a specific stock. For example, investors search for open contracts on Apple or Microsoft stock. If they find them at their desired price point, they'll scoop them up. Secondly, investors search for open contracts in hopes of finding a good deal. Here, the company itself is not the target. Instead, the target is the contract itself. The company then becomes a secondary target. Naturally, if the company is not worth the risk, then it makes sense to pass on the contract.

So, let's explore how investors stand to profit under this approach.

Scenario #1:

An investor is interested in purchasing stock in a company. This company's current share price sits at $12.50 per share. As such, the investor looks for options to find a lower price point for the stock. The investor finds an open contract for the stock at $12 per share. The contract has a premium of $5 with 10 days remaining on a 30-day expiration. The investor purchases the rights to the contract for $2. Then, executes the contract. The investor gets the shares at $12 apiece. Then, they turn around and sell the stock at the current market valuation. They profit $0.50 per share minus the cost of the premium.

Scenario #2:

An investor is bargain hunting. They find an option that's about to expire. This is a call on a corporation that is currently valued at $13 a share. The option has a strike price of $12.75. The contract was two days left on its duration. So, the investor scoops up the contract for a fraction of its original value. Since the stock is currently valued above the strike price, the investor sees the potential for a quick profit. So, they scoop up the call paying a modest premium. Then, they immediately exercise the option. Once they have bought the stock at $12.75, they promptly sell at $13. The profit is $0.25 per share minus the premium.

In both of these scenarios, the investor needs to move quickly. The investor is keen on time. They know that acting quickly will maximize gains. Unlike the traditional "buy and hold" strategy, the "buy low, sell high" strategy requires investors to act fact. Otherwise, market shifts may zap their profits altogether. As such, the investor needs to take advantage of an expiring option while also cashing in on the current market valuation.

Using Options for Speculative Purposes

In the stock market, speculation is like gambling. Investors make bets on what they hope will or will not happen. In such cases, investors can use options contracts to place their bets. Options provide investors with the opportunity to make risky deals without exposing themselves to unwanted consequences.

Speculation consists of what you, as an investor, believe will happen even when you are not sure, if or when it will actually take place. When speculators hit a home run, they clean up. When they strike out, they can be wiped out.

Let's consider an example.

A corporation's stock is currently trading at $16 a share. Historically, this company's stock has traded between $14 to $17 a share. However, investors are anticipating a breakout as the company is set to unveil a new product line. If all goes well, the company's stock will soar. As such, investors are looking to get in now before the stock takes off for the moon.

So, investors are prepared to get in now. However, there is no telling when the price will take off. Buying the stock now and waiting for it to take off would imply using the buy and hold strategy. However, investors are never willing to tie up their money for longer than absolutely necessary. Consequently, investors can use options to both buy and sell stocks.

In this example, an investor can use a combination of call and put options. For example, the investor can use a call option to buy the stock at $16 and sell at $20. But here's the tricky part. It is unclear when the stock will take off, and most importantly, it is not clear if the stock will take off at all.

A savvy speculator purchases the options contracts to ensure that they will hedge their position. That way, they won't commit their money without being sure of what will happen. If the stock doesn't take off, the investor doesn't have to exercise any of the options. If anything, they will simply lose the money on the premiums. This is a small change compared to getting wiped out on a downturn. However, if the deal goes as expected, the profits will easily offset the cost of the contracts.

This is the reason why speculators live and die by their options. Since they clearly understand the way that options work, they can leverage them to their advantage. Moreover, if you plan to plan the speculation game, then you must use options in your favor. Otherwise, using the buy and hold strategy on long shots will cause you to miss a lot of opportunities. It is worth noting that the buy and hold strategy is great for blue-chip stocks, that is, companies that are certain to perform at or beyond expectations. Since these stocks are highly coveted, you can be sure that you can sell them at any time. Thus, they are the closest thing you'll find to a sure bet. Anything that isn't considered as blue-chip would best be treated as a speculative investment. Therefore, options must become your go-to option.

Writing Contracts

Writing options contracts is an alternative best employed by seasoned traders. The reason for this is that writers must have stock and/or cash on hand. Writing options can be attractive for investors and traders as most contracts are often unused. This means that you can basically keep the premium contract holders pay. However, you cannot assume that the contract will go unused. You must always assume the contract will be used. That way, you need to be ready. Otherwise, you'll run into trouble.

There are two ways in which you can make money as an options writer. The first is to agree with another party beforehand. That way, you draft up the contract based on the specific agreement you have with the counterparty. This type of arrangement is quite common with exotic options. The second way is to write up a contract and put it out there. That way, other investors can come along and buy it from you. To make that work, you need to look for the right terms. Often that means making the contract attractive so that other traders find value in it.

For example, you are holding stock in a corporation. As such, you are looking to sell it. In that case, you can write a call option. A buyer that's interested in purchasing stock in that corporation will find it and buy the rights. If the premium you have assigned makes sense to the buyer, then you have a deal. If the buyer exercises the contract, then you make the transaction.

So, please bear in mind that when you write the contract, you don't have the right to exercise it. You sell that right to the other party. That's why you can't assume that it won't be exercised. You must always assume it will be.

Also, you can write a put option. In this case, you are looking to buy stock in a company. You write up the contract and then an interested party will buy the rights. That gives them the option to sell you the stock if they choose to. That means you must be ready to pay for the stock in case the contract is exercised.

Chapter 23: Options Strategies

The next thing we need to look at is some of the different strategies you can use when you want to trade-in options. Everyone needs to enter the market with some good strategies ahead of time. This makes it easier for them to make sure they enter the market at the right times, and that they can pick the right times to exit the market as well.

The Long Call

This is a strategy that bets the asset will rise above the strike price before the expiration date. If you look at the underlying asset and the market and you think the price will rise before the options contract ends, then the long call is a good one to use.

If you do this call well, then the upside on this call can provide you with an infinite number of profits until the expiration, as long as that asset sees an increase in the price. Even if you see that the stock is moving in the wrong way, it is possible to salvage at least part of the premium that you have by selling the call before it expires. The downside is a complete loss of the premium paid if the stock does not go up or if it starts to go down, but this is less risky than purchasing the stock outright.

The Long Put

The long put is going to be worth the most when you see the stock reaches $0 per share, so the maximal value will be the strike price times 100 times the number of contracts that you decide to do. You also get the benefit that if the price of the asset goes up, you can still sell the put and then save up some of the premium, as long as you still have a bit of time before your expiration. The most you can lose is all the loss of your premium based on how much you spend.

The reason that we want to use this one is that the long put is a good way to wager on the asset declining. If you can stomach that you may potentially lose the whole premium, you can do this one. If you do see a big decline in that asset, then you will earn more with the puts than you would by short selling that stock.

The Short Put

The short put is basically seen as the opposite of the long put. The investor will sell their put, or they will go short. With this one, the investor is betting that the stock will stay flat, or it will continue to rise until it reaches the expiration date. Remember that with this one, the other person is betting the price will go down and you hope it doesn't. Like the long call, this short put can be a wager on a stock rising, but it has some big differences that go along with it.

While a long call will bet that there will be a big increase in the value of a stock or other asset, the short put is going to be more modest and can pay off more modestly, though it can work in some situations.

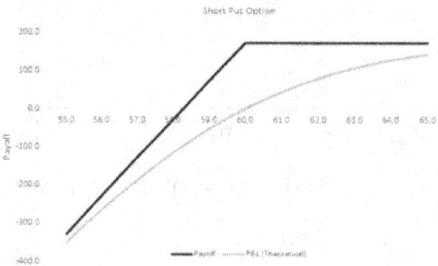

Covered Calls

The first thing that we want to look at is the covered call. This is a good strategy because it will help to reduce your risks of being all alone on a stock that is long while making sure you can get some income in the process.

The trade-off that we will get with this one is that you need to be willing to sell off the shares you have at a price that is set, which will be the short strike price. Not sticking with this will cause you to lose money in the process. To help you execute this one, you need to purchase the underlying stock on the options contract, just like we talked about before. Then at the same time, we need to write, or sell, one of the call options on that exact same share.

Married Put

We can then move on to the second type of strategy that we can use within our options, and this one is known as the married put. In this strategy, the investor will purchase an asset, such as some shares of a chosen stock. And then, at the same time, they will purchase the put options for the same number of shares in that same stock. The holder of the put option will then have the right to sell, within the time limits of the option, to sell the stock using that strike price, no matter what the value of the stock is all about.

The reason that you, as an investor, would use this one is that it can help to protect them against any downside risk when they hold onto the stock. Then this strategy will work just like an insurance policy and will help to establish the price floor if the price of the stock decides that it wants to turn and fall quickly.

Bull Call Spread

Now we can move on to a great strategy to learn about because it works well with options and in the stock market if you decide to purchase the stocks outright. With this strategy, known as the bull call, spread, the investor is going to buy calls of an asset at a specific strike price, and then at the same time they will also buy the same number of calls, but at a higher strike price. Both of these will come with the same asset, so don't try to do it with two different ones, and they will have the same expiration with them.

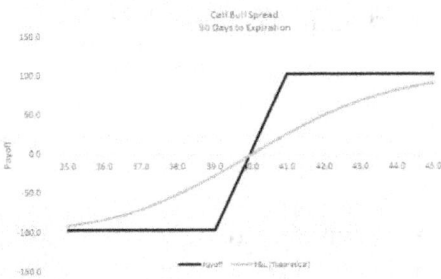

Bear Put Spread

We spent some time talking about the bull call spread and how to use it when we think the market is bullish. But there are times when the market will go in the opposite direction, and we will end up with a bearish market instead. This is why working with a bear put spread could be the best option to help you out here.

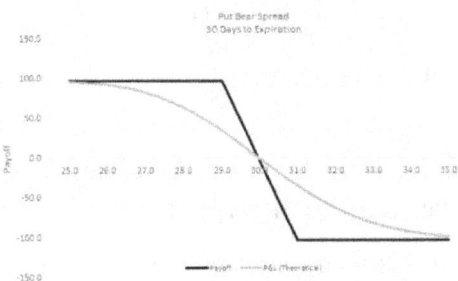

Protective Collar

Sometimes it is a good idea to find ways to protect yourself in the market. It would be nice if the stock market, or any other underlying asset that you use with options, would follow a pattern that made sense and always stayed the same. But if that happened, then everyone would get into the market, and you would not be able to make the money that you want. The good news is the protective collar strategy will be able to help you get this done, ensuring you are protected in the market.

The Long Straddle

You can't look much at the world of investing without looking at some of the straddle options that are out there. This is a great strategy that you can use that will provide you with lots of choices and can make it easier for you to stay protected and make as much money as possible. And we are going to spend some time looking at how to complete what is known as a long straddle.

The long straddle strategy will be one where the investor can purchase the put and the call option at the same time. You want to do this with the same asset underneath the option, with the same strike price and the same expiration date. Everything has to be the same on this one, except that you do one put option and one call option.

The Long Strangle

In the long strangle strategy, the investor will spend their time working on an out of the money call option, while also going through and doing an out of the money put option at the same time. We need to make sure the underlying asset of both is the same and that we keep the expiration date the same as well. This can help you to protect yourself if you are not certain which direction the market will go.

Long Call Butterfly Spread

This is a fun one that allows you to stay in the market a bit longer and can make it easier for you to really see some results with what you are doing here. However, we have to make sure that we use it well and that we are getting in and out at the right parts along the way. The strategy we will talk about here is known as a long call butterfly spread.

All of the other strategies we have taken a look at so far in this guidebook were a combination of two contracts or two positions. With this one, though, we will want to use the call options. With this one, the investor will combine both the bear spread and the bull spread strategies that were earlier in this guidebook. You would also need to make sure you work with three strike prices that are different. You will still stick with the same expiration date and the same underlying assets along the way to make this happen.

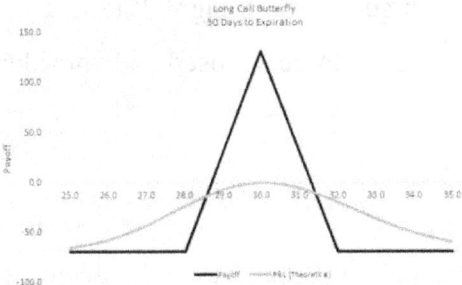

Iron Condor

The next choice that we are going to add to our list is known as the iron condor. This one is really interesting and allows us to work on a lot of different things at once to see some results.

The way to construct the iron condor is to sell one of your out of the money puts, and then we go through the process of selling one out of the money call while also buying one out of the money call, making sure we do this last one at a higher strike price.

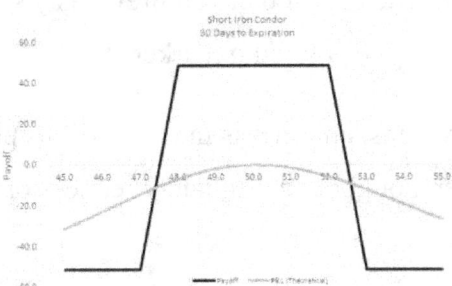

Iron Butterfly Strategy

Then it is time to move on to a strategy that is known as the iron butterfly strategy. We talked about the iron condor and the butterfly spread, so now we get to have some fun and work with the strategy of the iron butterfly. To make this one work, the investor will need to sell one of them at the money puts, and then they can buy an out of the money put, while also taking the time to sell one of them at the money calls and purchasing an out of the money call. This is a lot of steps, so make sure you really know the market and how it is supposed to work before you start.

Chapter 24: Successful Trading Tactics

One successful essential thing and another successful thing will lead to a successful outcome. Let's get acquainted with some of the ways we need to be exposed and consider how our options transactions can be successful.

Which Trade is Profitable?

There are several basic types of options trading that a novice and even experienced investors should know and master their options trading that will bring a lot of profit. Here are some of the cost-effective ways.

1. Buy to open. This requires the initiation of a new order to secure the new option and final improvement of the existing trading position, as assessed based on previous trading activities.

2. Sell to open. Selling for opening means selling a specific option that you do not necessarily have and eventually gaining a new position or an improved position in your options trading business.

3. Buying to close. This is buying a specific option that you previously sold on the market, and ultimately reducing your position in the options trading market.

4. Closed sale. In these types of transactions, an order is made to sell a specific option in which everything you sell has previously been bought and ultimately reduces or leaves the existing position in the transaction market.

How to Be a Thriving Option Investor

Below are some ways in which we can shine in this options trading field.

1. Risk management. Life itself is a risk, which means that risk will always be presented. The option trader must master all possible ways to minimize the number of risks that may arise and learn from each of them for proper future management. For example, in the capital sector, the entrepreneur should have an extensive plan with detailed information on the strict use of capital. Losses are also part of the consequences of trading options, and with poor capital handling, everything can fall over. Think about how lousy market volatility can be, which leads to large amounts of capital and substantial losses.

2. Be the boss in numbers. Options trading involves extensive use of names. Do you know the implied volatility? Is money an option or not? For beginners who do not have a single trace of what

is happening, kindly engage in in-depth research and try to pay attention. For brokers and experts, keep learning about the different numbers in options trading. Life stops when you stop learning.

3. They have great discipline. We encourage self-discipline when you engage in options trading. It is a driving force that will push you in line with the plan with so much determination. You can follow your specific plans and strategies, learn a lot from trading activities, and gain the right skills and experience to trade options more effectively. Remember that your plan strategies are the primary objects at this time.

4. Great patience. Every aspect of life is a process led by continuous growth. Trade during several market moves and learn from it. During these commercial travel options, you will be exposed to various situations that you need to learn and master. Find out about the potential risks, some market tricks, and so on. Well, get the best experience because it's always the best teacher.

5. Have your trading style. The intended trading style is usually used in the trading plan. Your trading style should be strictly followed and updated with new skills and information as you engage in various options transactions. Follow the program without any other impact and watch how you grow by trading options.

6. Trading plan. Unplanned planning for failure. This means that the loser will only be reflected if no planning occurs. Successful entrepreneurs have big plans. Great ideas include the right strategies, features, discussions, in-depth research, great self-discipline, goals, and reasonable goals. Establishing good trading plans is a clear reflection of the great success in options trading.

7. Emotionally stable. Emotions can be very distracting when we get involved in various aspects of our lives. Losing trade should be treated as a bad day, which is useful with good educational experience and knowledge for a bright future. Winning days should also be a learning day, appreciating the right moves expressed that day.

8. Intensive learning and proactivity. Life always remains stagnant when you stop learning. Knowledge is good and evil, including master and learn every possible expressed move

Also, subscribe to a variety of channels and blogs to get the extensive knowledge you need in trading options. Learning allows you to inform and educate about actual trading activities that are usually involved in options trading.

9. Secure, accurate business records. We encourage you to learn from past mistakes and strategic development to become a successful options investor.

10. Determination and commitment. This entails a lot of thrusts that should rule a beginner or an experienced trader to get what is best for him in options trading and getting down learn some tips on how to succeed as an options trader.

11. be flexible. Another thing to add is that when you feel it, the market does not suit you at all during this particular period of options trading, find something constructive to do. Master every possible market move that will likely occur in options trading and master it.

12. Basic understanding and interpretation. The trader should be familiar with the necessary market terminology to understand the primary activities of the market and learn the different ways to start and handle options trading. The interpretation consists of the analysis of actual commercial transactions on the market and obtaining the necessary information in each of the commercial activities. This helps the investor always pay attention to the reality Market, not hype, depending on significant market terms.

13. be aggressive. Being aggressive in options trading means that there is a desire for great success, and the chances of getting big profits are so high. A dynamic option trader most often participates in in-depth scientific research, learning new and learning new lucrative trade moves. This gives the trader extensive experience and skills to face all kinds of risks that may be involved in the market, and in a short time, the trader accredited a great expert in options trading.

14. Emotionally stable. Different feelings on the market should not control an investor engaged in options trading. Lost days should not in any way discourage the trader from deciding to stay with the market hype. It is recommended that investors follow their plan and always stick to it down their different strategies.

15. Excellent choice of goods. The option trader must select the appropriate sell option. Weigh are you able to handle the right inventory and manage the necessary risks that are highly involved in them? Most importantly, will the shares benefit the investor in making large profits?

16. Good capital management. When money is important this comes to trade. Monitor and plan any amount of capital that you plan to use on the market. Always be careful with the amount of money you put into each option. Accepting losses is still an alternative when it comes to options trading, a failure that can knock you down and lead you to bankruptcy. Plan the capital that you plan to invest in the company.

17. Powerful trading platforms. The platform on which various commercial activities take place is essential in all types of involvement in option transactions. Your best platform should consist of fantastic navigation tools, learning sources, and other amazing features.

18. Selling options are most often preferred than buying options while practicing buying and selling strategies that ultimately help the investor to make a large amount of profit.

19. Correct time. As an entrepreneur, you should be informed about good and bad times. Enter the market when the time is quite favorable. Bad timing leads to significant losses in the options trading market, which leads to a substantial decline in finance.

Strategies That Are Successful in Options Trading

Good strategies set out in the options trading plan should be a priority.

Use the appropriate period. A longer period, for example, five years is recommended during in-depth research and analysis of various sources to establish good strategies. Remember to choose a fairly long period to get up-to-date information and to report it as part of learning.

Covered connection. This type of strategy includes both, trading in underlying shares and options contracts. The ultimate goal of a secured connection is to collect income through premiums and mainly sell inventory that you already own. Here are some ways to consider when creating a program connection:

Buy shares and buy in the form of shares. Sell a purchase contract for every 100 shares you own. Then wait for the connection to be made.

The risk associated with secured connections maintains a cautious inventory position that may fail over time. Large parts of the profits from this particular combination are equal to the price of the specified call option and the lower purchase price of the underlying shares.

We are introducing to the market. This strategy consists in the fact that the investor has made two purchases on the stock exchange and a put option. The advantage of this is that as an options investor, you can protect yourself against several losses. Launching is also considered beneficial when buying a security that has an optimistic attitude. The market launch strategy is also necessary to protect the depreciation, in particular of share prices.

Market sales are also called the synthetic long call because of the similarities in the number of potential profits on both sides.

Spread options. This strategy was established by selling several options and purchase options of the same class and from the same collateral with different exercise prices and expiry dates.

Butterfly spread. Butterfly includes four calls to buy and sell and is also considered a market-neutral strategy that can pay the majority of its underlying shares without worrying about expiration dates.

There are several varieties of butterfly spreads that usually use four types of options with three different strike prices. To add, different types of butterflies have different levels of maximum profit amount and maximum loss amount, which usually occur when trading options.

Chapter 25: Tips to Become a Successful Trader

As you must have understood by now, that in the world of the stock market, one of the most versatile financial instruments are options. You can boost your net profit by leveraging their versatility, but you also have to deal with the potential for loss despite all these advantages.

Every tip mentioned below is equally important, and only when you master all of them will you be able to produce a cumulative effect that will help in your future trades. Beginners are mostly in a hurry to know how they can maximize the profits, but they miss out on the more important details in between. Make a Trading Plan

A trading plan is something that every trader should have. It is a plan that will have all the specifics clearly written, and this includes your entry, exit, and also criteria for managing money in the best way possible. There is a myth in the market that trading comes naturally to some people, and thus, they do not need any trading plan, but this is so wrong. Trading is something that you have to learn – what comes naturally is your ability to work hard and learn something new. People might have an innate skill with numbers or identifying patterns, but even then, you have to learn the strategies and what should be used when. Some skills and traits cannot be built overnight and require experience.

If you ask any professional options trader, they will tell you how important it is to always work on building an in-depth base of knowledge and then find out your cognitive biases that hamper your decision-making skills. You can then figure out ways to fight your biases and overcome them. But all of this is possible only when you have a trading plan. You need not have the same trading plan month after month or year after year. Every month you might come across something new that can be incorporated into your plan. In that case, you can tweak your plan according to your newfound knowledge. But before you apply anything from your trading plan on a real-time trade, you must test it on the historical data that is available to you.

When you have a fixed strategy in place, you don't have to worry about when or what decisions you need to make. The entire process of decision-making becomes much more simplified. The trading plan will not only have all your goals clearly written but also the strategies you plan to undertake to fulfill those goals and the amount of risk you are comfortable taking in the process. According to experts, you should try keeping a maximum of only 1% of your total account at risk in a single trade. Another important thing to keep in mind while designing your trading plan is that it should clearly point out where you are going to enter a trade and when you are going to do that; you should also mention the possible indicators that will signal you and similarly, you also need to have a fixed exit point.

But the key point here is that even when you have a trading plan, you have to promise yourself that you will stick to the plan no matter what. Some people deviate from it far too much and make trades outside the plan, which only causes even more loss.

Start Thinking of Trading Like a Business

If you want to be a successful trader, you cannot take it lightly; you have to treat trading as if you are running a business. It shouldn't be a hobby. The difference is that when you are approaching the subject as a hobby, you don't really feel obligated to learn new things or improve your skillset, which is important to be successful. Also, if you treat it like a job, then after a certain point of time, you will only be thinking of the paycheck and otherwise get frustrated. Thus, trading should be treated more like a business where you are going to have to pay taxes, incur losses and expenses, handle risk, and overcome stress. When you start trading, consider yourself as a small business owner, and then with proper planning and strategizing, you can upgrade your business to the next level.

If you are wondering as to in what other ways can you treat trading like your business, then here is what else you can do –

- Have a Vision – Just like you have a vision for your business; it is important to have it for trading too. But if you don't know how to, then think about why you started options trading in the first place, and from there, it would be easier for you to find your vision. Once you have figured out your vision, print or write it in bold letters on a paper and then hang it somewhere where you can spot it easily throughout the day.
- Have Proper Funding – You need to keep trading funds ready before you jump into the market. In today's world, you can start trading with as low as $50 or $100, but even though that will get you started, will it be enough to sustain you in the long term? If you want to be in the market for a long time, then proper funding is necessary. Thus, prepare your starting capital.
- Always Think Long-Term – When you are strategizing your trades or thinking of anything related to options trading, think about what you are going to do in the long-term.
- Prepare a Daily Trading Routine – You need to be disciplined to be a successful options trader. And one of the most important things to do is to have a daily trading routine. This means you will set a time every day when you will analyze the market and when you are

going to stop trades as well. Also, your routine should perfectly match your everyday lifestyle. It shouldn't seem like a burden.

Maintain a Trading Journal

A trading journal is a very powerful tool and something that every trader should have to be successful. It also instills in you the art of discipline. It is not anything fancy but just a written record of all the trades that you are making and what happened when you made the trade. Some things worth noting are market conditions, expiration time, size of the trade, notes on your emotions during the trade, and whether the trade was a successful one. The entries might not be the same for everyone. The entries should be customized based on your trading style so that it suits your ways.

I know what you might be thinking – keeping a trading journal is time-consuming and tedious. Even if it is so, when you maintain a trading journal, it helps you become disciplined and consistent at what you are doing. In the long run, both these qualities will help you a lot in the world of trading.

So, make sure you note down the patterns and charts you are watching and how your trade has been impacted by certain events. When you keep noting these things down over a certain period, you will be able to spot your mistakes and then work on rectifying them. For example, a trading journal often helps option traders figure out whether it was too early for them to exit the trade or whether they fell into the trap of a false signal.

When you have a detailed record of everything that you did, it helps in coming up with better strategies. In fact, this is why noting down your emotions is essential. This will help you understand whether you have a pattern of allowing your emotions to affect your trade.

Moreover, the journal will help you monitor your progress over a while. You should also write down your trading goals in the journal because often, writing down your goals is what helps you or gives you the extra push in achieving them. With time, you will understand how the trading journal can boost your confidence. And when you realize the benefits, it will no longer seem like a chore.

Make the Best Use of Technology

There is a lot of competition in trading, and you have to make this assumption that the person who is on the other side of the trade has access to the latest technology and is making the best use of it too.

Today, you can get access to plenty of charting platforms and other tools that will help you perform an in-depth analysis of the market conditions, and there are infinite ways in which you can view the market with the help of these tools. If you do not take the help of these things, you might make some wrong decisions that would turn out to be way more costly than you'd ever imagine. There is plenty of historical data available on these platforms that you can use for backtesting your strategies. In fact, some of these platforms will also give you the option of receiving real-time updates on your smartphone so that you can stay notified about everything that is happening on the market even on-the-go and keep monitoring your trades.

So, if you have been taking this technology for granted all this time, you need to gear up and make the best use of it because others are already going ahead of you. Once you start using these technological advantages, you will be able to see for yourself how your trading performance enhances drastically. You will stay current with every new product that launches and realize your hard work's proper rewards.

Understand Yourself

Did you know that before you start trading, it is very important to understand yourself, and sometimes it is even more important than understanding the market? Yes, there is no need to shy away from this because to become successful in options trading, a little bit of introspection into who you are is of utmost importance. You will be able to study your biases and figure out what you can do to overcome them. Strategizing your trades is one thing and understanding your mind and your emotions that affect those trades is a completely different thing altogether.

In Chapter 6, we have already spoken at length as to how you can keep your emotions in check while trading so that they do not affect your trading decisions. In fact, sometimes, all you need to do is maintain a positive attitude, and you will easily be able to spot the profitable trading opportunities that come your way. Be realistic while examining yourself and see whether you possess the qualities required to be a successful trader. If not, then there is no need to beat yourself up for it. Own your shortcomings and start working on them from today.

You also need to judge your abilities to manage things and regulate your emotions when it comes to an uncertain condition. No matter how much chaos there is, a successful trader can look past all of that and make the right decision.

You need to be able to evaluate risks instantly and determine what you need to do to minimize those risks and maximize your profits.

Make Peace with Losing a Trade

You have to understand that no matter how successful you are, there will be some trades that you cannot win. So, when you see that things are not working your way and the market is going in the opposite direction to what you predicted, you have to make yourself understand that you need to get out of the trade before your losses start escalating even more. This is what trading discipline is all about. No matter how disastrous things have become, you have to learn to take your losses and step out. Every loss that you encounter in the market will teach you something, and you must learn the lesson and promise yourself not to repeat the same mistake.

If you speak with any successful trader, you will realize that they have faced failures too, but they did not let their failures determine their life course. So, you shouldn't let your failures make you feel bad or lay you low. A part of trading is owning your losses. But the key factor is ensuring that your total gains are always more than your total losses.

Avoid Buying Options that Are Out-of-the-Money

This is because if we are to follow statistics, then these types of options have proven to be the least profitable. To overcome time decay, the price of the stock will have to move in your favor, and that has to be fast enough. Don't ever forget that options are decaying assets. That is why it is advised that you sell options that are out-of-the-money and not buy them.

Be Patient

Patience is a very important virtue that is necessary for traders. You cannot become a successful trader in a day. If you are a beginner who only started trading recently, then your first couple of years are going to be about learning different things about the market, and the learning curve is going to be quite steep. With time, as you get exposed to the different conditions of the market, you will keep learning more. And even if you make a mistake, note it down so that even if that market condition returns, you know what not to do. Sometimes, it is even more important to stay patient and not to do anything to make your trade successful.

If you become impatient and you exit a trade before it's time or enter a trader too late, you might lose a lot of potential profit. That is why having a clear idea of the trading strategy is very important so that your bottom line is not affected by rookie moves.

Another meaning of having patience is that even if you faced huge losses, you would not give in to the urge to do revenge trading and use the loss as an opportunity to brush up on your basics and then gain a better understanding of the situation.

These were some of the most important tips to keep in mind if you want to be a successful trader. But apart from this, there is one more thing that I would like to remind you – always stay updated with the news of the day and don't believe everything right off the bat. You need to be able to differentiate between reality and the hype and understand what a promising piece of news for your trading strategy might be.

Conclusion

When it comes to trading options, there's a lot of different options that you can choose from when it comes to your approach. Options are a great way to make money in the stock market. A lot of people don't understand options trading, and they think that it's too complicated. That's not true. For most people, options trading is the best way to make money on the stock market.

Options trading is a great way to gain exposure for your company, learn the ins and outs of options trading, and make a little extra money. Options trading is a great example of how simple it can be to make money. In options trading, you sell an option contract to buy or sell a certain quantity of something at a set price within a certain period. In conclusion, options trading is a great way to make money quickly without putting in huge amounts of time and effort. Every beginner should start by buying cheap puts and calls on stocks that they already have an interest in.

The most important thing about options trading is to make sure that you're getting the best possible price on your options. Options trading is a great way to make money if you're willing to learn about the options and know what they are. Options trading is about making decisions at the right time. It's important to be prepared for each situation to ensure you're able to make good decisions on what you want to do in a trade.

Options trading is a great way to make money, but it's also one of the riskiest investments you could make. Being an options trader can be really fun and exciting. However, it can also be dangerous if you don't understand the basics of options trading. These basics can help you make more informed decisions about your trades and protect yourself from taking unnecessary risks. This is an area of finance that may be new to you, but it's a great way to make money. Options trading is pretty simple, you buy a call option on an asset and people can only sell it to you.

Options are one of the most complicated investment vehicles to understand and invest in. If you don't understand how options work, then you're going to end up losing a lot of money. Options are a great way to diversify your investment portfolio. If you're trading options, don't just look at the stock price when you make a decision. There are many different kinds of options trading, but the most common type is covered calls. For this kind of trade, a trader can buy a call option with an expiration date as far out as the trader chooses.

Options trading is a way to speculate on the market but it's important to know the risks involved when you're making this type of investment. Options are a form of derivatives, which are contracts that derive their value from underlying assets. The options you trade will be based on some underlying asset such as shares, bonds, commodities, currencies, or indices. This is a very simple strategy that anyone can do. If you want to be able to buy or sell options, you have to be able to identify when they're reasonably priced.

OPTIONS TRADING STRATEGIES 2021

THIS BOOK PRESENT SOME BASIC KNOWLEDGE ABOUT THE DIFFERENT TERMS AND CONCEPTS USED IN OPTIONS TRADING THAT YOU NEED TO BE PROFITABLE ENOUGH

**WRITTEN BY
DAVID MATTHEWS**

Introduction

Options trading really is a field of specialty unto itself. There is a ton to learn and a great deal of terminology that can be confusing without the proper background. In this book, we will try to provide you with some basic knowledge about the different terms and concepts used in options trading.

Options trading is an important part of trading. With options trading, there are two different types of positions that you can take in the market. These positions are called a call option and a put option. A call option gives you the right but not the obligation to buy a specified quantity of assets at some price and within some time periods. On the other hand, a put option gives you the right but not the obligation to sell a specified quantity of assets at some price and within some time period. When you purchase an option, this means that if the option is able to make a good profit for you (if it is "in-the-money"), then it will give you this profit automatically. If the option is "out-of-the-money," then the option will expire and you won't be able to use it anymore.

Main Concepts of Options Trading

There are several main concepts that you have to understand about options trading so that you can take advantage of this type of investment. One of these concepts is known as "Time Value." To explain, if an asset is selling for $100 a share, then if I offer someone $5 as a premium to purchase a contract, then they will not accept it because they can just go out and buy the shares for $100 each. But after the option expires, if I am able to sell back the shares for $100 each, then you can say that I have made a profit.

The benefit of this time value is that it gives you a chance to make money without having any risk. The only thing that you have to do is to wait until expiration and then if there is a good price (higher than the premium that you paid), then you will make a profit.

Advantages of Options Trading

1. You can trade against the market. How you do this is when you purchase say a call option, then if the market goes down, then your value of the call option will be higher and then you will be able to sell it back at a higher value.

2. You can also trade in both bull and bear markets. If stocks are going up and there is no way that they will go down (bull market), then you can still use options to make money because they can still go down in price in which case your options will be very expensive for the buyer so he has to give more premium for them.

3. In options trading, there is leverage. With leverage, it means that if you put less amount of capital in, then you will get more money. For example, if I only have $300 and I want to purchase an option at $5 premium for a call contract, then I will be able to purchase 10 call options because with the regular stocks where I would have to put in at least $3000 to purchase the same 10 call options.

4. The final advantage is that they are cheaper than the stocks themselves. Due to this reason, you will have more opportunities than high-priced assets.

Chapter 1. Fundamentals of Technical Analysis

Technical analysis is turning into an inexorably mainstream way to deal with exchanging, thanks to a limited extent to the headway in diagramming bundles and exchanging stages. In any case, for an amateur dealer, understanding technical analysis—and how it can help foresee patterns on the lookout—can be overwhelming and stressing.

Technical analysis is the investigation of value developments in a market, whereby merchants utilize notable outline examples and pointers to foresee future patterns on the lookout. It is a visual portrayal over a significant time span execution of a market and permits the dealer to utilize this data as value activity, pointers, and examples to direct and advise future patterns prior to entering an exchange.

This technical analysis novice's guide will acquaint you with the fundamentals of this exchanging approach, and how it very well may be utilized to exchange in the monetary business sectors.

Understanding Technical Analysis

Technical analysis includes the understanding of examples from outlines. Broker's utilize notable information, in view of cost, and volume and utilize this data to distinguish exchanging openings dependent on normal examples on the lookout. Various markers are applied to outlines to decide passage and leave focuses for brokers to augment an exchange's potential or avoid great losses to rewards.

The following diagram is an illustration of a graph with the utilization of the MACD and RSI pointer.

Graph 2

While promoters of essential analysis accept that monetary components are the principal supporters of developments in the business sectors, technical analysis merchants keep up that past patterns can help with foreseeing future value developments. Albeit these exchanging styles can shift, understanding the contrasts among basic and technical analysis—and how to join them—can be very useful.

How Technical Analysis Can Help Traders

Numerous dealers have discovered technical analysis to be a valuable instrument for executives to identify hazard which can be a key hindrance. When a merchant comprehends the ideas and standards of technical analysis, it very well may be applied to any market, making it an adaptable logical instrument. Where key analysis hopes to distinguish characteristic incentives in a market, technical analysis hopes to recognize patterns, which helpfully can be brought about by the basic fundamentals.

Advantages of utilizing technical analysis incorporate the following:

- Can be applied to any market utilizing any time span.
- Technical analysis can be utilized as an independent technique.
- Permits merchants to distinguish patterns on the lookout.

Utilizing Charts in Technical Analysis

The diagram below is an illustration of a candle graph for the EUR/USD cash pair.

Graph 3

Diagrams are critical to technical analysis. This is on the grounds that the main proportion of a market's past and the current exhibition is simply the value; this is the beginning stage while digging into investigating the capability of an exchange. Value activity that can be addressed on an outline as this is the clearest sign of what the cost is doing.

Outlines help with deciding the general pattern, regardless of whether there's an upward or descending direction, either over the long or present moment or to recognize range-bound conditions. The most well-known kinds of technical analysis diagrams are line graphs, bar outlines, and candle diagrams.

When utilizing a bar or candle graph, every period will give the technical expert data on the cost from where it opened, the high or low of the time frame just as the nearby. Candle analysis is particularly helpful as the examples and relationships inside them can help with making conjectures about the future heading of the cost.

When a merchant has dominated the essentials of diagramming, they would then be able to utilize pointers to help with deciding based on the pattern.

Technical Analysis Indicators

Pointers are utilized by technical dealers whenever searching for promising circumstances on the lookout. Albeit numerous markers exist, merchants often utilize volume and valued based pointers. These help with figuring out where the degrees of help and obstruction is, the manner by which they are often kept up or penetrated to finding out the length of a pattern.

A broker can see the cost or some other pointer utilizing various time period analyses, going from one second to a month which gives the dealer an alternate point of view of the value activity.

The more famous markers for technical analysis include:

- Moving averages
- Relative strength file (RSI)
- Moving normal intermingling dissimilarity (MACD)

The EUR/USD diagram below tells the best way to utilize various pointers.

Moving midpoints and MACD are often used to distinguish patterns on the lookout while the RSI is regularly used to decide conceivable passage and leave focuses. Pointers help brokers in breaking down the market, approving exchange setups, and deciding passage focus.

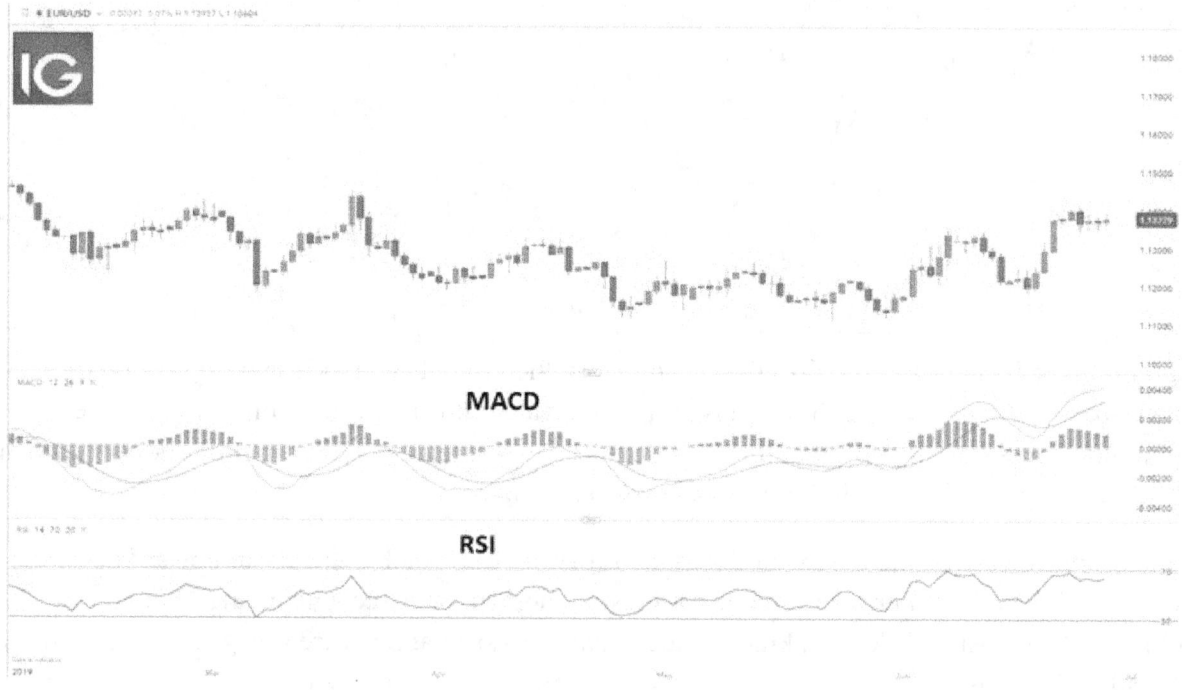

Graph 4

Chapter 2. What a Beginner Needs to Know

This section will zero in on the tips that can help a novice to accomplish while taking part in options trading. While participating in options trading, you are doing this antagonistically in a way that your danger is spread broadly. As such, you can screen your danger. While accepting a position trading, you do this politely. This is on the grounds that the position that you expect has a drawn-out impact on your business. The positions might be accepted in a drawn-out nature, nonpartisan nature, or transient nature. At the point when you are sufficiently adaptable, this can be an in addition to one with regards to overseeing hazard.

When contributing, you need to foresee hazards. This is on the grounds that no sort of adventure will be smooth as far as possible. You should foresee hazards if by, any means, you have any desire for succeeding. Dangers will happen, and they will be averse to the business on the loose. How best you minimize the danger will decide how far you will rise. Before, options trading has been identified with betting. This is on the grounds that this sort of adventure includes accepting up a business open door without a sharp inside and out about what it involves. This is the very definition that betting has been given.

A few components prove to be useful when trading in options. These components can be convenient to a novice who is considering taking up the endeavor of options trading. The dissemination of dangers across different fields is on its own preferences and impediments.

Adaptability Is Key

A long way from the antiquated strategy for options trading where the sole point was to sell at a high, options trading involves a great deal of choice that is adequately adaptable to suit your case. This implies that to catch them, you need to think deftly.

Options trading involves that a dealer can make a profit by flourishing in figures of stagnation, upswings, slumps, and unpredictability as a rule. With these sorts of options set up, this implies that it will be inconspicuous for a novel broker to discover their way around the market. This implies that they must be sufficiently adept to take advantage of a lucky break when they see one. The adaptability should be adequately sharp to ensure that it doesn't bring about control.

The term adaptability implies that you are causing yourself to conform to the overall conditions. There will be new examples and plan for progress that you should change yourself, too. There is an example that gives merchants profit about the instability of a stock. Regardless of the upswing or slump of the stock, the broker will consistently wind up in success when they utilize this sort of example. This sort of example is known as the ride design, and is accessible for merchants in options trading, while, in different types of exchanging, it neglects to surface.

Options as a Mitigating Factor

With options trading, a broker is in a situation to restrict their dangers. Take this example where you are not in a situation to decide the area of a particular stock. Options trading will guarantee that you can accept a mitigatory position. Along these lines, you are in a situation to deal with your dangers. There is a typical strategy that has been utilized time and again in an offer to limit hazards.

This sort of strategy includes the acquisition of stock in the way of a put choice. With this kind of strategy, you are in a situation to discard the stock generated loss regardless of whether its value chooses to fall.

This strategy as well as other different alternatives, can be utilized when alleviating hazards.

Options trading equips a trader with an assortment of options that can be used as a shield against the always existent dangers. This is probably the greatest value of options trading that can cause you to choose this specific kind of exchange. In any case, trading in options is certifiably not a definite arrangement that you won't take part in the misfortune. The effect is limited somewhat, however, the broker is as yet in a situation to feel it. This involves the pooling of dangers. At the point when dangers are pooled, for example, in protection conspire, it turns out to be not difficult to revoke a bad deal once a misfortune has happened.

Control the Game

With the options in position, you are blown to pick the one that will best suit you. This will include leading the broad investigation into the field that you wish to be engaged with. This regularly includes a wary examination. This alternative will at that point give you the approval to sell or buy the option to participate in the exchange. The buy and offer of stocks from an assortment of fields will make sure that you boost your benefits and limit your misfortune. Options, as a rule, can be utilized as a technique whereby you can rate your ventures, make a few enhancements for them, and cease from those that lead you into misfortunes. This endeavor of options trading is to a greater extent an active task. This is on the grounds that it includes a few examples, like money insurance about and covered calls, which give a trader greater rawness over the span of the business.

Purposes of Even-Breaking

All the options that you may have decided to choose have focuses that are known as equal to the initial investment focus. This kind of point is the place where you understand that the stock won't lead you into a benefit yet rather a descending bend of a misfortune. At the point when this occurs, you should be sufficiently prepared to ensure that you have an authentic perspective on your missteps. Along these lines, you will have the option to limit your dangers. To earn back the original investment point is a point that is specific to a stock. With this point, the stock needs to hit it before the dealer beginning making income.

These sorts of focuses are a mixture of two elements. These components remember the value of commissions for the exchange and the price that was paid to get the specific stock. These focuses are imperative to note in light of the fact that these are the focuses that sound good to the entire cycle of exchange.

Go Beyond the Option Chart

Prior to taking up this endeavor, you need to ensure that you lead a far-reaching inside and out on the different options. To accomplish this, you need to counsel different sources that are not restricted to the options outline. Restricting yourself to the options diagram will imply that you are not receiving a wide perspective available. The options graph works in an offer to give the exemplary behavior and the developments of the price. This is critical, in spite of the fact that it doesn't go further to feature the sort of resource that is encountering the developments in price. Prior to plunging into the exchange adventure, it is of key significance that you have an earlier appreciation of the stock that you wish to enjoy. The outlines are key perspectives not to be forgotten about, despite the fact that while utilizing the diagrams, you should do this with a meeting of the stock graphs. The essentials of trading necessitate that you study your stock before you begin.

Follow the Trend

With options trading, you should give sharp consideration to the pattern and ensure you embrace it since it is among the couple of patterns that you may experience in this. At the point when you are choosing a specific stock, you should cease from gauging the stock's character. This incorporates an upswing, decline, or stagnation. This is on the grounds that you may never take care of business.

The chances of options trading rest with the pattern. Rather than making your own fantasies and deciding to follow them, you need to embrace one that is now in presence, and then proceed. The equivalent applies when there is a plunge or stagnation.

Leave Plan

In any trading adventure, you need to remain without your feelings. This is on the grounds that nobody will place them into thought. With the correct arrangement set up, ensure that you can execute it. In this arrangement of yours, you should be sufficiently sharp to place into thought an arrangement that will pull you out of the mud in tough situations. Having a getaway plan is of key significance since it sets you up for the most noticeably awful unforeseen development. At the point when a specific sort of exchange is headed to the base, you need to escape from so that you need to experience misfortunes. To accomplish the most in income, you need to ensure that you follow your plan strictly, to the last minimum detail.

Chapter 3. Determining the Option Price

As an options dealer, you need to find out about the factors that can influence the price of an option and the intricate details of executing the correct system. A stock merchant who is comfortable and acceptable with foreseeing future stock price development may imagine that moving to options trading is simple, however, it's most certainly not.

There are three changing boundaries that an options dealer should manage—the hidden stock's price, the time factor, and instability. An adjustment in any of these components will influence the price of the option.

The price of an option is additionally called the premium and the evaluation is per share.

The option vendor gets the premium, which, in that way, gives the purchaser a condition that joins the option. The purchaser is the one paying the premium to the vendor and they can practice this privilege or simply permit the option to terminate with no value eventually. The purchaser is obliged to pay the top-notch if the option is practiced, which implies the dealer will keep the premium, eventually, regardless.

We should have a straightforward example. A purchaser paid a dealer for buying rights to stock ABC 100 shares and a strike price at $60. The agreement lapses by June 19. On the off chance that the option position becomes beneficial, the option will be practiced by the purchaser. On the off chance that it doesn't appear to bear benefit, the purchaser can just allow the agreement to terminate. The vendor at that point keeps the premium.

There are different sides to the premium of an option—its inherent and time value.

You can process for an option's natural value by getting the contrast between the strike price and the stock price. For the call option, it is the stock price less the strike price. For the put option, it is the strike price less the stock price.

To value an option, at any rate hypothetically, you should consider numerous factors, for example, the fundamental stock price, instability, practice price, time to termination, and financing cost. These variables will give you a decent gauge on the reasonable value of an option that you would then be able to fuse into your procedure for the greatest increases. We may be examining the time and unpredictability factors in detail. The essential objective for option evaluating is to register the likelihood that a specific option will be "in the money" or practiced when it lapses.

The value of puts and calls are influenced by hidden stock price developments dictate. That implies when the price of a stock raises, there should be a relating ascend in call value too since you can buy the hidden stock at a scaled-down price contrasted with the market's, while there is price decline input. On the other hand, there should be an expansion in the value of put options when the price of the stock takes a plunge and a lessening in the value of call options since the holder of the put option has the option to sell the stock at above-market prices. This pre-set price at which you can sell or purchase is known as the strike price of the option or its activity price. In the event that the option's strike price gives you the benefit of selling or purchasing the stock at an expense that gives your prompt benefit, that option is considered "in the money".

With the hidden stock price and strike price far removed, we would now be able to talk about the other two main considerations that can fundamentally influence the price of an option—time and unpredictability.

Time

Time is money. This aphorism actually remains constant and even applies to options trading. Along these lines, seeing how the Greek theta works is vital because it has a meaning for the estimating of options. On the off chance that you actually buy back the share, the Greek letter theta addresses the impact of time decay on the value of an option. All options, call or put, lose their value as the agreement lapse approaches- However, the value of an option contract is an element of the measure of time staying before it terminates.

The outward piece of the value of an option is the lone factor influenced by time decay. That implies an option that is 'in the money' will have a similar inborn value until the agreement lapses. For instance, if stock exchanges at $3, a require at 30-strike price will hold its natural value of $3 from the beginning until lapse however any value that surpasses $3 is viewed as outward value and will be influenced when time passes.

Theta addresses the deficiency of value over time so it's commonly addressed by a negative value. Furthermore, since time is irreversible, time just declines and never stops or returns. For instance, if theta is set to -0.28, the comparing option contract loses $0.28 in value every day.

Be that as it may, theta changes over the long run. We should accept that a stock's price stays unaltered, a $2.75 "out of the money" option with a -0.15 theta will have a scaled-down value of $2.60 quite soon. The theta at that point may just be set to -0.12 which implies the expense of the option will be down to $2.48 the succeeding day if stock prices stay unaltered. The option's value will bit by bit move toward nothing while it's actually "out of the money."

You likewise need to remember that the impact of theta turns out to be increasingly more clear as the termination approaches. You should envision a fast speeding up of the time decay inside the leftover few days before the agreement lapses.

Options that are 'at the money' have the most elevated value, extraneously.

That is the reason these options have their thetas set to most elevated. Options that are somewhere down 'in the money' or 'out of the money' have their thetas lower in light of the fact that contrasted with 'at the money options', they have lower extraneous values. Also, the less outward value an option has, the less they will lose with time decay.

The solitary path for the theta position to be positive is to have short options.

This is on the grounds that short options positions work best when the market is steady.

Wide swings both up or down hurt option positions and just time will help as it cruises by. Different methodologies likewise advantage from time's section, for example, impartial systems, or long butterfly. The less time there is before the agreement lapses, the less likely it for the fundamental stock to raise or go down and arrive at unfruitful domains.

Unpredictability

Instability influences most venture structures somewhat and as an options dealer, you should be acquainted with this component and what it means for options valuing. By definition, unpredictability is the propensity of something to vacillate or change altogether. By and large speculation, instability alludes to the rate that a monetary instrument's price rises or falls.

A low instability monetary instrument has a price that is moderately steady.

Alternately, a high instability monetary instrument is inclined to emotional price changes, in any case. By and large, monetary market instability can be extensively estimated. So when the market gets hard to anticipate and prices keep on routinely and quickly changing, the market is unpredictable Volatility can influence option estimating essentially. Many starting options dealers will in general overlook the ramifications which can prompt colossal venture misfortunes.

Prior to entering any sort of exchange, options trading included, it very well may be helpful to have a thought regarding its instability. For options, unpredictability is a critical factor by the way they are valued and priced. There are two instability types that are important—chronicled instability and suggested unpredictability.

Chronicled Volatility

Recorded or factual unpredictability is utilized to quantify the adjustments in the price of the hidden option so it depends on genuine information. We should allude to it as HV for the rest. HV shows how quickly the stock price has moved. The higher HV is, the more the stock price has moved during a specific period. So when a stock has a high HV, the price is bound to move, in any event hypothetically.

It's to a greater extent a future development sign and not a genuine assurance.

Then again, a low HV may show the stock price hasn't moved a lot however it very well may be going one way consistently.

You can utilize HV to some degree to anticipate how much a security's price will change depending on how quickly it changed previously, yet you can't utilize it to foresee a genuine pattern.

HV is estimated over a specific period, for example, seven days, month, or year and you can register for it differently.

Suggested Volatility

Another sort of unpredictability that options dealers should know about whenever suggested instability or IV. Though HV estimates a security's previous instability, IV is a greater amount of a gauge of its future unpredictability.

IV is a projection of how quick, and how much the stock price is probably going to change in price. Many starting dealers center on the benefit (contrast in strike price and stock price) and the agreement termination while considering an option's price, yet IV additionally assumes a significant part.

You can decide on option IV by considering elements, for example, the stock and strike prices, a period of time before termination, current financing cost, and HV. Since an option's IV may show how much the stock will change in price, the price gets higher when the actual IV increments. Since hypothetically, more benefit can be acquired when there are sensational developments in the price of the basic stock. The price of an option can likewise change fundamentally in any event, when the price of the actual stock remaining moves as before and is generally brought about by its IV.

For instance, ABC is going to deliver another item and hypotheses are developing that the organization is going to announce it. The options IV for stock ABC can be extremely high since there are assumptions for a huge development in the price of the hidden stock. The announcement may be gotten well and the price of the stock may go up, or the crowd will be baffled with the new item and stock prices can drop rapidly. In this situation, the price of the stock probably won't move altogether since speculators will be sitting tight for the official statement prior to purchasing or selling stocks. There will at that point be increments in extraneous value for the two puts and calls, as opposed to development in the stock price. This is one way that IV can influence option evaluating.

In case you're wagering that a stock's price will significantly increment once that announcement has been made, you may buy "at the money" call options to expand plausible additions for that increment. In the event that after ABC made the announcement and was gotten well making the stock prices shoot up, at that point there would have been critical additions in the call options' characteristic value. After the official statement and the stock price development, IV will at that point be lower since it's anticipated that the stock price won't change very soon. There will at that point be a significant fall on the calls' extraneous value and that would counterbalance a large portion of the benefit you acquired with the expanded inherent value.

Chapter 4. Getting Started With Options Trading

You Needed Thought of What Options Exchange Is. Mull over the different wordings utilized in this field. This may incorporate terms, for example, a holder, an author, a striking spot. And so forth, it is fitting to think of an accounting page with these phrasings and put forth an attempt to contemplate them inside and out. This will contribute a ton to your comprehension of what options trade spins around. By and large, options exchange can be characterized as an agreement that permits you or another purchase to buy or sell a stock at a specific strike price for a predetermined timeframe. With this information, you have just begun making your way towards options trading. You understand that options trading generally spins around the call option just like the put option and subsequently the need to guarantee that you comprehend what they involve inside and out. The options as a rule assume a basic part; they control the value of the stock. You should likewise comprehend that the options are inclined to terminate, particularly in situations where the agreement is finished. For this situation, you may wind up losing your investment.

While continuing with how to begin options trading, you will need to gather some essential tools. This alludes to different strategies and knowledge that will be sufficiently adequate to take you through the whole cycle of an options trade.

Your capital assumes an extremely basic part in guaranteeing that you can buy an option that best suits your methodology and be in a situation to reap many benefits. However, you must be prudent. In the situations where you plan on including a representative, you can easily provide their payments; just request them to employ their best administrations.

You Must Understand that Options Exchange Includes High Risks. The dangers here are as a rule in two measurements. One is the measure of money you lose when contrasted with the benefits you would have expected. The other measurement is the likelihood of obtaining benefits when contrasted with the likelihood of getting a misfortune. The high risks can happen, particularly when the options have been bought theoretically. In the event that at one point you are not cautious, you may wind up losing every one of your benefits. You can without much of a stretch gain high benefits in the event that you have an inside and out comprehension of the stock's price development. Exploiting the options in such situations can disappear up into ensuring your investment past a sensible uncertainty. For this situation, you just remain to lose the charges and a tiny level of the speculation, as you had portrayed in the agreement.

Getting to the most basic parts now, you should open a money market fund either on the web or customarily through a representative. Here there are different variables to consider prior to settling with the most dependable financier organization.

Guarantee that You Know About Their Expenses and Motivators. A portion of the business organizations might be offering limits to their clients to draw them in, and you can exploit this and advantage from the limits they offer. You can likewise beware of the accommodations and administrations that different financier organizations offer prior to choosing all things considered. These might be administrations, for example, money transformations or giving sufficient data on the stock estimations. Having listed the upsides and downsides of every one of the business firms, at that point you can choose one that best suits your longing. It is likewise fitting to guarantee that your business organization has an adequate type of money move, particularly for online records. A portion of the organizations will furnish you with Electronic Money Transfer frameworks, henceforth improving comfort.

You Can Get the Important Endorsement Application From Your Business Organization Before You Can Begin Purchasing Options. You understand that a large portion of the financier firms set cutoff points for their clients; they generally do this so they can keep you from getting wrong dangers that might have been dodged. They additionally do this as they have their own advantages that they are such a lot of ready to secure, particularly on issues to do with the legalities.

Acquaint Yourself With the Different Specialized Examination of Options. You understand that options are generally present moment. Inability to comprehend trchnicalities like the opposition and backing levels, the Fibonacci retracement, the significance of volume, and some fundamental information on the moving midpoints will make it very difficult to experience the interaction easily.

At the Point When You Get Into Genuine Trading, It Is Unseemly to Begin Trading Right Away. All things considered, attempt to run some demo accounts and acquaint yourself with them for one month. By doing this, you can attempt to assess your demo returns for certain months and, when you locate some degree of consistency in it, you would now be able to assemble the vital certainty and start genuine trading. At least with this training, you will have some premise under which you can base your investigation. Thusly, you will save yourself from enduring high dangers as you know that in the demo account, there are no charges included at all.

At the point when you get to trading currently, attempt, as reasonably as possible, to dodge market prices since they may shift after purchasing or selling the options. This may bring about high yet avoidable misfortunes. All things being equal, set a breaking point request that you find advantageous. For this situation, the exchange might be executed if, by any possibility, the market price arrives at your breaking point or is stunningly better contingent upon whether it's downstream or upstream.

Guarantee That You Occasionally Reconsider Your Technique. This guarantees that you endlessly learn from any misstep that you may have made during the exchange. In the situation where some of your strategies give great returns, attempt however much as could be expected to use them while at the same time attempting to amplify their productivity. Guarantee that you get accostumed to new market strategies that may appear to be very productive. You can likewise associate with others who have strategies that might improve yours. This should construct your security, particularly after you endure misfortunes. Having similarly capable individuals in a similar field as you, somewhat, makes you positive about your own self with the end goal that you don't need to beat yourself after you make colossal misfortunes. They assist you with proceeding onward and keep on target while simultaneously minding your technique and making vital changes at any place essential. This association additionally gives you a feeling of the local area; with this, you can accomplish a specific knowledge into the exchange.

Regardless, it would be astute on the off chance that you remain much centered around your strategies as opposed to differentiating such a huge amount on them. This saves you from wandering off-track as you continued looking for new strategies that may, over the long run, fizzle.

When you feel that you have gotten familiar with your present trading strategies, you can attempt to get into some more unpredictable strategies that, over the long run, procure higher benefits in the event that you will get them. At the point when this is introduced to you, don't be so careless to join the market without attempting a demo represent a few months, this will empower you to improve comprehension of how they run. With this step, you will have the option to pick whether to proceed with your past strategies or maintain the more perplexing ones. One of these strategies that you can really attempt is the ride system. In this procedure, you purchase the call and the put option at the same time; it shows up as though it is a nonpartisan options technique. Both the call and the put in this offer a similar strike price just as the expiry date. For this situation, you get your benefits for the situation where the prices either go above or underneath the strike price by a sum that is higher or preferably moreover that of the premium.

This technique is to some degree very hazardous as it possibly applies when the market is going here and there; in any case, on the off chance that it runs a similar way, just that side will be exercisable.

When you have completely dominated the craft of taking care of even the intricate strategies, don't stop there or lose sight, there is even more to learn. Attempt to boost your benefits however much as could reasonably be expected by acquainting yourself with the measurements which different options dealers use to harvest more benefits. They call it finding out about the Greeks. For this situation, you can utilize the measurements that consider the productivity of benefits. The benefit alludes to the chance of making, in any event, a $0.01 benefit on a given exchange. The likelihood of benefit is generally influenced by perspectives as purchasing options, selling options, or the general decrease of stock, or time. This would require cautious and top-to-bottom knowledge to understand it completely and use it as your procedure to receive the greatest rewards.

Chapter 5. Development of the Options

Options have a place with the gathering of monetary subordinates, which are normalized trading instruments. The price advancement of essential security is the measure at the latest cost. On account of subordinates, values, files, monetary standards, or even the actual subsidiaries may frame the fundamentals. At the point when exchanged on the stock trade, speculators regularly experience subordinates as options or prospects. These types of ventures are among the most exchanged items on the stock market. In any case, what is it precisely, and how did the option create until the speculative subordinate arose as the present substantial trading device?

- Options are exchanged on the stock trade.
- The option is a variation of the subordinate.
- Subordinates might be founded on various titles.
- The fundamental title is legitimate at the latest cost.

The exemplary option offers the option to exchange an item at a price called the strike price. Both the obtaining (call) and the deal (put) might be thought of.

Trading doesn't establish a commitment, which implies that the broker doesn't have to purchase or sell the stock or some other basic resource. It is only a matter of defending the option to exchange a business item at the established price sometime in the future. To gain the option, the speculator pays the vendor, who is likewise called the author, a superior, in particular, the option price. A call warrant subsequently secures the option to purchase the basic resource. On the off chance that you exchange the American variety, you, as a purchaser, can exercise your option directly at any time until due date.

Then again, you can practice your privilege in the European form only on the due date. Much of the time, speculators will possibly exercise the call or put if the price of the stock, at a given time, is above or underneath the base value. Something else, the financial specialist should exchange the stock at a superior price on the lookout. For call and put, there are the accompanying profiles:

- Call: Purchase Option—Right to purchase the hidden resource.
- Put: Put option—Right to sell the basic resource.
- Long: Viewpoint Buyer—purchaser position.
- Short: Viewing Angle Seller—Verkaufs position.

Note: Buyers and sellers allude to the option and not to the fundamental resource.

The Purchase Warrant (Call)

Set on rising prices, they can best be explained with an example: A speculator secures a warrant of procurement from a bank, otherwise called a backer, on a Siemens AG security. This has a base price of 109 euros. The option type is American for this situation, and the term has been set to a half year. The merchant subsequently has the option to request from the bank the conveyance of the portion of Siemens AG at the price of €109. In the event that the paper of Siemens AG is currently recorded at €120 after some time, it is beneficial for the financial specialist to purchase the offer at the price of €109. Nonetheless, should the Siemens share tumble to €90, it is less expensive for the speculator to purchase the security available. Consequently, he turns into the option to lapse and purchases the stock straightforwardly on the stock trade.

Be that as it may, it stays sketchy whether this activity additionally brings the speculator a benefit. The response to this inquiry relies essentially upon how high the option premium was. Put the case, and the purchaser paid a premium of €5 on the option to purchase the paper by the due date for €109. On account of options lapse, the dealer has, at any rate, made a deficiency of €5. When making a buy, notwithstanding, he possibly makes a benefit when the fundamental resource transcends €109 in addition to the premium, i.e., to in excess of €114.

Under such conditions, financial specialists might have the option to benefit uncertainly from rising prices through such a warrant. On the off chance that the price falls, the misfortune stays restricted to the option premium.

How Are Warrant Options Different?

The two options, just as warrants, are monetary instruments with which future exchanges are completed. That is the thing that they share practically speaking with prospects.

Financial specialists act in these exchanges, in a manner of speaking, on the improvement of the option or the warrant. Since exchange alludes to a delimited period, these two subordinates depend on a similar rule. The purchaser of the call option hypothesizes that the price of the basic resource will raise inside a predefined period or until the due date. This places the merchant in the situation to purchase the hidden at a small price. The financial specialist makes the real benefit on the off chance that he quickly exchanges the fundamental resource in a at a higher value. In this way, he can strike the distinction of the market value toward the start of the lawful exchange from the value on the due date.

Interestingly, the vendor of the call option hypothesizes on a falling price. Simultaneously, he expects that the purchaser of the instrument doesn't profit himself of the chance to secure the basic resource. Subsequently, the vendor procures a benefit with the premium and the further maintenance of the fundamental.

Options and Warrants—A Comparison

Options are normalized items. These are exchanged as agreements on the prospects trade. Paradoxically, warrants are among the protections. They are given by the backers (for instance, the banks). Be that as it may, the backer doesn't normally theorize on a falling price. The backers issue another warrant, which should have an opposite impact. Along these lines, the bank gets away from the occasion of accepting a danger as the price either falls or rises. The bank produces its benefits from the commissions it gets for the given warrants.

Warrant:

- Is given by a guarantor who all the while sets the price the danger of indebtedness borne by the seller.

- Just long call or long put is conceivable.

Option:

- Is given by each market member.
- No danger, as the lawful exchanges are supported.
- The price is dictated by the options trade, for example, EUREX.
- The conditions are normalized.
- The sky is the limit, for example, long call, short call, long put and short call, just as blends thereof.

On a fundamental level, options and warrants are very comparative: both are forward exchanges dependent on a formerly settled hidden resource. This value is likewise frequently called a basic. For the two varieties, fundamental of the accompanying monetary instruments might be accessible:

- Offers
- Monetary forms
- Lists
- Crude Materials
- Bonds
- Fates

Note: Options are exceptionally advantegous as their fairly estimated worth is distributed on the stock trade each day. On the other hand, warrants have less reliability.

Trading Based on the Acquisition of Rights

The root of these theory items can be found in the Netherlands in the seventeenth century. At that time, the main tulips were grown there. Sometime after its presentation, the tulip turned into a mainstream bloom in Holland. Energetic blossom cultivators set out to develop explicit assortments that would acquire a great deal of money.

Increasingly, more intrigued tulip buyers requested the specific sorts from the flower specialists, despite the fact that they had not at this point been brought to advertise. To give their activity a firm security, they paid for the tulips beforehand. Consequently, the flower vendors offered a specific measure of tulip bulbs at a fixed price on a particular date.

This made the reason for the beginning of options.

On a fundamental level, the purchasers would not like to put away their money by any means, however, their will was completely coordinated to the activity of the lawful business. In any case, that could change if the tulips had lost critical value by the activity date. For this situation, the blossom purchasers were as yet obliged to buy at the concurred price, and the tulip dealer made an arrangement.

Note: The advancement of the option implied that the shipper had no way out during the time the options were made. He needed to get the tulip bulbs at the recently agreed price if he needed it. That could mean an immense win or liquidation for him.

The Exercise Right Then and Now

The advancement of the option went on for the long call. Specifically, the activity commitment has changed throughout the long-term. In the good 'old days, the purchaser needed to practice his obtained right. On the off chance that he had been approved to purchase 20 tulip bulbs at the price of 200 guilders, he could reclaim them on the concurred date of procurement. In the event that the tulips price had raised, in light of the fact that the species and class of this assortment had abruptly acquired prevalence, the vendor profited by this bit of leeway. He was then ready to sell the tulip bulbs with net revenue of 100%.

Assuming, notwithstanding, the interest for this assortment of tulips has declined meanwhile, at that point the tulip bulbs may have been just worth a large portion of the buy date. However, regardless of whether they had not been worth anything, the money manager of the time had an obligation to remove the tulips. The bloom bulb purchaser was not permitted to demonstrate that he needed to revoke the exchange. He needed to pay the concurred measure of money to the flower vendor and take useless products home. The present condition has totally changed right up until today. For the current options offered available, the speculator can choose whether he needs to practice his entitlement to end the term or not. The speculators appreciate these advantages today: if the monetary item doesn't proceed as wanted, the most elevated conceivable misfortune is the danger of losing the option premium. The default hazard is in this way sensible since there is no business commitment. Merchants can in any case profit from better prices in the event that they wish.

Note: Financial items because of the exchange of a correct currently offer brokers a few points of interest over other trading openings. On the off chance that you find that your exchange is not the same as you might want, you would now be able to acknowledge the deficiency of the option premium and let the exchange terminate. You can ascertain your risks ahead of time and act appropriately.

Preferences and Disadvantages Compared to Warrants

Options have a few points of interest over warrants. This is particularly obvious as far as the danger in question. With both speculative instruments, merchants with little capital can likewise exchange through a record the speculator isn't obliged to work out. Then again, he can utilize the agreement that the lawful exchange has lapsed. Additionally, he has the chance to sell the monetary subsidiary, in the American variation even before the development date.

Accordingly, the speculator doesn't really have high monetary holds really to put resources into the instance of need. Options and warrants are tradable without purchasing the hidden resource. Nonetheless, there is an exceptional element in the warrants. These are seldom really exercised. Its motivation serves over all the theory on a benefit advantage after a resale.

Chapter 6. Options Trading: The Language

This section zeros in its radar on the phrasings of options trading. As we have lerned before, options trading is the cycle by which a merchant takes part in an exchange with different options about an exchange. Options trading has, in the recent past, been believed to be generally good as far as the risks are adressed. This is on the grounds that it takes part in the pooling of dangers. Numerous phrasings have been utilized time and again while participating in options trading.

With a comprehension of the different phrasings that are available to an options trader, one can exchange in a way that is normal. The different wordings include:

Ex-Dividend Rate

In the process whereby a company chooses a profit margin; it does this along with the presentation of a date known as a record date. This record date is the date whereby a speculator is taken up into the books of the organization as an investor who is qualified to get the profit. Soon after the record date, at that point comes the payable date. The payable date is the particular date when profits accumulaed are paid. In the wake of choosing the two days, at that point follows the way toward setting the ex-date or as it is officially known as the ex-profit rate. This frequently includes two business days, which are regularly before the record date. Acquisition of stock before the ex-date places you in the shoes of being obligated for receipt of the forthcoming installment. Then again, the acquisition of stock on the ex-date will make sure that you don't build on the profit.

Lognormal Distribution

From its phrasing, this sort of wording alludes to the logarithms that are related to the everyday price changes. On a drawn-out premise, when you notice the behavior of prices, you will find that there are shifts that will in general happen every day. This wording controls itself from the financial value of the change and zeros in its radar on logarithms as it were. At the point when we go number-crunching, the ramifications of this are that the price of the stock must be resolved between factor zeros to boundlessness. Coming to the real world, we locate that the circumstance is somewhat not the same as the past insight. Inferable from this, we can reason that lognormal appropriation is bullish in nature. In reality, a stock can take a decline of 100%. This is a disturbing value. At the point when the stock value expands, you will find that it can defeat the neighborhood's furthest reaches of 100%. More or less, we can say that a measrue of the price behavior, later on, is definitely centered on this sort of wording to decide its advanced instability.

Typical Distribution

The commonality of this kind of phrasing includes a numerical viewpoint in it. The appropriation of the final stock prices should be in an orderly fashion inside the normal distribution. The ending stock prices are what structure the irregular numbers. When attracting a diagram to catch this sort of information, more often than not, you will find that it accepts a shape known as a bell. In this bell, you will locate the numbers that have been registered as often as possible; subsequently, the prices that have been utilized often are supposed to be close to the normal structures. This is regularly at the specific focus on the bell. Since the circulation happens evenly, the numbers on the bell are a portrayal of the everyday changes of the prices in stock. This implies that for each current impact, there must be a counter-current impact. At the point when the price on the balance reflects upwards, there must be an inverse descending impact. When in the monetary world, the stock could just tumble to nothing and transcend any nearby cutoff points. Hypothetically negative effect on the stock is regularly felt.

Short Stock

This is a place that isn't in the drawn-out nature but instead centers on the present moment. This position is opened when offers are discarded in a commercial center that anybody doesn't claim. This is regularly alluded to as a short deal. Since this stock doesn't have anybody, it is frequently acquired from either a vendor or a merchant. This relationship is regularly started on the premise that offers should be purchased and restored to the intermediary or seller. This is regularly a nook of the short relationship that had been opened when the offers were gained from the vendor. At the point when the offers are discarded at a rate that will in general be lower than the underlying deal, at that point a benefit will impact. At the point when the occasions are turned, and the offers are sold on a high, at that point the impact of this is an outright misfortune. While expecting a stock position, it is typical that you will encounter misfortunes that are limitless in nature.

Model of Option Pricing

This is a kind of equation that is numerical in nature. It is utilized when you need to locate the hypothetical value of an option. You need to choose an option, however, you don't know of its value. The equation will help in an offer to make sure about a scrappy value of the option that you wish to wander into. This kind of equation places into thought a few variables, which include: hazard-free interest, profit sum, fundamental stock unpredictability, and the stock price.

The option Greeks are the experts who attempted to create this kind of model.

Spread

At the point when you take part in an exchange that has a similar security premise, you are said to have occupied with the spread. A spread involves the deal and acquisition of two unique options whose premise of security is the equivalent. With the spread, the two options might be purchasing from a similar put, and it very well may be from various puts.

Inferable from this, their strike prices may be the equivalent or in error. When executing a spread request, this is done in a way that resembles a bundle. This implies that the two sections are discarded all the while.

Time Value

A put or call is alluded to as the level of the option's top-notch value.

This option is frequently one that outperforms the characteristic value. The natural value alludes to the measure of money that is found in the stock. Changing the instability of loan costs and profits is the thing that negatively affects time value. Time decay additionally will in general influence an incredible arrangement.

Compose

This alludes to the offer of an option contract that has not been bought. The initial deal exchange is the thing that comes accordingly and influences the short situation of that specific option. The vendor, in this point of view, is otherwise called the author. This merchant is frequently at risk to be given a task on any date before the termination. At the point when this occurs, the individual in question should take up the agreement and satisfy it. This agreement regularly infers to arrange at whatever point a short call and obtain at whatever point a shot put.

Edge Requirement

This sort of necessity includes a sum that should be in the record of a broker to deal with its exchanges when in the securing of a short position. A short position frequently works in the way that you get stock without possession dependent on an intermediary or a vendor and sell it making installments to the seller. The short position has additionally been alluded to as a stripped situation as such. This is on the grounds that the situation right now isn't known and is along these lines, it isn't covered by anybody. This kind of monies has time and again been seen as a security to the representative for the broker to participate in the exchange. This security is of key significance to the merchant if there should be an occurrence of a put or a call. The broker will control the base stock regarding the task that has been given to the person in question.

Mean

In the ordinary world point of view, the mean is the number of factors that have been separated by the number of factors to choose a stand that is equivalent to all the current factors. In this viewpoint, the mean includes two factors. This is the additional up times of perceptions and the recurrence of this perception. The recurrence of perception is the number that is isolated into the number of perceptions. At the point when this occurs, you find that you show up at a mean. The central point of the information is presented by the mean. The mean will in general be estimating the scope of events that are probably going to occur.

Chapter 7. Basic Investment Strategies

According to the Oxford English Dictionary an investment strategy "is a plan, or course of action, taken in an attempt to achieve a specific goal." Investment strategies are commonly used for financial investments. However, they are also applied to other activities such as acquisitions, mergers, and divestitures, and M&A. This article will focus on equity investment strategies.

One of the earliest existing equity investment strategies is the "Stock Selection Policy" I developed (see "The Stock Selection Policy"). This is based on the principle of valuation. The purpose of this strategy is to identify undervalued securities that should be purchased and sold in a timely manner. It combines price point analysis with volatility.

The selection phase is where you identify undervalued securities that have strong fundamentals but are not overpriced. The pre-purchasing phase occurs immediately before purchase when you buy enough shares to reach your targets for selling, or to accumulate more shares to first cover your losses before cutting losses short or to avoid breaking even at all. The selling phase is where you sell off your stake in the security to realize your gains.

The Stock Selection Policy is designed to seek the excess return from stock price appreciation and dividends, and not from capital gain. The foundation of this strategy is the principle of valuation, meaning a company's assets are worth more than its shares in the long run.

Investment strategies are commonly used for financial investments. However, they are also applied to other activities such as acquisitions, mergers, and divestitures, and M&A. Investment strategies can be broad or narrow. They can be market-neutral (both long and short), based on company fundamentals or a combination of both.

These strategies are normally executed only for short periods, such as when the investment capital is available or has become available.

The goal is to make the maximum profit with minimal risk. There have been many developments in investment strategies and some have been successful. However, there are many classic equity investment strategies that are still prevalent today. These include fundamental analysis, contrarianism, and momentum strategies. All of these were developed at least 50 years ago by researchers from both academia and practitioners.

Fundamental analysis is based on analyzing the power of a company to generate sales and profits and is a combination of fundamental and technical analysis. Fundamental analysis involves a detailed examination of the historical financial performance, as well as the future prospects of a company. The most common criteria used in valuing companies include earnings per share, dividend payout ratio, return on equity (ROE), return on assets (ROA), and sales growth.

In a contrarian investment strategy, an investor does not follow conventional wisdom. This investor may be characterized by having "a tendency to think ahead; an independent mind; and courage in taking risks." This type of investor may also have bullish or bearish views about individual securities or the market in general. A contrarian investor will only buy equity security if he believes that it will underperform the market (or underperform a benchmark).

This type of investing strategy is understood in a variety of ways. In some cases, the investor may hold several securities in the portfolio. He may have few holdings (such as 2–3) and each one is held for different lengths of time or at different prices. In other cases, the investor may only hold single security for long periods of time, such as six months to two years or more. Many investors also use this strategy by selling short in the market by borrowing stocks and selling them short. Short selling is where an investor borrows a stock from a broker and sells it in the market but never takes possession of the stock.

Momentum investing strategies are based on investor preferences for momentum pro-cyclicality, i.e. investment in stocks with higher price momentum and lower price momentum (i.e., more volatile). This strategy involves following the crowd to buy a stock at low prices or sell a stock at high prices and is based on the theory that if investor sentiment is strong, then it will continue to be strong even after setbacks or news of bad performance.

Momentum investing strategies are also known as market-neutral strategies. The momentum effect is the tendency of any trend to continue when it has already begun. Momentum investors believe that the performance of a stock will stabilize after an initial surge in prices, and thus, buy a stock when it has risen sharply over short periods of time or followed by a decline of less than 20% from its high point.

This strategy is used by those who do not believe in fundamental analysis because it advocates that the best way to invest in the market is to wait for other people to make mistakes and then sell their shares at an opportunity.

These strategies are based on the belief that certain market conditions provide an opportunity to make money in the stock market. The strategies are typically used by professional investors, rather than retail investors. The research and development of these strategies are usually for short periods and it is not used as a long-term investment strategy.

The fundamental investor's basic strategy is to go long only when fundamentals indicate that the market will do well in the near term (for example, if company fundamentals are strong). Fundamental analysis involves valuing companies based on various indicators such as earnings per share, return on equity (ROE), ROA, sales growth, and so forth.

Value investing is a term that is used in the investing world to mean that an investor believes that the intrinsic worth of stock exceeds its market price on the day it is traded. Value investors are interested in finding companies with a higher current value relative to their assets and liabilities than they are currently trading for.

The basic strategy of value investors is to buy stocks when they are undervalued. They seek companies whose current assets (cash, marketable stocks, and real estate) represent a higher proportion of value than the price paid for it in terms of P/E multiple (NYSE: P/E).

The P/E ratio is calculated by dividing a stock's current share price by the last 12 months' earnings per share. Value investors tend to place more importance on the P/E multiple than on the overall market, as it reflects how much investors are willing to pay for each dollar of a company's net earnings. The higher the ratio, or multiple, it is believed that there is less potential for growth in future years. Low or depressed ratios may indicate that a company will do well in the near term.

Some analysts use an even more complicated method to compute their P/E ratios. They divide the stock price into EBITDA (Earnings before interest, tax, depreciation, and amortization). In this method, they account for the debt of the company and its depreciation expense to arrive at a conservative figure. An investor who uses the P/E ratio should consider other factors such as price to cash flow, price to book value, price to sales, earnings growth rate, and return on equity.

Growth investing is an investment strategy that emphasizes investing in companies with solid fundamentals (which usually means they have a good P/E ratio) but with strong growth potential. Growth investors want companies that will grow their earnings per share over the short term and long-term (more than 20% per year). Growth investors believe that companies growing at 20 to 30% will outperform the market on average.

The basic strategy of growth investors is to buy stocks that have good potential for earnings growth over a long period of time. Growth investors would prefer to buy high-quality, less volatile stocks with a promising outlook near their peaks. Basically, they are interested in buying low and trading them higher as long as they are not overvalued. The measures used by growth investors are P/E ratios and price-to-book ratios (P/B).

The P/E multiple is calculated by dividing the company's share price by its annual Earnings per Share (EPS) (NYSE: EPS). A higher multiple indicates that investors think there is more potential for growth in the company's future. The P/E ratio is a number that represents the forward price-to-earnings (P/E) ratio over an appropriate period, usually 1 to 5 years. In an ideal situation, P/E ratios should be below 15 and above 10 for stocks with a low to moderate growth rate.

A price-to-book (P/B) ratio is calculated by dividing the stock's market capitalization (number of shares multiplied by the current share price) by its book value per share (or net asset value). A lower P/B value indicates that the stock is undervalued.

Growth investors and Momentum investors may also employ valuations from other price-to-book (P/B) valuation ratios such as price to cash flow (P/CF), price to revenue (P/R), or price to book value (P/BV). These are commonly used by investors who want to buy low and sell high.

In this strategy, the investor selects a few key stocks in the market, then makes a buy and holds investment on those stocks. The stock is held for the long-term which is for a 5–10 year period. Although this strategy is similar to trend following, market timing, technical analysis, fundamental analysis, and value investing, it differs in its choice of investments. The main objective of the investor is to have simple portfolio management and reduce risk and volatility in his portfolio.

Chapter 8. Options Greeks

The "Greeks" is a term used in the options market to depict the different components of risks related to taking an options position, either in a particular option or a portfolio of options. These elements are called Greeks since they are routinely associated with Greek letters/images. Each risk variable is an outcome of imperfect speculation or the relationship of the option with another fundamental variable. Dealers use assorted Greek values, for instance, delta, theta, and others, to review options risk and manage option portfolios.

Delta

Delta (Δ) implies the pace of progress between the option's price and a $1 change in the basic resource's price. By the day's end, the price affectability of the option relative with the hidden Delta of a call option has a reach somewhere in the range of 0 and 1, while the delta of a put option has a reach among 0 and -1. For example, a monetary expert expects a call option with a delta of 0.50. Along these lines, if the hidden stock additions by $1, the option's price would theoretically increase by 50 cents.

For options brokers, delta moreover means the support extended for making a delta-unprejudiced position. For example on the off chance that you purchase a standard American call option with a 0.40 delta, you should offer 40 shares of stock to be totally supported. Net delta for a plan of options can in like manner be used to get the portfolio's fence extent.

Theta

Theta (Θ) connotes the pace of progress between the time and option price, or time affectability—now and again known as an option's time decay. Theta shows the aggregate an option's price would lessen as the time to termination reduces, all else same. For example, a monetary expert acknowledges a long option with a theta of -0.50; the option's price would decrease by 50 cents. All else being the same, in the event that three trading days pass, the option's worth would speculatively lessen by $1.50.

Theta increases when options are at-the-money, and lessens when options are in-and out-of-the-money. Options nearer to end in that have animating time decay. Long puts and long calls will for the most part have negative theta; short puts and short calls will have positive theta. Conversely, an instrument whose value isn't broken down by time, for instance, a stock, would have zero thetas.

Gamma

Gamma (Γ) means the pace of progress between the fundamental resource's price and an option's delta. This is called second-request price affectability.

Gamma shows the entirety of the delta would change given a $1 move in the fundamental security. For instance, what we expect from a monetary trained professional or financial specialist is one long call option on theoretical stock XYZ. The call option has a gamma of 0.10 and a delta of 0.50.

Vega

Vega (V) implies the speed of progress between the fundamental resource's inferred instability and an option's value. This is the option's affectability to unpredictability. Vega shows the amount of an option's price changes given a 1 rate change in suggested instability. For example, an option with a Vega of 0.10 shows the option's value is depended upon to change by 10 cents if the inferred instability changes by 1%.

Since extended unpredictability infers that the fundamental instrument will undoubtedly experience ludicrous values, a rising in instability will correspondingly construct the value of an option. Then again, a decrease in unpredictability will unfavorably impact the value of the option. Vega is at its generally outrageous for at-the-money options that have longer times until the end.

Minor Greeks

Hardly any different Greeks, with aren't discussed much of the time, are Epsilon, Vomma, Lambda, Zomma, Vera, Speed, Ultima, Shading.

These are second-or third-subsidiaries of the evaluating model and influence things, for example, the adjustment in delta with an adjustment in instability, and so forth They are continuously used in options trading philosophies as PC programming can quickly measure and record for these perplexing and sometimes slippery risk factors.

Benefits and Risk From Buying Call Options

The call options let the holder buy hidden security at the communicated strike price by the termination date called the expiry. The holder doesn't resolve to buy the resource in the event that they would not really like to purchase the resource. The danger to the call option buyer is confined to the exceptional paid. Changes in the hidden stock don't influence.

Benefits and Risk From Selling Call Options

Selling call options is known as creating an arrangement. The author gets the top-notch expense. Toward the day's end, an option buyer will pay the premium to the merchant—or author—of an option. The most outrageous benefit is the premium gotten when selling the option. A financial specialist who sells a call option is bearish and acknowledges the basic stock's price will fall or remain respectably close to the option's strike price during the existence of the option.

In the event that the transcendent piece of the pie price is at or under the strike price by expiry, the option lapses uselessly for the call buyer. The option trader pockets the premium as their benefit. The option isn't drilled in light of the fact that the option buyer would not buy the stock at the strike price higher than or comparable to the prevalent market price.

Benefits and Risks From Buying Put Options

Put options are investments where the buyer accepts the fundamental stock's market price will fall below the strike price prior to the lapse date of the option. The holder can offer offers without the obligation to sell at the communicated strike per-share price by the expressed date.

Since buyers of put options need the stock price to get lower, the put option is beneficial when the fundamental stock's price is below the strike price. In the event that the overarching market price isn't actually the strike price at expiry, the speculator can rehearse the put. They will sell shares at the option's higher strike price. Should they wish to replace their holding of these offers they may buy them on the open market. Their benefit on this exchange is the strike price less the current market price, notwithstanding costs—the premium and any business commission to present the orders. The result would be expanded by the number of option contracts purchased, by then increased by 100—expecting every understanding/contract addresses 100 offers.

Benefits and Risks From Selling Put Options

Selling put options is generally called creating an understanding or an agreement. A put option creator acknowledges the essential stock's expense will stay proportionate or expand over the existence of the option—making them bullish on the offers.

Here, the option buyer has the advantage to make the dealer buy parts of the hidden resource at the strike price on expiry.

On the off chance that the hidden stock's price closes over the strike price by the termination date, the put option slips by uselessly. The trader's most prominent benefit is the premium. The option isn't exercised on the grounds that the option buyer would not sell the stock at the lower strike share price when the market price is higher.

On the off chance that the stock market's value drops underneath the option strike price, the put option author is resolved to buy shares of the fundamental stock at the strike price. All things considered, the put option will be acquired by the option buyer.

The buyer will sell their proposals at the strike price since it is higher than the stock market's value.

The danger for the put option holder happens when the market's price falls under the strike price. As of now, at termination, the vendor is constrained to purchase shares at the strike price. Dependent on how much the offers have been recognized, the put author's misfortune can be colossal.

The put author—the shipper—can either hang on to the offers and expectation the stock price rises above the price tag or sell the offers and accept the misfortune. Regardless, any misfortune is counterbalanced reasonably by the premium gotten.

Sometimes a monetary expert will make put options at a strike price. That is, they see the offers being a nice value, and would buy at that price. Exactly when the price falls, and the option buyer rehearses their option, they get the stock at the price they need, with the extra bit of leeway of getting the option premium.

Geniuses

A call option buyer has the advantage to buy resources at a price that is lesser than the market when the stock's price is expanding.

The put option buyer can benefit by selling the stock at the strike price when the market price is below the strike price.

Option shippers get a premium from the buyer for forming an option.

Cons

In a falling business sector, the put option vendor may be constrained to buy the resource at a higher strike price than they would consistently pay on the lookout.

The call option creator faces interminable danger if the stock's price rises by and large and they are constrained to buy shares at an excessive cost.

Option buyers should pay a straightforward premium to the creators of the option.

True Example of an Option

Expect that Microsoft shares are trading at $108 per offer and you are sure that they are going to increase in value. You decide to buy a call option to benefit from a development in the stock's price.

You get one call option with a strike price of $115 for one month later for 37 cents for each share. Your total money cost is $37 for the circumstance, notwithstanding commissions and charges (0.37 × 100 = $37).

On the off chance that the stock climbs to $116, your option will be valued at $1, since you could exercise the option to get the stock for $115 per share and immediately trade it for $116 per share. The benefit on the option position would be 170.3% since you paid 37 cents and earned $1—that is much higher than the 7.4% extension in the fundamental stock price from $108 to $116 at the hour of expiry.

On the off chance that the stock tumbled to $100, your option would terminate uselessly, and you would be out $37 premium. The potential gain is that you didn't buy 100 shares at $108, which would have achieved an $8 per share, or $800, full-scale misfortune. As should be self-evident, options can restrict your disadvantage risk. In a manner of speaking, the benefit in dollar terms would be a net of 63 cents or $63 since one option contract connotes 100 offers ($1 -0.37 × 100 = $63).

Options Spreads

Options spreads are methods that use distinctive blends of buying and selling different options for an ideal risk and cut losses. Spreads are created using vanilla options and can use various circumstances, for instance, high-or-low unpredictability conditions, up-or-down moves, or anything in the center.

Spread frameworks, can be depicted by their outcome or view of their benefit misfortune profile, for instance, bull call spreads or iron condors.

Chapter 9. Intermediate Options Trading Strategies

Almost every trade has a strategy behind it. Every trade has reasons as to why it was made and how the traders expected the trade to move from one state to another. The problem, especially for the novice trader, is that they do not have enough experience or knowledge of the various options strategies that are at their disposal to help them understand what "type" of strategy best suits their trading goals. This article is here to help the inexperienced options trader in the most basic of ways by categorizing different options strategies and providing some information about each one. This will help the trader to understand where each category begins and ends so that they can make educated decisions as to which option strategy is right for them on any given trade. The objective of this article is not to teach you how to trade—in fact, we hope it causes you to rethink and re-evaluate your trading strategy (it's much easier if you do this yourself as opposed to hearing about it from someone else).

Strategies and Their Uses:

Buying Straddles and Strangles: The basic rule of thumb for buying straddles is "don't make a trade unless you can afford to lose half your capital." This may seem like sound advice, but it isn't always as simple as that due to various scenarios that could arise during a trade. For example, if the stock price increases by 10 points at some point during the course of a trade (i.e. look at this price chart of MSFT), a 10 point increase could potentially turn a 20 points loss into a 2 point gain (i.e. +20 / -10) if the straddle is still in the money at expiration. Suppose you bought the 20/60 call spread, but the stock price increased by 40 points before your trade is even exercised. In this case, with MSFT at $30 per share, your loss would only be 20 points instead of 60 because you have made money on the calls you owned (remember that each option has value as soon as it is in-the-money).

An important thing to remember is that you should not let the position you're in discourage you. A 20 point loser of a stock trade could potentially become a 10 point winner with a little luck. Remember that when trading options, it's not always about making money on every trade, it's about making the most money possible from each and every trade while still remaining realistic and flexible.

Another option strategy is buying strangles. The basic rule of thumb for this strategy is "don't make a trade unless you can afford to lose both your initial investment and your "premium." This may seem obvious, but is it really true all the time? I mean what if you bought the 20/60 strangle and MSFT was trading at $27.50 when your contract is in-the-money? You now have a 25 point gain—you can't lose on that trade, even if nothing else happens. A loss of only 25 points over your investment of $2,500 is not something to be scoffed at.

The option strategy called buying straddles and strangles is one of the most common strategies out there. It basically consists of buying a call spread to potentially profit from the movement of an underlying stock. The strategy itself is not really complex, but the execution can be. If you're looking for a general outline of this strategy and its strengths and weaknesses, we go over it in detail in our blog post about Call Spreads and Straddles.

Puts: A put is exactly what it sounds like—you sell a put option contract instead of having the right to buy the stock at some future time. However, it is important to keep in mind that puts are nothing more than insurance policies for your portfolio. If you sell a put option on a stock and later the stock goes up in price by the amount of your premium, then you've made money. If you sold it too early and the stock price doesn't go up enough, you could have lost money—so always know how long your puts are before expiration.

Some examples of puts include:

Buying a "buying a put" strategy is where you sell an option on XYZ to potentially profit from their movement over time. For example, suppose you're generally bullish on a stock such as MSFT and you sell the XYZ June 26 put at $1.60. If the price of the stock increases above $26 by expiration, then your trade is profitable. If not, then you've lost $1.60 plus commissions for a small price risk strategy (the risk involved with selling an option).

The potential problems with this strategy are that if the stock moves lower instead of higher, then you could be required to buy XYZ stock at $26 or above when it was trading below that price before (i.e. your trade would be exercised). Also, you could be subject to time decay over time which would eat away at the potential profits of your trade.

Buying a "selling a put" strategy is where you sell an option contract on XYZ in order to profit from their movement over time. Because selling puts requires you to buy the underlying stock (which in this case is MSFT) at a premium, this could result in large losses if the underlying stock (MSFT) falls below its breakeven price instead of moving higher. This trade is best used by the swing or long-term traders who are less worried about time decay and more concerned with making money on their stocks over time.

Puts and credit spread: A put and credit spread is a combination of a put and a credit spread. The advantage of this strategy is that the premium received for the put increases the potential profit. For example, if you sell an XYZ June 26 put option selling for $1.60 and you receive $2 in premium, then you have $3 profit in your pocket to use on your next trade. If you sell the same XYZ June 26 call option at $2.20, then your overall position is worth (the initial premium × 2) $4 ($2 debit).

The main problem with this strategy is that the amount of options required to execute this trade increases greatly. If you had $1,000 to invest, then you would have to buy 10 options (a put and a call) in order to make this trade work. Not only that, but since both options are time-based (i.e. they expire on the same day), then you're required to exit your position exactly on expiration day i.e. "option chain" open and close transactions occur in real-time which can be very expensive for the beginner trader using such strategies.

Don't get us wrong here though, credit spreads are great strategies and can be used to great effect for a large number of trades. The main point here is that you must have the capital available to make such trades i.e. if you don't have the money to buy both options in order to make this trade work, then it won't work period no matter how good an idea you think it is.

Vertical spreads: A vertical spread is essentially an option strategy where you can profit from buying a bullish/bearish stock option and selling a nearby option that has a higher delta, thus reducing overall risk because the position consists of two contracts that offset each other. The basic rule of thumb for this strategy is "don't make a trade unless you can afford to lose both your initial investment and your premium."

For example, if you sell the XYZ June 26 call option at $2.20 and the June 26 put option at $1.60, then you have created a vertical spread which will give you more bang for your buck when XYZ stock moves in either direction. If XYZ stock moves up by less than 10 points, then you're considered "flat" with respect to the price of the underlying stock, but if it moves higher by 10 points or more, then you've made money on this trade because all options have value based on their intrinsic value (i.e. the value at expiration) minus commissions.

Combinations: A combination is where you combine two of the other options strategies we've already covered such as a put & call spread or a vertical spread. For example, if you buy the XYZ June 26 put option selling for $1.60 and the June 26 call option at $2.20, then you have created a combination that will give you more bang for your buck when XYZ stock moves in either direction.

A combination transaction can be very difficult to execute at times since you're required to buy both options in order to make it work. For example, if you sell the combo of XYZ put and call, then you'll have to pay for two options commissions just for that one trade which can get very expensive. If both are in-the-money options at expiration (i.e. the stock price is above their breakeven price), then your position will be worth (the initial premium × 2) $4 ($2 debit).

Alternatively, if MSFT closes at $32 or above on June 26, then the combo only goes in-the-money (in this case 3 points) and we'd have made a profit of $4.60 (in this case the initial premium X 2). If MSFT closes at $28 or below on June 26, then the combo goes out-of-the-money (in this case 15 points) and we'd lose our entire investment by the time expiration comes around. In that case, if you sold the June 26 put option ($1.60) and the June 26 call option ($2.20), then you're required to buy MSFT stock at $26 or above in order for this strategy to work. Since MSFT is trading at $27.50 on June 26, then you'd lose money on this trade (i.e. we would have purchased MSFT at $26 per share, but if it was trading at $27.50, then we'd be required to purchase it for an additional 2points which means that we'd have lost $2).

Chapter 10. Iron Condor Strategy

What Is an Iron Condor?

An iron condor is a procedure made with 4 options involving two puts (one short and one long) and two calls (one short and one long), and four strike prices, all with a similar end date. The goal is to benefit from sudden low prices in the instrument.

The iron condor has a relative outcome as a typical condor spread, notwithstanding, it uses the two puts and calls as opposed to simply calls or simply puts. Both the condor and the iron condor are developments of the iron butterfly and butterfly spread, individually.

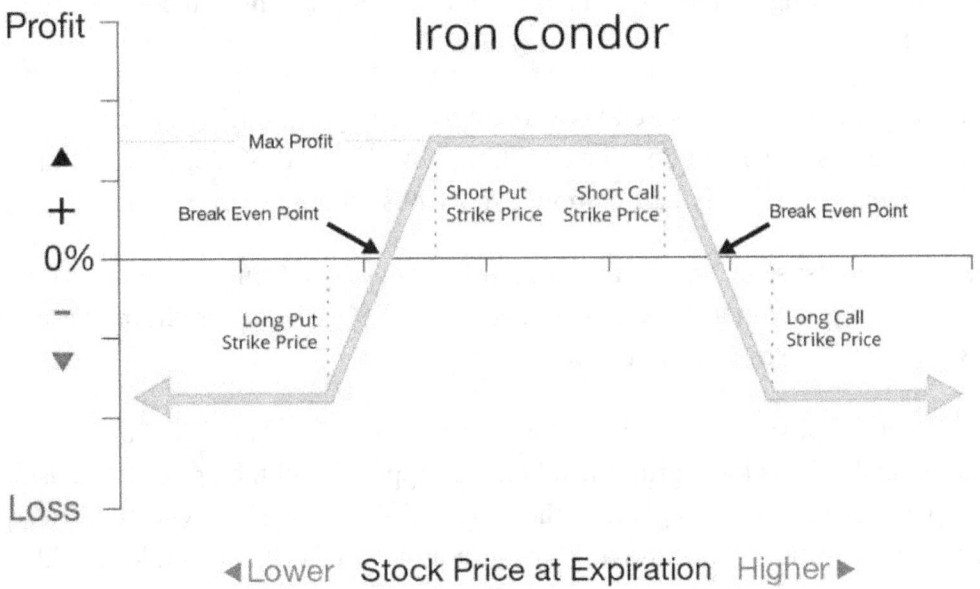

Graph 5

Key Takeaways

An iron condor is commonly a fair method and benefits the most when the basic resource doesn't move a great deal. Albeit, the procedure can be created with a bearish or bullish predisposition.

The iron condor is made out of four options: a bought put further OTM and a sold put closer to the money, and a bought call further OTM and a sold call closer to the money.

The benefit is topped at the top-notch gotten while the risk is, in similar manner, at the differentiation between the bought and sold call strikes and the bought and sold put strikes (less the premium got).

Iron Condor Losses and Profits

The most extraordinary benefit for an iron condor is the measure of credit, or premium, gotten for making the four-leg options position.

The most outrageous misfortune is low share prices. The best misfortune is the difference between the short call and long call strikes or the short put. Long put strikes reduce the shortage by the net credits gotten. Nonetheless, at that point add commissions to get the total deficit for the exchange.

The best misfortune happens if the value moves over the long call strike (which is higher than the sold call strike) or under the put strike (which is lower than the sold put strike).

The Example of an Iron Condor on a Stock

For instance, a financial specialist accepts that Apple Inc. will be for the most part level regarding price over the accompanying two months. They decide to complete an iron condor. The stock is as of now trading at $212.26.

They sell a call with a $215 strike, which gives them $7.63 in premium. They buy a call with a strike of $220, which costs them $5.35. The credit on these 2 legs is $2.28, or $228 for one agreement. The exchange is simply half complete, notwithstanding.

Additionally, the specialist sells a put with a strike of $210, which brings about a premium gotten of $7.20. They also buy a put with a strike of $205, costing $5.52. The net credit on these 2 legs is $1.68 or $168 if trading one agreement on each.

The whole credit for the position is $3.96 ($2.28 + $1.68), or $396. This is the best benefit the representative can make. This most prominent benefit happens if all the options end useless, which suggests the expense should be someplace in the scope of $215 and $210 when ends happen in two months. In the event that the price is above $215 or underneath $210, the vendor could in any case make a lower profit, or, in similar manner, lose money.

Iron Condors

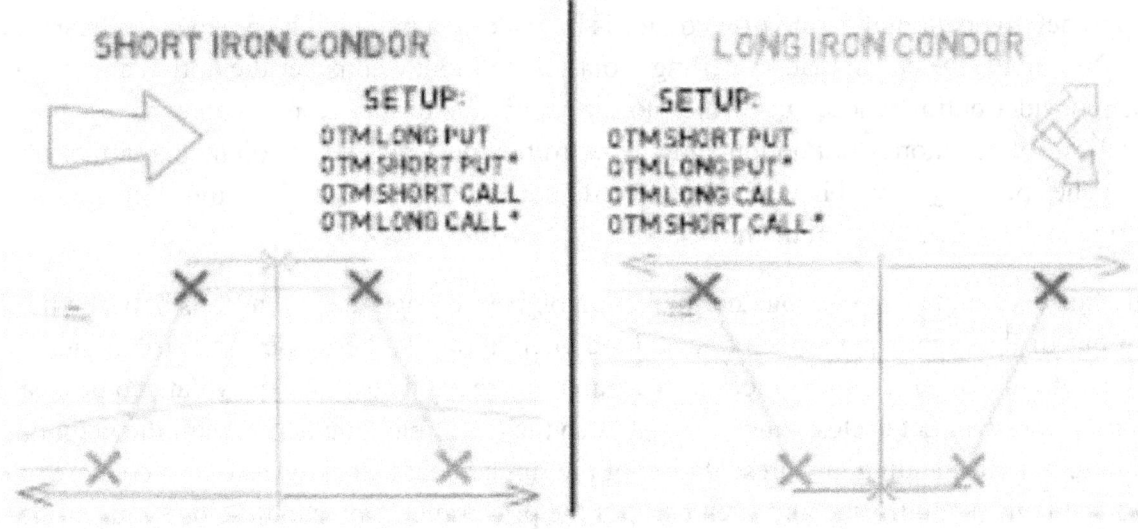

Graph 6

The misfortune gets greater if the price of Apple stock techniques the upper call strike ($220) or the lower put strike ($205). The most outrageous misfortune happens if the expense of the stock exchanges above $220 or underneath $205.

Accept the stock at the end is $225. This is over the upper call strike value, which suggests the dealer is confronting the most extraordinary possible misfortune.

The sold call is losing $10 ($225–$215) while the bought call is making $5 ($225–$220). The puts lapse. The agent/exchange loses $5, or $500 all out, however, they furthermore got $396 in charges. As such, the misfortune is topped at $104 notwithstanding commissions.

We should accept the expense of Apple rather dropped, however not underneath the lower put limit. It diminishes to $208. The short call is losing $2 ($208 - $210), or $200, while the long put slips are pointless. The calls moreover lapse. The seller loses $200 on the position, nonetheless, he got $396 in premium credits. Thusly, they actually make $196, and we still have to substract commission costs.

Long Iron Condor

The iron condor strategies are a high-level technique that, much the same as the butterfly, utilizes two vertical spreads. The traders open a call spread at a strike price higher than the current stock value of the basic resource and opens a put spread as well, at a strike price that is lower than the current stock value of the iron condor strategies, the Long Iron Condor is the most famous, and it is additionally perhaps the most favored progressed options purchasing strategies. Options trading teachers energetically suggest it.

Utilizing the long iron condor system is like making a "definite wager" despite the fact that it leaves space for some humble benefit and a couple of blunders. The system is intended to be utilized on stocks that are not unstable, and those that keep an impartial trading range. Also, in the event that the stock price moves excessively and the option arrives at its due date, the risks coming about are restricted.

The approach to opening the long iron condor is by making a bullish put spread and a bearish call spread. You make the call spread by selling 1 out-of-the-money consider the option and buying another consider option whose out-of-the-money position is further along. You make the put by selling 1 out-of-the-money put option and afterward buying 1 put the option that is farther of-the-money. The spreads you will have made are credit spread, and once the position is opened, you can hope to reap some benefit from them.

Having this exceptional spread together makes an objective price range that falls between the inward out-of-the-money put strike price and the internal out-of-the-money call strike price. On the occasion, the fundamental stock price stays around this reach when the expiry date comes, each of the four options will get useless, and you will keep the credit pay you had toward the beginning. Assuming, notwithstanding, the presentation of the fundamental stock turns out to be more unpredictable than you trusted and even escapes the price range, you should close your in-the-money positions right away. Shockingly, doing this will diminish your benefits and eventually, present to you a total deficit.

In contrast with other nonpartisan trading strategies, the long iron condor sticks out. In the event that you contrasted it with comparable strategies that manage non-unpredictable stocks like the Strong Strangle and the Long Butterfly, you would take note of the distinctions. For instance, if the price changes definitely, a dealer utilizing the Strong Strangle will endure limitless risks while a merchant utilizing the long iron condor will just experience some restricted greatest misfortunes.

In the event that the stock price stays at a similar situation with no development, under the Long Butterfly, the trader will appreciate the greatest benefit. Notwithstanding, the Long Iron Condor makes more space, with its broader price range, inside which the broker can appreciate the greatest benefit. This price reach can be controlled as well. In the event that you make it smaller, you make space to get more starting credit pay, yet this opens you to the danger of having the stock price arriving out of this reach.

One huge detriment of the long iron condor procedure is that it is comprised of four individual options, and this could mean higher commission costs, contingent upon the arrangements of your intermediary, in contrast with different strategies. Additionally, the greatest risk potential that a broker stands to bring about is regularly more than the underlying credit pay the dealer puts when opening this position. These two components are generous, and they cause the Long Iron Condor to show up less productive than individuals expect it to be.

Thusly, before you take it up, it would work well for you to plunk down and examine all components included, weigh out the circumstance successfully, and see whether the methodology is fitting for your trading objectives. Remember to incorporate the commission costs in your investigation.

Chapter 11. Advanced Options Trading Strategies

1. Covered Call

With calls, one strategy is essential to buy a bare call option.

You can similarly structure a central covered call or purchase compose. This is a renowned system since it creates pay and diminishes some threat of being long stock alone. The compromise is that you should be anxious to sell your shares at a set price: the short strike price. To execute the method, you purchase the basic stock as you ordinarily would, and all the while sell a call option on those equivalent offers.

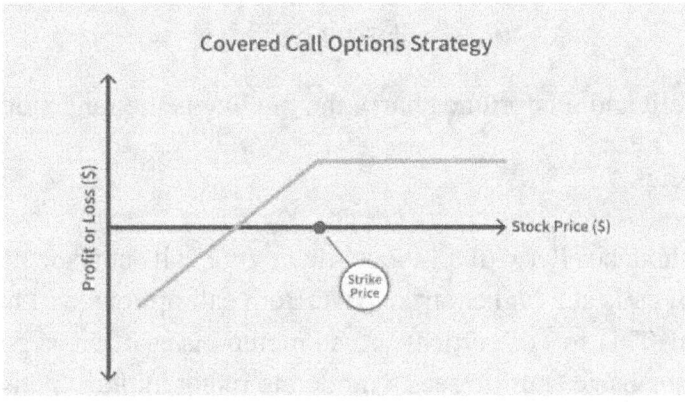

Graph 7

In the Profit and Loss outlined above, notice how as the stock price rises, the negative profit and hazard from the call balances the situation of the long offer. Since you get premium from selling the call, as the stock goes above the strike price to the potential gain, you can effectively sell your stock at a more raised level than the strike price (premium got + strike). The covered call's Profit and Loss diagram looks an extraordinary arrangement like a short exposed put's profit and risk.

2. Hitched Put

In a wedded put strategy, a speculator purchases a resource (in this model, portions of stock), and at the same time purchase put options for an equivalent number of offers. The holder of a put option has the option to sell the stock at the strike price. Each agreement implies a hundred shares. A theorist or financial specialist would consider this procedure essential to secure their disadvantage hazard when holding a stock. This methodology capacities simply act like a protection procedure, and sets up a value floor should the stock's value fall unexpectedly.

An occurrence of the wedded put would be if a seller purchases a hundred shares of stock and gets one put option simultaneously. This method is charming in light of the fact that a speculator is made sure about the disadvantage should a negative occasion occur. All the while, the financial specialist would participate in the aggregate of the potential gain if the stock increases in value. The essential disadvantage to the method/procedure happens if the stock doesn't fall, in which case the seller loses the superior paid for the put option.

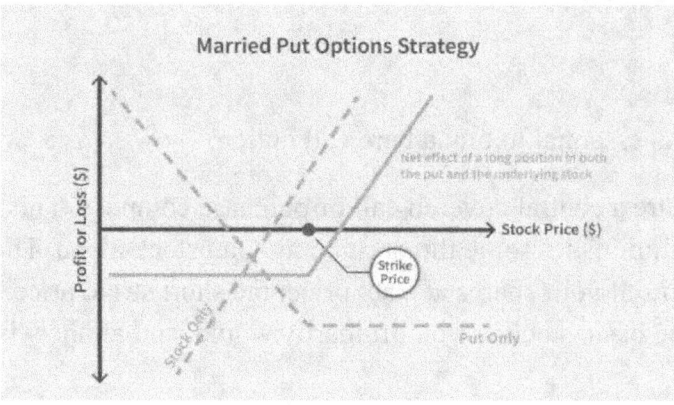

Graph 8

In the graph above (benefit and misfortune chart), the ran line is the long stock position.

3. Bull Call Spread

In a bull call spread method, a seller will all the while buying calls at a specific strike cost, can sell a comparative number of calls at a higher strike cost. Both call options will have a similar basic resource and termination. This sort of vertical spread method is as often as possible used when a speculator is bullish on the basic and foresees a moderate rising in the expense of the resource. The speculator compels his/her potential gain on the exchange, yet decreases the net premium, which appeared differently in relation to buying a bare call option all around.

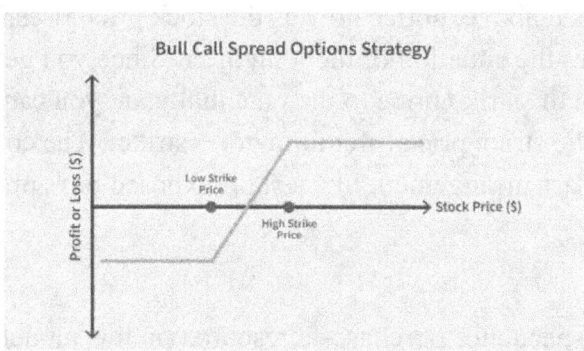

Graph 9

In the Profit and Loss outline above, you can see this is a bullish strategy, so the agent needs the stock to increase in expense to make a benefit on the exchange.

This is the manner in which a bull call spread is created.

4. Bear Put Spread

The bear put spread procedure is such a vertical spread. In this technique, the monetary expert will simultaneously purchase put options at a specific strike cost and sell a comparative number of puts at a lesser strike cost.

The two decisions would be for a relative end date and the same principal resource. This system is used when the seller/specialist is bearish and predicts the basic resource's expense to drop. It offers both confined gains and obliged risks.

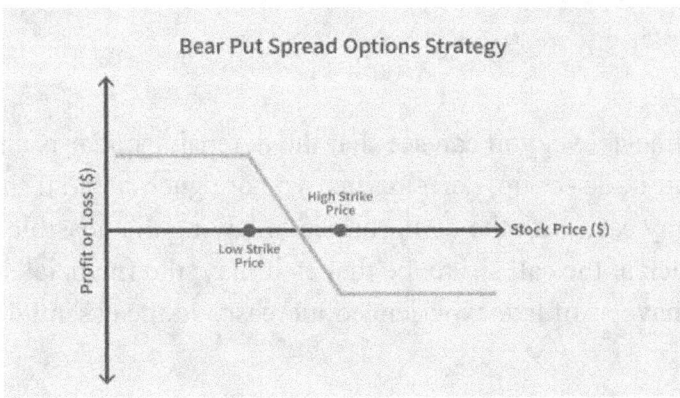

Graph 10

The Profit and Loss chart above is a bearish method, so you need the stock to lessen to profit. The compromise while using a bear put spread is that your potential gain is kept, regardless, your superior spent is diminished. On the off chance that total puts are constantly costly, one approach to manage to offset the high premium is by selling lower strike sets against them. This is the way a bear put spread is created.

5. Defensive Collar

A defensive collar technique is carried out by purchasing an OTM put option and working an OTM call option for a comparable fundamental resource and end.

This procedure is as often as possible used by financial specialists after a long situation in stock has encountered critical increases. These options blend license speculators to have disadvantage confirmation (long puts to make sure about benefits) while having the compromise of possibly being resolved to sell shares at a more critical price (selling higher = more benefit than at current stock levels).

An essential model would be if a speculator is long a hundred portions of IBM at $50 and IBM has risen to $100 as of the first of January.

The trader could build up a defensive collar by offering one IBM approach 15 March 105 and along these lines buying 1 IBM March 95 put. The seller is guaranteed beneath 95 USD until the fifteenth of March, with the compromise of maybe resolving to sell their offers at 105 USD.

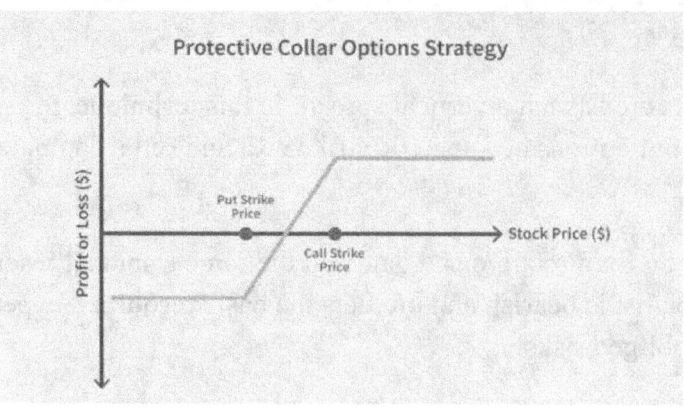

Graph 11

In the Profit and Loss outline above, you can see that the defensive collar is a mix of a long put and a covered call. This is a fair trade set-up, deriving that you are guaranteed if there should emerge an event of falling stock, in any case with the compromise of having the possible commitment to undercutting your long stock at the call strike. be that as it may, the financial specialist should be glad to do thusly, as they have as of late experienced increases in the essential offers.

6. Long Straddle

This methodology is where a financial specialist or a vendor at the same time buys a put and call option on the same hidden resource, with a comparable strike price and end. A monetary expert will as often as possible use this methodology when the individual acknowledges the cost of the hidden/principal resource will move out of reach, however, is dubious of which course the move will take. This philosophy permits the financial specialist to have the open entryway for theoretically boundless addition, while the most extraordinary misfortune is restricted unquestionably to the cost of the two options contracts solidified.

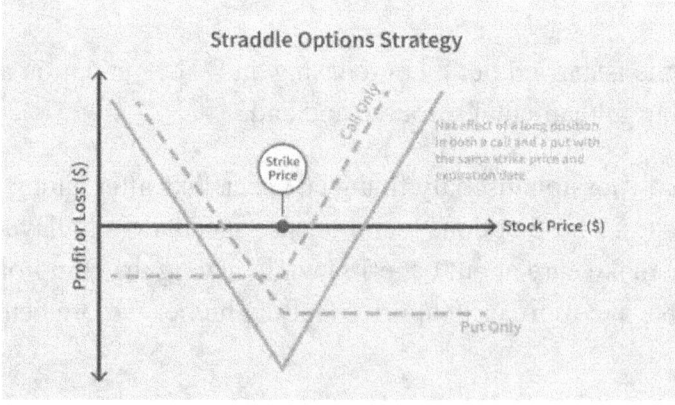

Graph 12

In the Profit and Loss diagram above, there are 2 breakeven focuses. This approach becomes beneficial when the stock takes a gigantic action, one heading on the other.

7. Long Strangle

The speculator purchases an OTM call option and an OTM puts on a similar pass, at the same time, and the same basic resource. A financial specialist who uses this methodology acknowledges the basic resource's price will experience a tremendous development; anyway it is questionable which course the move will take.

This could, for example, be a bet on a paid release for an association or an FDA occasion for a medical care stock. Risks are limited to the top-notch spent on the two options. Chokes will routinely be more moderate and sensible than rides on the grounds that the options bought are out of the money.

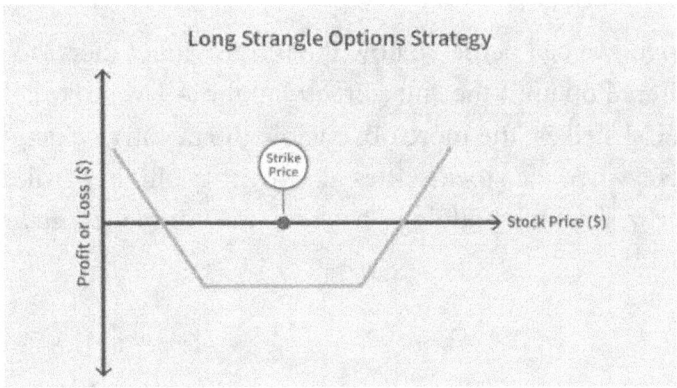

Graph 13

In the P and L chart above, there are two breakeven focuses. This system becomes profitable when the stock takes an especially colossal action without a doubt. Once more, the theorist couldn't ponder which course the stock moves just that it is a more famous move than indisputably the superior the financial specialist or examiner paid for the design.

8. Long Call Butterfly Spread

The entire methodology so far has required a mix of two remarkable agreements or positions. In this system, using call options, a speculator will join both a bear spread procedure and a bull spread methodology, and use three different strike costs. All options are for the same lapse date and fundamental resource.

For example, a long butterfly spread can be made by getting one ITM call option at a lesser strike cost, while getting one OTM call option, and selling two ATM call options. A reasonable butterfly spread will have close to wing widths. This model is known as a "call fly" and results in a net charge.

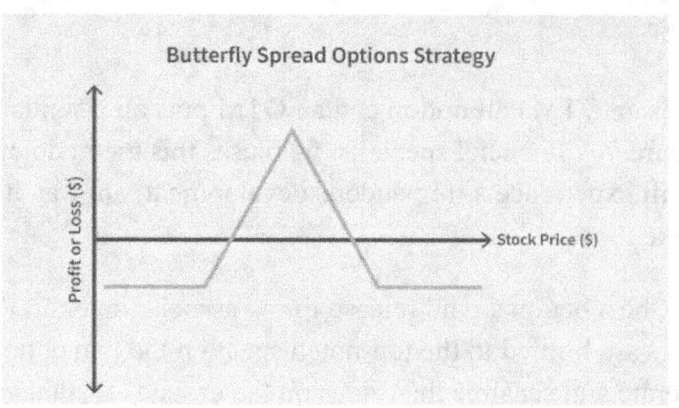

Graph 14

In the P and L graph above, we can perceive how the most evident increase is made when the stock remaining parts are unaltered up until the end (directly at the ATM strike). The further away the stock moves from the ATM strikes, the more observable the negative change in P and L. The most extraordinary risk happens when the stock settles at or over the higher strike call, or when it settles at the lower strike or below. This methodology has both the compelled downside and confined potential gain.

9. Iron Condor

An intriguing procedure is the iron condor. In this technique, the monetary expert holds a bull put spread and a bear call spread. The iron condor is created by selling one OTM put and getting one OTM call of a higher strike (bear call spread), and selling one OTM put and getting one OTM put off a lesser strike (bull put spread). All options have a near-end date and are on a similar fundamental resource. Customarily, the call and put sides have a practically identical spread width.

This trading procedure procures a net premium on the design and is expected to exploit a stock encountering low eccentrics.

Various brokers like this exchange for its evident high probability of acquiring a humble benefit in the premium.

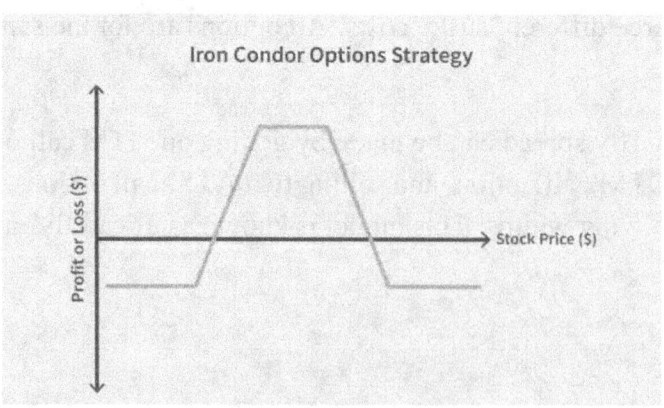

Graph 15

In the Profit and Loss graph above, we can observe how the greatest increase is made when the stock stays unaltered up until the end (straightforwardly at the ATM strike). The further away the stock moves from the at the money strikes, the more critical the negative change in misfortune and benefit. The most extraordinary risk happens when the stock settles at the lower strike or below, or if the stock settles at or over the higher strike call.

10. Iron Butterfly

The last option procedure we will show is the iron butterfly. In this methodology, an examiner will sell an ATM put and purchase an OTM put, while in a similar way, selling an ATM put and purchasing an OTM call. All options have a comparable termination date and are on the same basic resource. Even though it resembles a butterfly spread, this system contrasts since it uses the two puts and calls, instead of just one.

This methodology joins selling an at-the-money ride and buying defensive "wings." You can, in a similar manner, consider the development of two spreads. It isn't surprising to have a comparable width for the two spreads. The long out-of-the-money call makes sure about against limitless drawbacks. The long OTM put shields against hindrances from the short put strike to nothing. P also, L are both confined inside a specific reach, dependent upon the strike prices of the options used. Financial specialists like this method for the pay it produces and the higher likelihood of a little increase with a non-unpredictable stock.

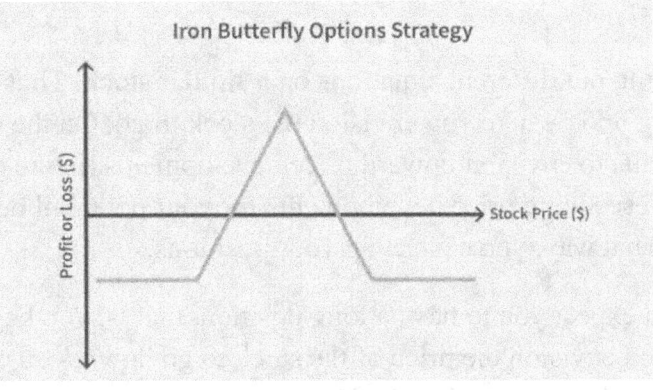

Graph 16

In the P and L framework above, notice how the most extraordinary increase is made when the stock remain unaltered up until pass. The further the stock moves from the at the money strikes, the more well known the negative change in P and L. The most noticeable risk happens when the stock settles at the lower strike, or if the stock settles above or at the higher strike call. This strategy has both the restricted disadvantage and restricted potential gain.

Chapter 12. How to Behave on Lateral Movements

The risks is a characteristic piece in any adventure. Unfortunately, there are no certain wagers. This implies that all investments convey a specific measure of danger.

Likewise, some are normally more dangerous than others. Consequently, you should know about the danger related to the sorts of investments you are making.

Utilizing a Trading Plan

There's a proverb that states, "When you neglect to design, you intend to come up short." In the realm of trading, this aphorism has stood the trial of time. At the point when you disregard to have a trading plan, you make yourself powerless. The explanation behind this lies in the absence of direction you may have. At the point when you need direction, you may wind up picking stocks aimlessly. Also, in the event that you base your choices exclusively on the suggestions of masters and savants, you may wind up coming up short on a strong establishment.

That is the reason having a trading plan will give your direction while likewise empowering you to expand on a sound methodology. Outfitted with this methodology, you can fabricate a steady approach. Kindly remember that consistency is the way to progress.

Utilizing Option Spreads

This system includes taking out different situations on a similar stock. Thusly, you are covering different positions relying upon where you envision the stock to go. On the off chance that you are bullish, you can utilize calls to envision upward price developments. In the event that you are bearish, you can utilize descending price developments for your potential benefit. Everything relies upon the hidden basics. That way, you can set up your positions.

To begin with, we should expect you to have a long position, that is, you begin possessing the stock. In the event that you envision the price of the stock to go down, you can take out a put in this way bolting at a more exorbitant cost point. At that point, you accept out a required similar stock at a much lower price point than it right now stands. At the point when the stock's price falls, you would then be able to practice the put at the greater cost point and afterward practice the call once the price has fallen. Eventually, you make a benefit by selling at a higher cost point and afterward re-buying a similar stock at a much lower cost. Now, you could either sell once the price bounces back or decide to purchase and hold.

Utilizing Diversification

Enhancement is a center precept of trading. Prepared speculators use options as a method for enhancing their portfolio, especially on the off chance that they are vigorously put resources into long positions. All things considered, options can be an extraordinary method of dealing with your resource investment. All in all, in the event that you own common assets, list reserves, or a 401(k), options can be an incredible path for you to enhance hazard. While options depend on a fundamental stock, the truth of the matter is that it gives you cover in the event that you need to balance hazards in long positions.

In addition, options are extraordinary when markets are violent or don't have an unmistakable pattern. Moreover, bear markets will in general create complex environments for financial specialists. Thus, it's consistently a smart thought to utilize expansion as a method for assisting you with trying not to contribute most of your investment capital into a solitary resource class.

Utilizing Automated Trading

By far most of the trading is finished by PC stages these days.

Thusly, you don't be on the trading floor to get bargains going.

You can set up your trading framework from the solace of your home with a couple of keystrokes. At that point, you should simply pause for a minute or two and let the framework deal with everything. We exceptionally empower that you utilize these highlights. For the most part, computerized trading maintains a strategic distance from deferred responses. This is imperative to consider as the response time of a human is definitely not exactly any PC framework. Subsequently, you might not get an opportunity to respond to showcase moves in time. With a strong trading stage, you can mechanize sections and leave focuses. Thusly, arrangements will happen right when you need them to.

One proviso is deciding to go into "manual mode." In manual mode, you are purchasing and selling continuously without the utilization of options. Informal investors do this constantly. In any case, they are sitting at their terminal watching the activity unfurl. On the off chance that you are not anticipating being an informal investor, at that point, it simply makes more sense to robotize exchanges. That way, you won't need to stress over being actually present at your PC constantly.

Utilizing Money Management

The money the board alludes to a bunch of rules that you can follow as a method for lessening risks. These are best practices that veteran speculators have created throughout the long-term. Tragically for a few, these principles have arisen as the aftereffect of the mix-up's speculators have made. Subsequently, these missteps have been refined into exercises learned.

Along these lines, you should investigate the central exercises you can use to decrease your danger openness.

Position Sizing

Position measuring alludes to the measure of money you can put into a solitary exchange. This is significant as sinking a lot of your investment capital into a solitary exchange expands your danger dramatically. The brilliant guideline here is to contribute close to 2% of your investment capital. This implies that on the off chance that you have $100, you should put close to $2 in a solitary exchange. Presently, this doesn't imply that you can't invest the entirety of your $100 simultaneously. It simply implies that you shouldn't put everything in just one instrument. Doing so would resemble betting everything at a poker game.

Multiplying Down

This standard alludes to the move a few speculators make when they lose money on an arrangement. For example, you invest $100 on an arrangement that turned out badly. Thus, the allurement here is to "twofold down," that is to put $200 in order to recuperate the lost capital. This is an exceptionally unsafe recommendation. In the event that you should end up losing on the subsequent exchange, you're presently out $300 rather than the first $100.

The most ideal approach to recover misfortunes is to spread them out over the course of the following exchanges. In doing as such, you recover your lost investment from the benefit you make in different arrangements. Indeed, it might take a few arrangements before you bring your money back. However, eventually, it's smarter to utilize different instruments to counterbalance the misfortunes from one.

Utilize Technical Analysis

Specialized examination alludes to the factual models that are utilized to follow and anticipate price activity. Specialized examination should turn into your go-to device from here on out. Set aside the effort to get familiar with diagrams and charts. These will help you acquire a decent comprehension of where price activity is going.

Moreover, graphs can furnish you with the data you need to base your choices on the present and as it were.

Without the utilization of any quantitative examination devices, you are putting together your choices with respect to hunches. Obviously, your senses are a significant resource.

Notwithstanding, putting together your investment choices exclusively with respect to emotional understandings can be a risky game. Thus, the utilization of examination is consistently an extraordinary method to discover backing for your choices.

You Can Weather the Storm

Options prices can move a great deal all through brief periods. So somebody who likes to see their money secured and not losing any won't be reasonable for options trading. Presently, we as a whole need to win out over the competition, so I am not saying that you must be glad about losing money to be an options merchant.

Options don't gradually value the way a Warren Buffett financial specialist would want to see. Options move largely on a rate premise and they move quickly. On the off chance that you are trading various agreements immediately, you may see yourself losing $500 and afterward acquiring $500 over a matter of a couple of hours. In this sense, albeit most options merchants are not "informal investors," in fact talking, you will be in an ideal situation in the event that you have a smidgen of a day trading outlook.

You Don't Make Emotional Decisions

Since options are, by their temperament, unstable, and unpredictable for some, stocks, coming to options trading and being enthusiastic about it's anything but a decent method to move toward your trading. On the off chance that you are passionate, you will leave your exchanges at some unacceptable time in 75% of cases. You would prefer not to take any unexpected actions with regard to trading options. As we have said, you should have a trading plan with rules on leaving your positions, adhere to those guidelines and should be fine.

Be a Little Bit Math-Oriented

To comprehend options trading and be fruitful, you can't be bashful about numbers. Options trading is a numbers game. That doesn't mean you need to roll over to the closest college and get an insights degree. Yet, on the off chance that you do get likelihood and insights, you will be a superior options broker. To be perfectly honest, it's difficult to perceive how you can be a decent options dealer without having a psyche for numbers. Some math is at the center of options trading and you can't get around it.

You Are Market-Focused

You don't need to set up a day trading office with ten PC screens so you can be following everything by the occasion, however in the event that you want to set up an exchange and apathetically return to check it three days later, that won't work with options trading. You do check your exchanges a couple of times a day. You additionally should stay aware of the most recent monetary and financial news, and you need to stay aware of any news straightforwardly identified with the organizations you put resources into or any news that could affect those organizations.

In the event that the news comes out, you will have to decide, if it's news that won't be great for your positions. Likewise, you should check the diagrams intermittently, so you have a thought of where things are setting out toward now.

Zero In On a Trading Style

As should be obvious, there is a wide range of ways that you can exchange options. In my assessment, adhering to a couple of strategies is the most ideal approach to move toward options trading. I got going purchasing call options, yet now, I center around selling put credit spreads and iron condors. You should pick what you like best and furthermore something that lines up with your objectives. I moved into selling put credit spreads and iron condors since I got inspired by earning enough to pay the rent from options trading with normal pay installments, as opposed to proceeding to purchase calls and expectation that the offer price would go up. There is no set-in-stone answer. Pick the trading style that is most appropriate to your style and needs.

Chapter 13. Options Trading Strategies Used by Hedge Fund Managers

We will introduce the most popular options trading strategies used by hedge fund managers in 2013, according to the Barclay Hedge Fund Index.

Hedge fund managers are not always out of touch with what retail investors are doing with their money. In fact, the most popular options trading strategies used by hedge funds in 2013 were similar to the most popular options trading strategies used by individual investors last year, according to a study by Barclay Hedge and Barclays Capital. This may be encouraging news for retail investors who seek to mimic the moves of sophisticated money managers without actually becoming one.

How did hedge fund managers play the options market in 2013? Here are the strategies and their popularity.

Sellers of Covered Calls

Sellers of covered calls were the most popular options trading strategy, favored by 42.4% of hedge funds that trade options. Selling covered calls require owning an underlying stock that is owned or shorted and writing a call option against it. If the stock price rises above the strike price, then the call option is exercised by the holder, leading to a sale of stock at a previously agreed-upon price, but if it doesn't rise above that level then nothing happens and the trader simply keeps on holding onto his stock and pocketing whatever dividends come his way.

This strategy is intended to produce a steady stream of income in the form of option premiums, with a reduction in losses due to stock price declines. The goal is to turn the potential for large gains from an upward movement in a stock's price into an attractive stream of income by selling covered calls against that stock. This strategy worked in 2013 for 46.5% of hedge funds that employed it, according to the Barclay Hedge Fund Index.

Sellers of Puts

Sellers of puts were the second most popular options trading strategy, used by 19.4% of hedge funds. Selling a put means the trader is obliged to purchase an asset at a price set by the contract if it is exercised. The risk here is that the underlying asset declines in value, which reduces or eliminates any profit from selling the put if exercised.

This strategy represents a bet that an asset will decline in price over time, and is intended to produce income with limited downside risk, provided that the stock doesn't fall too much below the level specified in the strike price. Selling a put was profitable for 29.9% of hedge funds that used it in 2013, according to the Barclay Hedge Fund Index.

Sellers of Bull Call Spreads

Sellers of bull call spreads were the third most popular options strategy, held by 10.7% of hedge funds that traded options in 2013. Selling a bull call spread is the selling of a call option against an existing long position in the base stock, and then buying a lower strike price call option at a price that is offset by the premium received from selling the original call option.

The goal is to produce income when a stock takes off, without having to take on unlimited losses if all goes wrong and the stock plummets. This strategy was profitable for 22.2% of hedge funds used in 2013, according to the Barclay Hedge Fund index.

Sellers of Iron Condors

Sellers of iron condors were the fourth most popular options strategy, used by 9.3% of hedge funds in 2013. An iron condor is the simultaneous selling of both a call option at a given strike price plus the sale of a put option at a lower strike price, while also buying an even lower strike price put option and an even higher strike price call option. The goal is to produce income when there is the limited risk from buying both legs if all goes well and the stock proceeds to move sideways or remains essentially flat in price.

This strategy was profitable for 26.9% of hedge funds that employed it in 2013, according to the Barclay Hedge Fund index.

Sellers of Calendar Spreads

Sellers of call calendars were the fifth most popular options trading strategy used by hedge funds in 2013 and were used by 8.6% of the funds. Selling a calendar spread involves selling a higher strike price call with an expiration date as far out as possible while simultaneously buying an identical option at a lower strike price with an expiration date as close to expiration as possible. This is done in order to avoid suffering large losses when a stock's price declines sharply after it has reached its designated level following expiration.

This strategy was profitable for 15.8% of hedge funds that used it in 2013, according to the Barclay Hedge Fund index.

Sellers of Straddles

Sellers of straddles were employed by 8.2% of hedge funds in 2013 and involved writing both a call option and a put option with the same strike price on the same underlying asset with the same expiration date. The goal is to produce income if the stock price moves without suffering large losses from buying an equal number of call and put options. This strategy was profitable for 21% of hedge funds that used it in 2013, according to the Barclay Hedge Fund index.

Sellers of Vertical Spreads

Sellers of vertical spreads were employed by 7.4% of hedge funds in 2013. This entails buying an option spread that is "in the money," and selling a second, higher strike price call option spread that is "in the money" plus the premium received from selling the original call option spread. This strategy is sometimes done to protect against large losses if stock prices decline sharply.

This strategy was profitable for 20% of hedge funds that employed it in 2013, according to the Barclay Hedge Fund index.

Sellers of Strangles

Sellers of strangles were employed by 4.7% of hedge funds in 2013 and involved selling both a call option and a put option with the same strike price but different expiration dates. The goal is to produce income if the stock price doesn't move by exercising one or the other, and is also intended to protect against large losses if stock prices decline sharply during the period prior to expiration.

This strategy was profitable for 19.9% of hedge funds that used it in 2013, according to the Barclay Hedge Fund index.

Chapter 14. Financial Leverage in Options Trading

Financial leverage is perhaps the greatest advantage of trading options. Leverage is made by making your investments turn out more enthusiastically for you to boost benefit. At the end of the day, leveraging is creating the potential for greater gains using a more modest measure of capital.

Financial leverage is generally made by using others' cash with an end goal to augment future benefits. Home loans are utilized to invest in land, and organizations acquire cash to extend tasks. The advantage of the leverage comes from increased property estimation, or higher organization income which raises the estimation of investors' offers.

For the investor, nonetheless, buying options gives inherent financial leverage. Without needing to utilize acquired capital, by investing in options, you can handle a bigger number of offers for a similar initial investment, than if you bought the actual offers.

Financial Leverage

For instance, on the off chance that you wish to invest $1000, you could buy 10 portions of IMAX stock (speculatively) esteemed at $100 per share. On the other hand, the alternative agreements may reasonably be esteemed at $200 for heaps of 100 offers ($2.00 per choice). For your investment of $1000, you could purchase five options contracts, increasing your financial leverage by allowing you to control 500 offers instead of only 10.

On the off chance that, during the alternative agreement, the estimation of those offers rises significantly, you may wish to purchase the offers that you reserve the option to purchase, at the concurred value (strike value), which by then is a lot of lower than the market esteem. You would then be able to exchange those offers at market esteem, generating a benefit on a lot bigger number of offers than the ones you would have bought originally on the off chance that you had purchased the 10 offers with your $1000. Clearly, however, to execute this exchange, you would have to approach much more capital in request to buy the offers that your options qualifies you for purchase, and be willing to face the challenge of the market cost out of nowhere dropping before you have the chance to exchange your offers.

Amplify Profit

The best wellspring of financial leverage in this investment, in any case, comes from the way that the rate increase on the alternative is proportionately higher than the increase of the underlying offer. This leverage likewise comes without the danger of investing a lot more noteworthy measures of capital in request to purchase and sell the offers that your options give you the option to purchase.

In the speculative buy referenced already, suppose that the estimation of the offers increases from $100 per share to $105 per share. On the off chance that you purchased those 10 offers, the benefit that this would produce on your investment of $1000 would be $50, or a 5% increase.

Then again, a sensible measure is that the estimation of the options you might have purchased is an increase from $2.00 to $2.80 per alternative. For your 500 options, this creates an increase of $400, or 40%. This a lot higher potential increase is a way that trading options can adequately make leverage.

It is essential to know, however, that the potential of risk is likewise higher. A deficiency of 5% incentive on offers could mean a 40% loss of significant worth on the same options.

Understanding financial leverage, the favorable circumstances, and dangers are vital in trading options. With great trading techniques, using leverage can permit you to augment your profits, while minimizing the danger.

Chapter 15. Trading Levels

Before you begin pondering trading options, you should know that financiers classify options traders by level. Since options trading is somewhat precarious and conveys some danger, financiers don't simply permit you to do anything in advance. The level you are relegated figures out what sorts of exchanges you are permitted to partake in. Explicit subtleties may change from dealer to handle, however, they will in general adhere to similar guidelines.

Level 1 Trading

The main level is prohibitive, indeed, it just permits you to offer to open options contracts under exacting conditions. In the principal case, you can do what is known as a covered call. This implies you will sell a considered option that is covered, which means it is supported by 100 portions of stock. All in all, you have to claim the portions of stock before you can sell a covered call. As we will see, numerous individuals who own portions of stock utilize covered calls to procure month-to-month pay from their investments.

Level 1 merchants can likewise offer to open a secured put. A secured put is an option that is upheld by the money expected to purchase the portions of stock should the option get worked out. While an ensured put has the advantage of giving monetary security should the option be worked out, it requires a lot of capital in your record. It turns out there are alternate approaches to sell puts with good profits, so it's difficult to envision numerous individuals selling secured puts.

Level 1 options brokers can't accept options, and they can't exchange options (that is, purchase an option, and afterward sell it for a benefit).

Level 2 Trading

A level 2 dealer can sell covered calls and secured puts. Likewise, a level 2 merchant can purchase calls and puts and exchange them available. Level 2 brokers can't participate in cutting-edge trading strategies like spreads. Additionally, they are not formally permitted to go into chokes and rides, in spite of the fact that they can do them by implication by buying options on an individual premise.

Most users are likely wanting to be at any rate a level 2 merchant. Turning into a level 2 merchant expects you to submit to a meeting interaction by the dealer.

Fortunately, the "meet" is done by means of PC nowadays, and it is quite simple to get endorsement as long as you most likely are aware of what to say. The two fundamental things you should know about prior to going through the meeting is that the agent will need to know your investment objectives and time skylines. Your answers should guarantee the intermediary that you see how options work.

Right off the bat, they will inquire as to whether your objectives are long haul capital appreciation or transient benefits. Regardless of whether you have a stock portfolio or IRA, you are overseeing for your retirement, you need to tell the specialist your investment objective is to make transient benefits. Also, they will inquire as to whether you are keen on hypothesizing or contributing. You need to disclose to them that you are keen on conjecturing. That implies that you are purchasing monetary protections with the expectations of selling them for a benefit in 1 year or less. Once more, what your genuine objectives are by and large isn't significant—you need to mention to the merchant what they need to hear in the event that you are anticipating trading options.

Level 3 Trading

In the event that you have not done any options trading, you are likely must put in a couple of months at level 2 and purchase and sell a few options before you are endorsed for level 3. Level 3 opens up some additional opportunities for you. As a level 3 merchant, most financiers will permit you to participate in specific options strategies that help limit danger and increment the chances of benefit. You will have the option to sell options even without money or possessing the stock—as a component of one of the pre-characterized strategies. The strategies that level 3 dealers can utilize incorporate credit and charge spreads, rides, chokes, and more muddled exchanges like an iron condor. A portion of these strategies include the concurrent deal and acquisition of options, and they can even include call and put options at the same time. Numerous specialists set them up for you and will give you the assessed benefit and misfortune for each situation.

Level 4 Trading

Level 4 is the most noteworthy trading level all things considered financiers. This permits you to take part in options trading, including selling "bare." This implies that you can sell options that are not upheld by any money or insurance.

In any case, that isn't carefully precise, as businesses require an edge record to take part in that sort of trading. To open an edge account, you should deposit $2,000 money. At that point, the specialist utilizes an equation to decide the negligible part of the capital you should have in your record to cover an exchange. Remember the money is rarely spent, it is kept in the record as protection. While an "ensured put" may expect you to put $10,000 in your record, for a "bare put" you may just need $1,500. The points of interest rely upon the particular strike price, basic stock, and different conditions.

Level 4 brokers likewise approach further developed trading strategies. These incorporate utilizing different legs and unique strategies, for example, a "butterfly" or iron butterfly.

Each extra degree of trading offers admittance to anything a lower-level broker can do, so a level 3 dealer likewise has the forces of a level 1 and level 2 merchant.

For junior dealers, it is ideal to exchange a few options a direct way at level 2, preceding climbing to cutting edge levels.

Chapter 16. Butterfly Options Trading Strategies

An elective system blending bull and bear spreads, and a fixed danger, and a restricted advantage is a butterfly spread. These spreads including four calls are proposed to be a market-unbiased procedure and address the best cost if the basic components don't move before the termination of the option.

Getting Butterflies

Butterfly spreads utilize four option arrangements simultaneously however three distinctive strike prices: the higher strike price, a money strike price, a lower strike price. The higher and lower strike price options are similar separation from the financial options. On the off chance that the money options are at a strike price of $60, the upper and lower options should have strike prices equivalent to $60. For instance, at $55 and $65, these strikes are both $5 away from $60.

Puts or calls might be utilized to spread butterflies. By joining the options differently, unique butterfly spreads will be created, each intended to one or the other profit by unpredictability or low instability.

Long Call Butterfly

The long butterfly phone spread is cultivated by buying a low effect in-the-money call option, composing two on-the-money calls, and buying a higher caliber out-of-the-money call option. When the exchange enters, the net obligation is created.

The full advantage will be made if the fundamental price is equivalent to composed calls at termination. The general advantage rises to the composed right, less the lower call charge and other obligatory expenses. The total deficit is the absolute amount of the expenses charged and the charges got.

Short Call Butterfly

The short spread of butterflies is produced through the offer of one in-the-money call option, the acquisition of two out-of-the-money call options, and a higher strike price for out-of-the-money call options. When entering the position, a net credit is made. This put boosts its benefit when the fundamental price is above or beneath, or underneath the lower strike at termination.

The gross advantage is equivalent to the underlying premium acquired, less the commission price. The greatest risk is the effective price of the call bought shortly before the lower strike price, less the expenses got.

Put Butterfly

The durable butterfly spread is made by buying one at a lower price, selling two sticks, and buying a put at a greater cost. The net obligation is produced when the put is entered. This spot has the most noteworthy preferred position, as the long call butterfly, while it presents elevated cost for the options.

The greatest benefit is equivalent to the higher strike price, less the strike paid by the selling person. The gross exchange risk will be restricted to the underlying expenses and charges implied.

Short Put Butterfly

The short butterfly spread is made by composing a low-strike option, buying two money fillers, and composing a money option at a higher strike price.

The procedure accomplishes the full advantage, regardless of whether the fundamental price is above or below the base strike price at termination.

Expenses generated is the greatest benefit for the system. The general risk is the higher strike price less the bought price, less the procured charges.

Iron Butterfly

The iron butterfly spread is accomplished through the acquisition of an off-the-money call option at a lower strike cost, the composition of an in-the-money call option, and the acquisition of an all the more striking out-of-the-money call option. The impact is a net credit exchange that is undeniably appropriate for lower unpredictability situations.

The greatest benefit is gotten when the basic is at the mid-range price.

The most extreme benefit is the premium. The genuine risk is the strike price of the paid call, less the strike price of the submitted call, short the procured charges.

Switch Iron Butterfly

The converse spread of iron butterflies is made through the composition of an out-of-the-money call at a lower cost, the acquisition of an out-of-the-money call, and a more expensive cost of an out-of-money call. The outcome is a net charge exchange most appropriate to high unpredictability situations. The greatest advantage exists if the fundamental price is higher or lower than the high, or low strike rates.

The danger of the methodology is restricted to the exceptional paid for the position. The greatest advantage is the strike price of the composed call less the buy call value, less the expenses charged.

Illustration of a Long Call Butterfly

A speculator accepts that in the following situation, Verizon shares at present trading at $60 won't move essentially. They intend to apply a long butterfly to profit if the price remains where it is.

A financial specialist composes two call options on Verizon for $60 and purchases two more call options for $55 and $65.

In this situation, if Verizon's stock is priced at $60 at lapse, a financial specialist would acquire the greatest benefit. In the event that Verizon is beneath $55 or above $65, the speculator would understand its most extreme risk, which would be the expense of purchasing two (higher and lower strike) wing call options, which would be lower by the returns of both center strike options.

On the off chance that the hidden resource is somewhere in the range of $55 and $65, there might be a misfortune or benefit.

The superior charged to join the job is huge. Accept that entering the put costs $2.50. Along these lines, the job would lose if Verizon were priced anyplace beneath $60 less $2.50. The equivalent applies if the hidden resource is at the termination of $60 in addition to $2.50. In this situation, the put would profit if the essential resource were priced at an expiry somewhere in the range of $57.50 and $62.50.

This model doesn't include exchange costs, which can be applied to a few options while trading.

Chapter 17. Covered Call Strategy

A covered call implies trade in the money-related market in which the monetary expert selling call options has the indistinguishable proportion of the premium. To execute this, a trader holding a call, sells at an identical price or higher than the premium for making a compensation stream. The seller has a bit of leeway in the "spread" since it infers the trader can pass on the shares if he chooses to work out. In case the monetary expert simultaneously buys a stock and creates call options against that stock position, it is known as a "buy express" trade.

Note

An insurance about the call is a standard elective system used to make payments as decision charges.

To execute an insurance about the call, a monetary expert holding a share by then forms (sells) call decision on that identical asset.

It is consistently used by the people who intend to hold the central stock for a long time, yet don't anticipate an undeniable expense increase in the near term.

This procedure is ideal for a monetary expert who acknowledges the basic expense won't move much over the nearby term.

Understanding Covered Calls

Insurance about calls are an unprejudiced framework, which implies the monetary expert simply envisions a minor augmentation or decrease in the fundamental stock expense for the existence of the formed call decision. This system is every now and again used when a monetary expert has a transient unprejudiced view on the bit of leeway and hence holds the advantage long and, simultaneously, has a short position utilizing the decision to deliver compensation from the decision premium.

In the event that an expert monetary design holds the central stock for a long time yet doesn't anticipate an anticipated expense increase in the near term, at that point they can make compensation (charges) for their share. Simultaneously, they hold up the agreement.

An insurance about call fills in as transitory help on a long stock position and allows monetary experts to gain payment for the premium for making the decision. In any case, the monetary expert surrenders stock increments if the expense moves over the decision's strike cost. They are similarly dedicated to giving 100 shares at the strike cost (for every agreement made) if the buyer chooses to exercise the option.

An insurance about call philosophy isn't important for a bullish nor an uncommonly bearish theorist. In the event that a monetary expert is especially bullish, they are customarily more joyful, not forming the decision and basically holding the stock.

The choice elevates the advantage on the stock, which could decrease the overall advantage of the trade if its value spikes. Correspondingly, if an examiner is incredibly bearish, they may be in an ideal circumstance simply selling the stock, since the premium obtained for forming a call option will do little to adjust the adversity on the stock if the stock falls.

Most Extreme Profit and Loss

The most evident advantage of insurance about the call is indistinguishable from the strike cost of the short call decision, less the price tag of the fundamental stock, notwithstanding the premium obtained.

The worst risk is proportionate to the price tag of the major stock less the premium obtained. Made sure about call example:

A monetary expert case segments of hypothetical association TSJ. They like its drawn-out potential outcomes comparably its offer expense; notwithstanding, feel in the more limited term the stock will presumably trade general level, possibly inside a few dollars of its current expense of $25.

In the event that they sell a call elective on TSJ with a strike cost of $27, they get the premium from the decision bargain in any case, for the range of the decision, top their potential gain on the stock to $27. Acknowledge the first-rate they get for making a three-month call decision is $0.75 ($75 per arrangement or 100 offers).

One of two circumstances will work out:

TSJ shares trade underneath the $27 strike cost. The option will pass futile, and the seller will keep the premium from the decision. For the present circumstance, by using the buy make an approach, they have viably beaten the stock. They detest everything, own the stock yet have an extra $75 in their pocket, less the costs.

TSJ shares climb above $27. The decision is worked out, and the potential gain in the stock is topped at $27. In case the expense goes above $27.75 (strike cost notwithstanding superior), the theorist would have been outstanding off holding the stock. Despite the fact that, if they proposed to sell at $27 regardless, creating the call elective gave them an extra $0.75 per share.

Advantages and Risks of Covered Calls

We, all in all, understand that there is money to be settled on by creating premiums on the calls. You can for the most part find the people who will swear that it is the best technique that exists. Furthermore, subsequently, others won't go anyplace close to a premium on the call! in a similar manner, with any endeavor, there are threats and favorable circumstances collaborate with trading premiums on calls as well.

Since someone else has had achievement with a particular technique for trading, it doesn't suggest that it is a confirmation of advantages for you. Then again, on the off chance that you run over someone who won't consider selling, think about other options, it is anything but a sign that you should keep away from that technique.

There are focal points and threats included when deciding to sell premiums on calls. It doesn't suggest that you shouldn't contribute that way. It simply suggests that you should think about the favorable circumstances and drawbacks before you decide to sell your best option contract.

So since no one gets a kick out of the chance to hear horrendous news, we should discuss the focal points to your portfolio should you decide to form approaches stocks that you own.

Aces

Making made sure about calls can allow you to incorporate an extra installment every month. By selling a premiums on shares that you are basically holding in your portfolio, you can create an additional revenue stream over your benefits and stock appreciation. Various people just hold a stock for the benefits; nonetheless, think "why not make extra advantages from premiums on call selling as well!" By acknowledging when to sell call decisions (and if/when you need to repurchase them), you can elevate the rate at which your stock record creates in regard.

Premiums on call-making allows to profit by a stock that is slanting sideways. In the event that you will probably sell stock whenever it has risen two or three dollars, you can, at times, be disillusioned when one of your properties simply moves around a comparative value you at first paid for it. Made sure about calls can give you extra pay while you are believing that your stock will climb in value.

Selling call options gives you on various occasions the acquiring power. A stock that has choices allows the owner to repeat the premiums, bringing system over and over, after an apparently perpetual measure of time after month, all through the whole year. For the people who probably won't want to watch how their stock value changes every snapshot of the day, using the premiums on the call approach frees you to simply make 12 trades for every year.

The earning you accumulate from selling the call option(s) is all yours, notwithstanding. Whether or not you have not left out at the end, you, in spite of everything, grasp the money you got from opening the position. You, moreover ,don't have to auction the stock on the event that it doesn't close over the strike value you sold the decisions at.

A consistently ignored bit of leeway to selling a made sure about call is that it can cut down the cost of buying parts of the stock. In case you buy stock and all the while selling you're made sure about the call, this is the thing that's known as a buy make. On the off chance that you some way or another figured out how to buy stock and a while later sell made sure about calls at a later point in time, that would essentially be selling a made sure about the call.

Assume that you expected to purchase shares of stock that were as of now trading at $30 per share. The $30 call decision for that stock is assessed at $1.00. In the event that you some way or another figured out how to buy the stock and at the same time selling the call choices, buying the stock would just cost you $29 per share ($30 for the stock less the $1 you get for selling the call decision).

To be sure, even offer tied down calls to purchase stock, still altogether brings down your cost for each position.

Cons

Selling options against your stock normally beats your advantage potential should your stock distinctly rises in regard. On the off chance that you sell a premium on the call at the $20 strike value, you leave behind any advantage if the stock closes above $20 on end. This is conceivably the best impediment of the premium on call framework.

Opening a premium on a call putting doesn't shield you from having incidents all things considered. It does in any case help with making sure about your disadvantaged risk. The underlying investment at creating a call is the proportion of the option you sold deducted from the stock you paid for each share. In our past model, we bought the stock at $30 per share. We, by then, sold calls that were $1.00 each. Our profit to the underlying investment in the present circumstance would be $29. Should the stock close under $29 at the end, we would persevere through a setback in this position.

Should the stock drop and you need to adapt to the circumstance to prevent further adversities. You would have to repurchase your call options before you can sell any of the shares; which can moreover make further incidents in your portfolio.

To lay it out simply, premiums on calls can be a valuable technique in the event that you think about the perils being referred to. Keep in mind, there is no peril-free way to deal with put assets into stocks other than never buying any. You profit by your ability to manage possibility, not by keeping an essential separation from it.

The Danger of Covered Calls

Call traders need to grasp essential offers or arrangements, or they'll be holding uncovered calls, which have theoretically endless disaster potential if the fundamental security rises. In this manner, vendors need to repurchase options before they expire or they'll have to sell shares or arrangements, generating trade costs while cutting down net gains or extending general risks.

Chapter 18. Credit Spread Options

A credit spread requires a high top-notch option for selling or composing and, simultaneously, a lower premium option for buying. The prize acquired from the composed option is higher than the price charged for the long option, which brings about a reward credited to the dealer or financial specialist's record when the put opens. At the point when brokers or speculators utilize a credit dissemination methodology, the net premium is the general benefit they acquire. The spread of credit prompts a benefit when the options are thin.

For instance, by composing a March Call Option with a striking price of $30 for $3, a merchant applied a credit spread technique and, simultaneously, bought a March Call Option of $40 for $1. Since the typical value multiplier is 100, the net premium acquired for the arrangement is $200. Truth be told, if the spreading procedure recoils, the dealer will acquire the option.

A bearish broker anticipates that stock prices should fall and in this manner purchases call options (long call) and sells a similar number of call options inside one class at a given strike price (short call) at a similar expiry at a lower strike price. Bullish brokers, in the examination, anticipate that stock prices should increment, so they purchase call options at a given strike price and sell a similar number of calls inside a solitary class of a similar expiry at a higher strike price.

Put Credit Spread

The thought behind a put credit spread is to bring in cash from selling a put option. Yet, to relieve the danger, you purchase a put option at the same time.

This is not quite the same as selling an exposed put option, where you simply sell one option and that is its finish. Since the option that you purchase will relieve your danger a little, you are not held to similar principles as somebody who is selling stripped put options. All things considered, you actually must have a level 3 trading account to utilize this procedure.

The primary thing to acknowledge about the put credit spread is that you are offering to open the position. Along these lines, this is offering, not accepting exchange options.

Hypothetically, there is a danger of task, however as we'll see, it is anything but a genuine danger in viable terms, and on the grounds that the exchange is relieved constantly put which you purchase to open the exchange, the commonsense effect of this is negligible.

The two options are purchased and sold in one exchange, so this is viewed as a solitary exchange and isn't two separate exchanges. You can purchase a put charge spread, so the other party to the exchange is doing that when you offer to open your position.

The conviction that is behind this kind of exchange is that you are anticipating that the price of the stock should remain about where it is currently, just negligibly decline in price, or expansion in price. It is viewed as a "bullish" move, thus sometimes, passes by the name bull credit spread, yet put credit spread is undeniably more enlightening.

Second, it's not actually a bullish move, as in you are trusting that the stock price is going to increment by a great deal. Positively, you will be in an ideal situation if that does in fact occur. In the event that you set it upstanding, you will procure the greatest conceivable benefit first thing and give some space for the stock to fall before that circumstance changes.

One of the special properties of a put credit spread that we have not seen at this point in our assessment of options is that when the price arrives at a specific level, that is fundamentally it. A further expansion in offer price won't build our benefits. In the model beneath, consider a put credit spread for Amazon.

At the point when you offer to open the position, you get a worthy representative for your record of $4.92 (x 100 offers for $492 all out). The offer price is right now in the greatest increase zone. On the off chance that the offer price climbed by $100, it would surely affect the trader of this credit spread, other than having them inhale a murmur of help that they are unquestionably going to benefit from the exchange.

In this way, it's sort of a bullish methodology, however, how you are truly doing a put credit spread is you are trusting that the price doesn't fall. You are utilizing out of the money put options to set up the exchange, and the expectation here is that they will lapse out of the money and that you will take the net premium paid on the arrangement.

Call Credit Spread

A call credit spread is comparable to a put credit spread, however, this is an exchange that you would utilize when you feel that the stock price will drop. A call credit spread is an offer to a vacant position. You make a benefit by selling a call option, and you alleviate expected misfortunes by purchasing a call option with a similar date to end the agreement date yet an alternate strike price. For this situation, you sell a call with a lower strike price. The danger is moderated by buying a call with a higher strike price.

The greatest benefit is the credit gotten from selling the position.

On the off chance that the stock price goes over the lower strike price, at that point you will begin losing money. To perceive how this functions with a model, we will utilize Facebook. The current offer price is $199.27. You can go into a call credit spread by selling a call option with a strike price of $202.50 and purchasing a call option with a strike price of $210. The credit you would get for this exchange would be $3.30, or $330 for each of the 100 offers. The breakeven point is not difficult to figure. You do this by utilizing the lower strike price and add it to the credit got: $202.50 + $3.30 = $205.80.

However, long the offer price stays underneath the lower strike price call, for this situation, $202.50, the most extreme benefit is acquired. That is the credit got or $330.

The greatest misfortune happens if the offer prices transcend the higher strike price call, so for this situation, there is a $420 misfortune if the offer price transcends $210.

The greatest misfortune is given by the distinctions in the strike prices minus the credit obtained. For this situation: $210 - $202.50 - $3.30 = $4.20.

Chapter 19. Day Trading Options

Day trading is the demonstration of purchasing and selling a monetary instrument around the same time or even on various occasions throughout the span of a day. Exploiting little-value moves can be a worthwhile game—in the event that it is played effectively. However, it tends to be a perilous game for beginners or any individual who doesn't stick to a thoroughly examined technique.

Not all dealers are appropriate for the high volume of exchanges made by day brokers, in any case. However, a few dealers make profits considering the day trade. You can look at any list of the best intermediaries for day trading to see which representatives best oblige the individuals who might want to day exchange.

The online representatives on our rundown, Fidelity and Interactive Brokers, have proficient or progressed renditions of their foundation that include constant streaming statements, progressed outlining instruments, and the capacity to enter and change complex orders with hardly a pause in between.

Underneath, we'll investigate some broad-day trading standards and afterward proceed onward to choosing when to purchase and sell, normal day trading strategies, fundamental graphs and examples, and how to restrict misfortunes.

Key Takeaways

Day trading is just productive when dealers pay attention to it and do their exploration.

Day trading is a task, not a leisure activity; treat it accordingly—be persevering, engaged, objective, and keep feelings out of it.

Here we give some fundamental tips and the ability to turn into an effective day broker.

Day Trading Options Strategies

1. Information Is Power

Notwithstanding information on fundamental trading systems, day brokers need to keep up on the most recent securities exchange news and occasions that influence stocks—the Fed's financing cost designs, the monetary standpoint, and so on

So get your work done. Make a list of things to get of stocks you'd prefer to exchange and keep yourself educated about the chosen organizations and general business sectors. Sweep business news and visit dependable monetary sites.

2. Put Aside Funds

Survey how much capital you're willing to risk on each exchange. Numerous effective day dealers hazard under 1% to 2% of their record per exchange. In the event that you have a $40,000 trading account and will hazard 0.5% of your capital on each exchange, your greatest misfortune per exchange is $200 (0.5% × $40,000).

Put aside an overflowing measure of assets you can exchange with and you're set up to lose. Keep in mind, it might occur.

3. Put Aside Time, Too

Day trading requires your time. That is the reason it's called day trading. You'll have to surrender the majority of your day, truth be told. Try not to consider it on the off chance that you have restricted extra time.

The interaction requires a merchant to follow the business sectors and spot openings, which can emerge whenever during trading hours. Moving rapidly is vital.

4. Start Small

As an amateur, center around a limit of one to two stocks during a meeting. Following and discovering openings is simpler with only a couple of stocks. As of late, it has gotten progressively regular to have the option to exchange fragmentary offers, so you can determine explicit, more modest dollar sums you wish to contribute.

That implies if Apple shares are trading at $250 and you just need to purchase $50 worth, numerous representatives will presently allow you to buy one-fifth of an offer.

5. Maintain a Strategic Distance From Penny Stocks

You're most likely searching at arrangements and low costs however avoid penny stocks. These stocks are regularly illiquid, and the odds of hitting a big stake are frequently disheartening.

Numerous stocks trading under $5 an offer become de-recorded from significant stock trades and are just tradable over-the-counter (OTC). Except if you see a genuine chance and have done your examination, avoid these.

6. Time Those Trades

Numerous orders put by financial backers and merchants start to execute when the business sectors open toward the beginning of the day, which adds to value unpredictability. A prepared player might have the option to perceive examples and pick fittingly to make benefits. In any case, for amateurs, it very well might be better to peruse the market without taking any actions for the initial 15 to 20 minutes.

The center hours are typically less unpredictable, and afterward, development starts to get again toward the end ringer. In spite of the fact that the times of heavy traffic offer freedoms, it's more secure for novices to keep away from them from the start.

7. Cut Losses With Limit Orders

Choose what kind of orders you'll use to enter and leave exchanges. Will you use market requests or cutoff orders? At the point when you submit a market request, it's executed at the best cost accessible at that point—subsequently, no value ensure.

A cutoff request, then, ensures the cost however not the execution. Breaking point orders help you exchange with more accuracy, wherein you set your cost (not ridiculous but rather executable) for purchasing just like selling. More modern and experienced day dealers may utilize options strategies to fence their situations too.

8. Be Realistic About Profits

A procedure doesn't have to win constantly to be beneficial. Numerous brokers just win half to 60% of their exchanges. Be that as it may, they make more on their victors than they lose on their washouts. Ensure the danger on each exchange is restricted to a particular level of the record, and that passage and leave techniques are unmistakably characterized and recorded.

9. Stay Cool

There are times when the financial exchanges test your nerves. As a day dealer, you need to figure out how to keep avarice, expectation, and dread under control. Choices should be administered by rationale and not feeling.

10. Stay on Track

Effective brokers need to move quickly, yet they don't need to think quickly. Why? Since they've built up a trading system ahead of time, alongside the control to adhere to that methodology. It is critical to follow your recipe intently as opposed to attempt to pursue benefits. Try not to allow your feelings to defeat you and surrender your procedure. There's a mantra among day dealers: "Plan your exchange and exchange your arrangement."

Before we go into a portion of the intricate details of day trading, we should take a gander at a portion of the reasons why day trading can be so troublesome.

What Makes Day Trading Difficult?

Day trading takes a ton of training and expertise, and there are a few factors that can make the cycle testing.

To start with, realize that you're going toward experts whose vocations rotate around trading. These individuals approach the best innovation and associations in the business, so regardless of whether they fizzle, they're set up to prevail eventually. On the off chance that you get on board with the fad, it implies more benefits for them.

Uncle Sam will likewise need a cut of your benefits, regardless of how thin. Remember that you'll need to pay charges on any transient increases—or any ventures you hold for one year or less—at a negligible rate. The one proviso is that your misfortunes will balance any gains.

As an individual financial backer, you might be inclined to passionate and mental predispositions. Proficient dealers are normally ready to remove these of their trading strategies, however, when it's your own capital included, it will in general be an alternate story.

Choosing What and When to Buy

Day brokers attempt to bring in cash by abusing minute value developments in individual resources (stocks, monetary forms, prospects, and options), ordinarily utilizing a lot of funding to do as such. In choosing what to zero in on—in a stock, say—a commonplace day merchant searches for three things:

Liquidity permits you to enter and leave a stock at a decent cost—for example, close spreads, or the distinction between the offer and request cost from stock, and low slippage, or the contrast between the normal cost of exchange and the genuine cost.

Instability is just a proportion of the normal everyday value range—the reach where a day merchant works. Greater unpredictability implies more noteworthy benefit or risk.

Trading volume is a proportion of how often stock is purchased and sold in a given time span—most normally known as the normal day by day trading volume. A serious level of volume demonstrates a great deal of revenue in a stock. An increment in a stock's volume is regularly a harbinger of a value bounce, either up or down.

When you understand what sort of stocks (or different resources) you're searching for, you need to figure out how to recognize section focuses—that is, at what exact second you will contribute. Devices that can assist you with doing this include:

Continuous News Administrations: News moves stocks, so it's imperative to buy into administrations that disclose to you when possibly market-moving news comes out.

ECN/Level 2 Statements: ECNs, or electronic correspondence organizations, are PC based frameworks that show the best accessible offer and ask cites from different market members and afterward consequently coordinate and execute orders. Level 2 is a membership-based help that gives constant admittance to the Nasdaq request book made out of value cites from market producers enlisting each Nasdaq-recorded and OTC Bulletin Board security. Together, they can give you a feeling of requests being executed continuously.

Intraday Candle Outlines: Candlesticks give a crude investigation of value activity.

Characterize and record the conditions under which you'll enter a position. "Purchase during upswing" isn't sufficiently explicit. Something like this is substantially more explicit and furthermore testable: "Purchase when value breaks over the upper trendline of a triangle design, where the triangle was gone before by an upswing (at any rate one higher swing high and higher swing low before the triangle-shaped) on the two-minute graph in the initial two hours of the trading day."

When you have a particular arrangement of passage rules, filter through more graphs to check whether those conditions are created every day (accepting you need to day exchange each day) and usually produce a value move in the foreseen heading. Provided that this is true, you have a potential passage point for a methodology. You'll at that point need to evaluate how to exit, or sell, those exchanges.

Chapter 20. Day Trading Tips the Pros Don't Want You to Know

Day trading is speedy-paced. It requires a request and uncommonly fast reflexes to pull the trigger once a promising trading opportunity uncovers. It might be a worthwhile and empowering trading style if you get the foundations right.

That is the explanation we've made a summary of multi-day trading tips to remain by.

From hazard, the board to trend following, seek after these concentrations and see your primary concern creating.

1. Prepare for Your Trading Day

As a day dealer, availability is quite possibly the main endeavor you should start your day with. This joins not simply analyzing the market for potential exchange plans yet moreover mental and actual availability and exercise.

Set your caution instantly at the start of the day, so you can have the chance to do some short expanding exercises and plan for the trading day. Before the monetary exchange opening ringer or the beginning of the Forex meeting, glance through your frameworks and see whether there are some potential trade game plans that are as per your trading system.

Various day dealers check the market late around evening time to anticipate the going with trading day, which can similarly be a convincing technique in the event that you're an evening person.

2. Explore the Chief Trading Hour

The primary trading hour of any financial market reveals a ton about the current trading day. Forthcoming solicitations that were put by dealers the day going before get executed in the underlying couple of snapshots of the new trading day, which can give significant information into where the market is going.

Forex dealers much of the time seek after the value action of the early trading meeting to get a vibe of the market beat. On the occasion that there're enormous breakout candles, this every now and again sets up the speed for the remainder of the day. Comparable remaining parts steady for stock vendors—feel the market idea by keeping it together for the underlying 1-hour fire of the stock you need to exchange.

3. Check a Monetary Timetable

Monetary timetables fuse critical market events and reports that can make silly capriciousness on the lookout—and precariousness is essential for day trading. The greater part of the money-related timetables consolidates the stock or money that is likely influenced by the release, the foreseen number (also called street want), the previous number, and the genuine release.

Checking a monetary timetable for the main market reports got ready for the day should be a standard piece of your morning status plan. Record or recall the particular events of the releases to avoid any repulsive wonders not far-removed.

Markets will, all in all, be shaky if the certifiable number changes from the ordinary number to a gigantic degree. Dependent upon your market sees this unusualness can work either potentially on the side of you.

4. Examine Huge Market News

While most day brokers use specific examination in their trading, fundamentals have an essential effect in financial business sectors.

Basics can outline new examples, upset them, and cause huge assistance and block levels to break, which makes it basic to seek aftermarket news when day trading.

Various intermediaries pass through renowned budgetary entrances to stay to-date on grandstand news, for instance, Bloomberg or Reuters. While you don't have to examine any news that runs over, acknowledging what's going on in the market will help you with your market examination and produce new trading contemplations.

5. Find Oversold and Overbought Budgetary Instruments

The trading methods of day merchants can, when in doubt, be accumulated into three classes: trend following, breakout trading, and counter-trend trading.

Whichever technique you use, finding and trading overbought and oversold budgetary instruments can hugely affect your fundamental concern.

Overbought protections will, all in all, tumble to their ordinary trading range, while oversold protections will, by and large, rising to their typical trading range after some time. A notable gadget to recognize assurances that exchange at those remarkable levels is the Relative Strength Index, which comes worked in with most standard trading stages.

Simply apply the RSI to your diagram and read its value—an assessment of underneath 30 shows an oversold monetary circumstance, while an assessment of more than 70 banners an overbought financial circumstance. Avoid buying protections that are overbought and selling protections that are oversold.

6. Take Exchanges at the Course of the Trend

Trend following is perhaps the most popular trading framework among day dealers for clarification—it works. Trend following implies taking exchanges just the course of the arrangement trend. If the current trend is up, look for buying openings, and if the energy trend is down, look for selling openings.

To perceive the current trend, you can use a basic pinnacle and box assessment or a particular marker, for instance, the ADX (Average Directional Index). A market in an uptrend shapes consecutive higher highs and higher lows, while a downtrend market outlines nonstop lower lows and lower highs. You'll consistently find that, during a rise, protections become oversold unequivocally at the motivation behind a fresh higher low, which is the value level at which you should consider buying the security or money pair.

Basically, during a downtrend, protections normally get overbought straightforwardly at where another lower high is outlining, which banner a potential selling opportunity.

If you need to utilize the utilization of the ADX pointer to perceive and trade designs, by then, follow the assessment of the ADX line. A value underneath 25 shows that the market isn't slanting, a value someplace in the scope of 25 and 50 banners a floating business area, while values more than 50 sign an amazingly strong example. Use the –DI and +DI lines to perceive the course of the example—if the –DI line is over the +DI line, you're dealing with a downtrend, and if the +DI line is over the –DI line, you're dealing with a rise.

7. Counter-Trend Exchanges Can Be Perilous

The opposite method to manage trend following, counter-trend trading implies taking exchanges the alternate method of a fabricated uptrend. Counter-trend brokers hope to profit on transient value cures; for instance, they endeavor to sell at the most elevated purpose of higher highs during an upswing and to buy at the base of lower lows during downtrends.

Right when gotten together with trend following procedures, counter-trend trading can make all the more trading open entryways for dealers. In any case, recall that counter-trend exchanges are ordinarily less secure than exchanges that are taken toward the essential example.

8. Have Extreme Danger on the Board Frameworks Set Up

Without sound danger, the executive's rules, even the best trading system will, finally, lead to enormous misfortunes. Danger on the board urges you to accept accountability for your exchanges, position sizes, misfortunes, and advantages. No single exchange should be allowed to get out a colossal piece of your trading record, or you'll gain some hard experiences endeavoring to re-visitation or procure back the first investment.

For example, if you lose half of your trading account on a singular exchange or a few exchanges, it will take you 100% of benefits just to return to breakeven. That is the explanation you should separate the possible threat of any exchange course of action, use a fated danger for each exchange, take exchanges with an adequately high prize to-hazard extent, and cling to the 6% guideline.

9. Persistently Hazard a Fixed Level of Your Trading Account on Any Exchange

To dodge misfortunes to acquire out of influence, you should just chance a fixed level of your trading account on any single exchange. The splendid rule is to never risk more than 2% of your trading account on an exchange. Here is a model: if you have a $10,000 account, by then, you shouldn't chance more than $200 on any single exchange. Recognize your stop-misfortune decisively at the value level where your full-scale misfortune for that exchange would ascend to $200.

While 2% is the most extraordinary danger you should be taking on any single exchange, you can diminish this rate on the off chance that you need to. For brokers with greater trading accounts, it's altogether expected to chance simply 1% or even 0.5% of their records.

10. Separate the Prize To-Chance Extent of Potential Courses of Action

The prize to-chance extent of exchange suggests the expected advantage of the exchange partitioned by its possible misfortune. For example, in the event that you're taking an exchange that has an advantage capacity of $50, in any case, you're betting $100, the prize to-risk extent of that exchange would be 0.5. Figuratively speaking, you're betting $2 to get $1.

This is an instance of a foreboding prize to-hazard extent. You should never risk past what you can possibly get. The best exchange game plans have a prize to-risk extent of in any occasion 2:1 or fundamentally more; for instance, you're betting $1 to get $2 or more.

Chapter 21. Errors on the Application of Strategies and How to Avoid Them

Fundamental Options Trading Mistakes

In this part, we will assemble all our outstanding pointers and suggestion for keeping away from typical beginner botches on the whole.

It's common for fledglings to make blunders when purchasing and selling since it's fascinating and upsetting all simultaneously. How about we take notice of a portion of the missteps amateurs are at risk to and ponder thought on the most proficient method to keep away from them.

Freezing and Exiting Early

You need to have a standard for leaving a capacity that isn't venturing into your way. Be that as it may, you need to have a couple of adaptabilities since little activities inside the stock convert into enormous moves in another option. In this way, you may see your options show up at some $40 inside the red. That is a revolting possibility, nonetheless, implying that the stock would conceivably have dropped through something like $60. Presently, on the off chance that you think about thought on which you realize that it's currently normal at all for a stock to drop 60 or $70, after which bounce back inside the upper bearing by utilizing a dollar. Thus, to auction your option essentially because of the reality there might be a little plunge that way—until unmistakably it's a piece of the descending pattern—may be a stupid move. Realize that on the off chance that you ponder thought on that, it's not, at this point extraordinary in any regard for a stock to drop 60 or $70, after which bounce back inside the upper way by utilizing a dollar. So to auction your option basically because of the reality there might be a little plunge like that except if obviously, it's important for the descending pattern, would be a senseless film. Yet, we will excuse amateurs for committing an error of that nature. It's perfect to get panicky while you begin seeing your cash sneak away legitimately sooner than your own personal eyes.

To adapt to those assortments of conditions, it's fundamental to comprehend and chomped around specialized assessment and candle diagrams. These themes are past the extent of this book, however, you can find records about those subjects on the web, on YouTube, and obviously, in numerous books. The factor of acquiring information on this tool is so you can notice the diagram and measure wherein the stock is going. The stuff is some separation from best; else, anyone could be multimillionaires. Notwithstanding, they are really obvious at giving you a thought that I may name a learned bet. It's higher to make an informed bet than it is to frenzy and sell your option. At the point when I initially began, I made the mix-up of leaving positions some distance too soon and I may appear a little later and find that in the event that I had remained in, I could've made a huge benefit. Keep in mind, the stock commercial center is consistently fluctuating a splendid arrangement.

Engaging in Many Trades at Once

As we've said numerous cases extending yourself excessively far is a basically impractical notion regarding the matter of trading. The check what approach you choose to receive; my insight is that you should get mindfulness on a couple of extraordinary protections and no extra. Thus, what you may plunk down and do is select 5 shares that you have been essentially curious about. Ideally, those are colossal offers because of the reality you need liquidity inside the other options.

Something else you need is a moderately over the top offer charge with the goal that the options have a threat to benefit. Know in the event that you are advancing other options or credit spreads; you really need an unreasonable offer expense so you can acquire from the top class. When you choose your five organizations, you need to examine the entire parcel about the organizations and comprehend them all around. That implies looking at their fiscal summaries, knowing while their income calls are, and holding the tune of things simply like the unpredictability, and charge to benefits proportion. At that point, you need to consider the outlines of that business endeavor for as far back as a year. Acquaint yourself with the activities that the company has experienced during the most recent year. None of that is finished evidence; notwithstanding, you have been going much better because you have loaded yourself with knowledge instead of truly blindly going for it while purchasing and selling options.

All in all, what occurs in the event that you do extra than five associations? At a couple of components, you will extend yourself excessively far. On the off chance that you trade in excess of 5 immediately, it will be hard to keep in tune with the alterations in the share charges of companies that you are purchasing and selling. Also, to decide if to get in or out of exchanges you should watch out for the sum. Presently a couple of individuals are neurotics, and they might have the option to separate your consideration altogether and that they like a high strain. On the off chance that you are a so-alluded to as kind character that likes inordinate pressure, at that point possibly you can go along with as numerous as you need. In any case, my guidance for novices is which you are going to be work much better in fewer enterprises that you can essentially study and observe.

Utilizing Too Many Strategies

One of the principal things you should do is sit down and sort out what your point is with trading choices. You would prefer not to utilize an erratic technique and attempting to do that and that and seeing what happens. All things being equal, choose what your point is inside the pleasant way you need to accomplish that reason. At that point, take a gander at all of the exceptional strategies that possess and notice what is the most likeminded, alongside your objectives. At that point, apply possibly two or 3 unmistakable strategies all at once. There must be some adaptability since certain conditions will require one technique appropriately; different conditions require an unmistakable methodology.

Taking Too Much Risk

On the off chance that you saw with the strategies that we inspected, there are a couple of tradeoffs that must be made. The compromises regularly include a substitute off between the amount of benefit you can make and the degree of possibility.

Individuals are continually covetous, I can guarantee that, yet one issue that essentially does is get you into an issue with regards to purchasing and selling. You need to be focused and deliberate, which implies not taking an excessive amount of threat while it could stay away from. It's smarter to be attempting to discover little benefits in little nibbles that can transfer up instead of attempting to hit a homer.

Set It and Forget It

This is a serious mix-up the fledglings make. They accept purchasing options is a cool thought, thus they purchase another option. Yet, at that point, they don't go through every day dissecting it and following it. Possibly they heard on the news that the stock drop by five dollars. At that point, on the off chance that they go to check their options, they may find that it lost $65 in the charge. Absolutely never take to set it and disregard its strategy. Each option that you substitute, you should know about in detail every day.

Disregarding Time Decay

Time decay is one of the fundamental properties of options. Consistently an option is losing outward or time cost. However, some people withdraw their options for the long haul trusting that the stock goes to move an ideal way. At that point, does not move the slightest bit, and they wind up losing cash while the option lapses useless. So you should keep up as the main priority that an option has time decay and that the options go to lose expense because of this. In the event that it's not, at this point inside the cash, which means it's dropping expense generally.

When Selling Options, Stop Looking at Probabilities

One factor that likewise can be enticing is to continually be objective for the most noteworthy top class that you could acquire while advancing a credit spread. That is an awful technique. Indeed, even in spite of the fact that you may get a major FICO rating, you may furthermore place yourself in a high possibility of the task. The reason must be to introduce exchanges that have an extreme likelihood of progress. Would you as an option have a change that would make $200 anyway it has a 65% threat of disappointment, or would you rather have a substitute that made $75 and had a 95% danger of accomplishment? I believe the last may engage the greatest individuals. The factor is the $75 is only one change. You can do 10 or 20 of those exchanges.

Not Paying Attention to Volatility

Each time you are up to an option, I propose you investigate the suggested unpredictability. This is essentially a measure of unexpected movements of the stock that underlies the option. In the event that the inferred unpredictability is disorderly, it means higher charges as a rule. In case you're advancing other options, you will have to sell options wherein the suggested instability is better. That is something that a lot of people disregard; once more, beginner appears to just acknowledge on the rate they get hold of for the option.

Not Having a Training Plan

Other than defining standard objectives, you should have a trading plan set up. The initial segment of your preparation plan may be to set up how much cash you're slanted to danger on each change. One more segment to examining is: does the next technique you will apply figure out which exchanges to enter? For instance, you may get it done spontaneously while it seems like the stock goes up.

That is the means by which most extreme individuals see the business sectors. Nonetheless, you may adopt an exceptional strategy as opposed to doing that. What you could do is have a specialized examination based on absolute reason to enter a trade. For instance, on the off chance that the stock rate has been dropping nonetheless, at that point there's a brilliant cross. This implies that a fast period of moving regularly has gotten over on the zenith of the yard. Moving normal, this is a brilliant sign which you should include a substitute. In this way, you may begin your week by choosing the stocks which you're keen on for that week. I advocate running with a little assortment of stocks at some random time, so you could choose 3 comprehensives of Facebook, Lucky Martin, and Amazon. At that point what you do is you considered the graphs and anticipate the correct second to go into the substitute.

Chapter 22. The Mindset of an Options Trader

Realize When to Go Off-Book

While adhering to your arrangement, in any event, when your feelings are advising you to disregard it, is the sign of a fruitful trader. This, not the slightest bit implies that you should aimlessly follow your plans 100% of the time. You will, unquestionably, wind up in a circumstance occasionally where your strategy will be delivered totally pointless by something outside of your control. You should know enough of your tactic's shortcomings, just as changing economic situations, to realize when following your predetermined strategy will prompt disappointment rather than progress. Knowing when the circumstance truly is changing, versus when your feelings are attempting to hold influence is something that will accompany practice. However, in any event, monitoring the uniqueness is a tremendously positive development.

Keep Away From Exchanges That Are Out of the Cash

While there are a couple of strategies out there that make it a state of getting options that are at present out of the cash, you can have confidence that they are assuredly the exemption, not the standard. Keep in mind, the options market doesn't care for the customary financial exchange which implies that regardless of whether you are trading options dependent on hidden stocks purchasing low and selling high is simply not a suitable system. On the off chance that a call has exited the cash, there is for the most part not exactly a 10% chance that it will recover satisfactory levels before it terminates. This implies that in the event that you buy these kinds of options, you are showing improvement over betting, and you can discover approaches to bet with chances in support of yourself of a lot higher than 10%.

Try Not to Hold Tight to Your Starter Methodology

Your center trading technique is one that should consistently be continually advancing as the conditions encompassing your trading propensities change and develop too. Also, outside of your essential system, you will need to, in the long run, make extra plans that are all the more explicitly custom-made to different market states or explicit strategies that are just valuable in a thin band of circumstances. Keep in mind, the more set you up are before beginning a day of trading, the more prominent your general benefit level is probably going to be, it is similarly straightforward as that.

Never Begin Without an Unmistakable Arrangement for Entry and Exit

While finding your first arrangement of enter/leave focuses can be troublesome without experience to control you, it is critical that you have them secured before beginning trading, regardless of whether the stakes are moderately low. Except if you are amazingly fortunate, beginning without an idea to get away from the battleground will do nearly nothing however lose your cash. In the event that you don't know about what restrictions you should set, start with a summed up pair of focuses and work to calibrate it from that point.

More significant, than setting passage and leave focuses, nonetheless, is utilizing them, in any event, when there is as yet the presence of cash on the table. Probably the greatest obstacle that new options dealers need to get over is the possibility that you need to wring every single cent out of every single effective exchange. The truth is that, as long as you have a productive trading plan, and afterward, there will consistently be more beneficial exchanges in the future which imply that, as opposed to agonizing over a little additional benefit, you should be more worried about ensuring the benefit that the exchange has just gotten you. While you may sometimes make some additional benefit overlooking this exhortation, chances are you will lose definitely more than you acquire as benefits will be surprisingly common and start dropping again before you can viably pull the trigger. On the off chance that you are as yet struggling with this idea, think about this: options trading is a long-distance race, not a run, gradual will consistently dominate the race.

Never Twofold Down

At the point when they are up to speed seemingly out of the blue, numerous new options brokers will wind up in a situation where the most ideal approach to recover a genuine misfortune is to twofold down on the hidden stock being referred to at its freshest, essentially brought down, cost with an end goal to make a benefit under the suspicion that things will pivot and afterward keep on doing as such to the point that everything is totally beneficial indeed. While it tends to be hard to let a basic stock that was once amazingly beneficial go, multiplying down is only very seldom going to be the right choice. On the off chance that you end up in where you couldn't say whether the exchange you are going to make is really going to be a decent decision, you should simply inquire as to whether you would make a similar one in the event that you were going into the circumstance visually impaired. The appropriate response should reveal to you all you require to know.

On the off chance that you wind up in a second where multiplying down seems like the correct decision, you will have to have the solidarity to calm yourself back down and to cut your misfortunes as altogether as conceivable given the current circumstance. The sooner you cut your misfortunes and proceed onward from the exchange that finished inadequately, the sooner you can begin placing energy and interests into an exchange that actually can possibly make you a benefit.

Think About Nothing Literally

It is human instinct to assemble stories around, and thusly structure associations with, all way of lifeless things including singular stocks or cash sets. This is the reason it is totally normal to feel a nearer association with specific exchanges, and potentially even consider tossing out your arrangement when one of them takes a sudden plunge. Contemplating and following up on are two totally different things, notwithstanding, which is the reason monitoring these propensities are so critical to maintaining a strategic distance from them no matter what.

Not Paying Attention to Your Decision of Trader

With such countless interesting points, it is straightforward why numerous new option traders essentially choose the primary intermediary that they find and continue on ahead from that point. The truth is, notwithstanding, that the merchant you pick will be a tremendous piece of your general trading experience which implies that the significance of picking the correct one ought not to be limited on the off chance that you are praying fervently experience conceivable. This implies that the main thing that you will need to do is to burrow past the well-disposed outside of their site and get to the basics of what it is they really offer. Keep in mind, making an eye-getting site is simple, filling it will genuine data when you have sick expectation is significantly more troublesome.

First of all, this implies investigating their set of experiences of client support as a method of not just guaranteeing that they treat their clients in the correct manner, yet additionally of verifying that nature of administration is the place where it should be also.

Keep in mind, when you make an exchange each second check implies that in the event that you need to contact your trader for help with an exchange you need to realize that you will be talking with an individual who can take care of your concern as fast as could really be expected. The most ideal approach to guarantee the client care is adequate is to call them and note the amount of time it requires for them to hit you up. On the off chance that you stand by in excess of a solitary business day, take your business somewhere else as though they are this impartial in a new customer, consider what the assistance will resemble when they as of now have you right where they need you.

With that out the way, the following thing you should consider is the expenses that the merchant will charge in return for their administrations. There is next to no guideline with regards to these expenses which implies it is unquestionably going to pay to look around. Notwithstanding expenses, it is critical to consider any record essentials that are needed just as any charges having to do with pulling out assets from the record.

Discover a Mentor

At the point when you are hoping to go from causal dealer to somebody who exchanges effectively on the standard, there is just such a lot of you can learn without anyone else before you need a genuine target eye to guarantee you are continuing properly. This individual can either be somebody you know, in actuality, or it can appear as at least one individual on the web. The fact of the matter is you need to discover someone else or two who you can ricochet thoughts off of and whose experience you can profit by. Options trading shouldn't be a single movement; exploit any local area you can discover.

Information Is the Key

Without some kind of data that you can use to evaluate your exchanges, you are essentially playing at the roulette table. Indeed, even poker players appear at the table with an approach. They can adjust to the conditions and figure out how to peruse different players. That way, they can tell the competitors from the actors.

Options trading is the same. In the event that you can't utilize the data that is out there for your potential benefit, at that point what you will wind up with is a progression of suppositions that might possibly work out. In view of the theory of probability, you have a 50/50 possibility of bringing in cash. That may not seem like awful chances, however, a line of helpless choices will take off from you in the helpless house right away.

Thus, it is significant that you become acquainted with the different examination and devices out there which you can use for your potential benefit. Remember that everybody will be taking a gander at similar data. In any case, it is dependent upon you to sort out what can, or may, occur before every other person does. This infers truly learning and examining the numbers with the goal that you can distinguish examples and see where patterns are going, or where patterns may switch. The ideal antitoxin to that is vision and premonition. Work on building situations. Attempt to envision what could happen are patterns proceeding. Or then again, what might occur if patterns switched? What requirements occur all together for those patterns to proceed or turn around?

At the point when you ask yourself such extreme inquiries, your insight and understanding start to extend. Your psyche will unexpectedly have the option to handle more noteworthy measures of data while you create your own emergency courses of action dependent on the numerous uncertainties. That may appear to be a lot of data to deal with, however toward the day's end, any time spent in improving your trading discernment is unquestionably worth the exertion.

Chapter 23. Additional Information on Options Trading

Investors who buy call options are bullish that the asset's price will raise and close over the strike price by the option's expiration date.

Options are accessible to trade for some financial products, for example, bonds and products but, equities are one of the most mainstream for investors.

Options give the purchaser the chance—however, not the commitment—of purchasing or selling the underlying security at the agreement expressed strike price, by the predetermined expiration date. The strike price is the execution price or transaction value for the portions of the underlying security.

Important: Options trading can be incredibly volatile, particularly in the midst of noteworthy market changes, for example, with enormous scope macroeconomic events like economic plunges, natural disasters, and other such events.

In-the-Money Call Options

Call options consider the acquisition of the underlying asset at a specified price before the specified date. The premium becomes possibly the most important factor while deciding if an option is in the money or not, however, it can be deciphered in an unexpected way, contingent upon the sort of option included. The call option is in the money if the current market price of the stock is higher than the option's strike price. The amount that an option is in money is known as the intrinsic value, which means the option is at least worth that amount.

For instance, a call option with a strike of $25 would be in the money if the underlying stock was trading at $30 per share. The contrast between the strike and the present market price is commonly the amount of the premium for the option. Investors hoping to purchase a specific in the money call option will pay the premium or the spread between the strike and the market price.

In-the-Money Put Options

While call options permit the purchase of an asset, a put option achieves the contrary action. Investors purchase these options that enable them to sell the underlying security at the strike price when they anticipate that its value should diminish. Put option purchasers are bearish on the movement of the underlying security.

An in-the-money option means that the strike price is above the market price of the total market value. An investor holding an ITM put option at expiry implies the stock price is below the strike price and it's conceivable the option merits exercising. A put option purchaser is trusting the stock's price will fall far enough below the option's strike to at least cover the expense of the premium for purchasing the put.

Out of the Money (OTM)

This is an articulation used to depict an option contract that just contains intrinsic worth. These options will have a delta lesser than 50.0.

An OTM call option will have a strike price that is greater than the market price of the underlying asset. Then again, an out of the money put option has a strike price that is lesser than the market price of the underlying asset.

Out of the money, options may diverge from ITM options.

Key Takeaways

Out of the money is known as OTM, which implies an option has no intrinsic value but has extrinsic value.

If the underlying price is below the strike price, a call option is OTM. However, if the underlying's price is over the strike price, a put option is OTM.

An option can be at the money.

OTM options are more affordable than ATM or ITM options. This is because ITM options have intrinsic value and ATM options are near having intrinsic value.

Implied Volatility—IV

What Is Implied Volatility—IV?

Implied volatility is a metric that catches the market's perspective on the probability of changes in a given security's price. Investors can utilize it to extend future moves and demand and supply, and regularly utilize it to price options contracts.

Implied volatility isn't equivalent to historical volatility, otherwise called statistical volatility of realized volatility. The historical volatility figure will measure past market changes and their real outcomes.

Key Takeaways

Implied volatility is the market's estimate of a probable development in a security's price.

Implied volatility is regularly used to price options contracts: High implied volatility brings about options with higher premiums and the other way around.

Demand/supply and time value are major deciding elements for figuring implied volatility.

Implied volatility increments in bearish markets and diminishes when the market is bullish.

Understanding Implied Volatility

Implied volatility is the market's prediction of possible development in a security's price. It is a measurement utilized by investors to assess future variances (volatility) of a sdtock's price dependent on certain prescient components. Implied volatility, symbolized by the symbol σ (sigma), can frequently be believed to be an intermediary of market chance. It is ordinarily expressed utilizing standard deviations and percentages over a predefined time line.

When applied to the stock market, implied volatility by and large increments in bearish markets, when investors accept value prices will decay after some time. IV diminishes when the market is bullish, and investors accept that prices will ascend after some time. Bearish markets are viewed as unfortunate, henceforth more risky, to most equity investors.

Implied volatility doesn't foresee the direction the price change may take. For instance, high volatility implies an enormous price swing, however the price could swing upward—high—descending—exceptionally low—or change between the two directions. Low volatility implies that the price likely won't make expansive, eccentric changes.

Implied Volatility and Options

Implied volatility is one of the main factors in the pricing of options.

Buying Options Contracts allows the holder to buy or sell an asset at a specific price over a specified time.

Implied volatility approximates the future estimation of the option, and the option's present value is additionally thought about. Options with high implied volatility will have higher premiums and the other way around.

It is critical to recall that implied volatility depends on likelihood. It is just an estimation of future prices as opposed to a sign of them. Although investors consider implied volatility when settling on investment choices, and this reliance has some effect on the prices themselves.

There is no assurance that an option's price will follow the anticipated pattern. Be that as it may, while thinking about an investment, it helps to consider the moves different investors are making with the option. It is straightforwardly associated with the market opinion, which does, thus, influence option pricing.

Implied volatility additionally influences the pricing of non-option monetary instruments, for example, an interest rate cap, which restricts the amount of an interest rate on an item that can be raised.

Option Pricing Models and IV

Implied volatility can be dictated by utilizing an option pricing model. It is the main factor in the model that isn't legitimately noticeable in the market.

Rather, the mathematical option pricing model uses different variables to determine implied volatility and the option's premium.

The Black-Scholes Model is a generally utilized and notable options evaluating factors in options strike price, current stock price, time until expiration (indicated as a percent of a year), and risk-free interest rates.

The Black-Scholes Model is fast in computing any number of option prices.

Notwithstanding, it can't precisely compute American options, since it just considers the price at an option's termination date. American options are those that the proprietor may excersice at any point in time, including the expiration day.

The Binomial Model, then again, utilizes a tree graph with volatility figured in at each level to show every conceivable way an option's price can take, then works in reverse to determine one price. The advantage of this model is that you can return to it anytime for the chance of early exercise.

Early exercise is executing the contract's action at its strike price before the contract's termination; it just occurs in American style options.

Be that as it may, the figuring involved with this model set aside a long effort to determine, so this model isn't the best in rushed circumstances.

Factors Affecting Implied Volatility

Similarly likewise with the market, all in all, implied volatility is dependent upon volatile changes. Demand and supply are major deciding variables for implied volatility. At the point when an asset is popular, the price will in general ascent. So does the inferred volatility, which prompts a higher option premium due to the risky nature of the option.

The inverse is likewise true. When there is a lot of supply, however, insufficient market requests, the implied volatility decreases, and the option price get less expensive.

Another premium affecting variable is the time value of the option, or the measure of time until the option terminates. A short-dated option regularly brings about low implied volatility, though since a long call outdated option will in general outcome in high implied volatility. The distinction lays in the amount of time left before the expiration of the agreement. Since there is a lengthier time, the price has an all-inclusive period to move into a great price level in contrast with the strike price.

Pros and Cons of Using Implied Volatility

Implied volatility assists with evaluating market sentiment. It assesses the size of the movement an asset may take. However, as referenced earlier, it doesn't show the course of the movement. Option authors will utilize computations, including implied volatility to price options contracts.

Additionally, numerous investors will take a look at the IV when they pick an investment. During times of high volatility, they may decide to put resources into more secure products or sectors.

Implied volatility doesn't have a premise on the essentials underlying the market assets, yet depends entirely on price. Additionally, adverse events or news, for example, natural disasters and wars may affect the implied volatility.

Pros

- Quantifies market uncertainty, sentiment
- Help set options prices
- Determines trading procedure

Cons

- Based exclusively on prices, not basics
- Sensitive to unforeseen components, news events
- Predicts development, but not heading

Real-World Example

Investors and traders use graphing to analyze implied volatility. One particularly well-known instrument is the Chicago Board Options Exchange (CBOE) Volatility Index (VIX). The VIX is a real-time market index. The index utilizes price data from near-dated, near-the-money S&P 500 index options to extend desires for volatility throughout the following 30 days.

Investors can utilize the VIX to contrast various protections or measure the stock market's volatility all in all, and structure trading techniques accordingly.

Chapter 24. Advantages and Disadvantages of Options Trading

What Are the Advantages of Options Trading?

There are various reasons why options trading can be an uncommon supplement to your present contributing approach. They fuse the going with:

Options give you an impact on your contribution. An options arrangement can give you more affordable openness to a stock than buying shares altogether, enhancing the two misfortunes and profits if the stock value moves.

Options can moreover decrease risk in your overall portfolio. For instance, you can join buying a put choice to sell stock at a predetermined cost with duty regarding shares themselves.

The defensive put exchange gives you the potential gain if the stock price raises; shielding you from a piece of risk if the price lowers.

Options can offer a wellspring of portfolio procuring/pay. By offering options instead of buying them, you're the one to get the installment for the alternative. Whether or not the alternative goes unexercised, you get the chance to save that portion as payment for having acknowledged the commission for the agreement.

What Are the Risks of Options Trading?

Offsetting these advantages are some veritable risk to options. As an issue of first significance, options, as often as possible, pass useless, achieving an outright loss of whatever the buyer paid for the alternative. For those used to seeing stock moves of even 5% to 10 % as an enormous arrangement, the instability of options can come as a gigantic daze.

Second, there is an expectation to absorb information associated with options trading.

Various financier associations offer options trading, be that as it may, you'll need to meet some extra managerial essentials before your specialist will allow you to exchange options. For instance, you'll need to scrutinize some enlightening material about the options market similarly as sort out how your intermediary handles tolerating orders for options. Moreover, you'll need to perceive what you need to do to exhort your representative that you need to practice or exercise an alternative—similarly to what'll happen on the off chance that you sell a choice and the buyer decides to practice it against you.

At long last, there are a couple of options procedures that perhaps work honorably when you make various exchanges simultaneously. Since options markets aren't by and large as fluid as the securities exchange, those simultaneous exchanges don't for the most part work eminently—and that can present the risk that your technique will not work how you arranged or trusted.

Chapter 25. Difference Between Binary Options Trading and Real Options Trading

Perhaps the best difference between real options trading and binary options trading is that the latter, for the most part, has uncommon short terminations—of even down to just 60 seconds—while real options trading cas last as short as a week and as long as a year. This has a colossal impact in that you have the chance to fittingly dissect an exchange and dealing with the exchange along the way, giving time at the expense of the underlying asset, be it stock or various assets, to move your anticipated heading. Keeping it short, let's say that, if you are a particularly master trader, from the time you put on an options exchange, costs can just honestly and rapidly move as you anticipate it to—something even prepared specialists can't guarantee.

Professional real options trading is tied in with giving the underlying asset time to change to the arranged or anticipated bearing. Having incredibly short termination suggests that you are putting on a 60 seconds electronic bet without significant examination behind each "bet." That has the effect between investing and gambling.

Differences Between Binary Options Trading and Real Options Trading—Limited Profit vs. Unlimited Profit

Another enormous differentiation between binary options trading and real options trading is that you can simply win a limited measure of "payout" in binary options trading while when you buy a real options contract, the potential payout is unfathomable. This infers in binary options trading, you ordinarily win a fixed payout, routinely 75% of what you put into the options exchange, paying little mind to how far the cost of the underlying moves on the side of you. For any situation, when you buy a real options contract, anything is possible. However, long as the cost of the underlying stock continues moving in support of yourself, the choice will continue yielding profits. In this manner, it isn't outstanding even to see profits of beyond 1000% in real options trading, while in binary options trading, you get your 75% despite the fact that you are an expert investigation and the cost of the underlying asset moves vehemently in support of yourself. A couple of individuals say, taking everything into account, basically, continue purchasing more binary options as the cost increases... The issue with that will be that even in a strong upswing (or downtrend) cost doesn't go straight up (or down), you may be caught in one of those little one minute or two minutes or even five minutes pullbacks, which are normal even in a strong pattern and get your record gotten out on the losses. You consistently lose more on a losing exchange than you can win on a winning exchange. That takes us to the following difference.

Differences Between Binary Options Trading and Real Options Trading—85% Loss vs. 100% Loss

In binary options trading, when you lose an exchange, they give you back 15% of the money you invested, making it an 85% loss while in real options trading, you can lose up to 100% of the money you put in, truly, the entire thing.

From the beginning, this makes binary options trading look outstandingly appealing contrasted with real options trading until you remember the last distinction, that there is a breaking point to the profit you can make on binary options trading, which is frequently tinier than the measure of money you can lose. All in all, on the off chance that you stand to win 75% or lose 85% in a 50/50 exchange, ok win as time goes on? Regardless of whether you stand to lose 100% in real options trading, two significant differences make up for it; one is the endless profit referred to above, conceivably returning you way higher profits than the 100% loss, and second, it will, in general, be offered to cut loss before you lose the whole thing! This takes us to the following difference between real options trading and binary options trading.

Differences Between Binary Options Trading and Real Options Trading—Cannot Be Traded vs. Can Be Traded

Binary options "trading" in fact isn't trading in any way. Trading infers having the choice to buy AND sell. So when you buy something for one cost and sell it for another that is trading. Be that as it might, in binary options trading, you can buy yet you genuinely can't offer it to another options dealer. At the point when you "buy" a binary choice, you should hold it to its conceivable outcome; it's difficult to offer it to rescue any outstanding worth when things begin to look wrong. Along these lines, it is exceptionally far-fetched to "stop-loss" to talk. You either win or lose as indicated by the measures so there's no "trading" needed in anyway shape or form, just "betting." Real options trading of course can be traded on the open exchange to another options broker or market creator at whatever point before it terminates. So when things begin to turn out seriously, you could offer it to safeguard remaining worth basically like trading stocks. There is a genuine market with genuine buyers whom you are trading in and trading within real options trading. This takes us to the following difference.

Differences Between Binary Options Trading and Real Options Trading—Unlisted Instrument vs. Listed Instrument

Another difference between binary options trading and real options trading is that Binary options, the advertised ones, don't commonly even exist. It is anything yet a money-related instrument that is recorded on a regulated open exchange like a protection trade or the forex market. In any case, it exists similarly as a PC program you are placing bets on which is equivalent to a game or an online casino. Real Options Trading on the other hand exchanges a genuine options contract that is recorded on a coordinated open exchange and gets become tied up with your record as a values asset when you buy real options. This suggests in real options trading, you are purchasing a real options agreement of the genuine financial trade and possessing it as an asset in a real values account.

You own an asset when you buy a real choice yet when you "buy" a binary alternative, it's an expensive thing that you bought utilizing your charge card just like game credits.

Differences Between Binary Options Trading And Real Options Trading—Trading Against Binary Options

Broker Vs Trading Against Other Traders

In Binary Options Trading, you are genuinely trading just against the broker, or in more careful words, "wagering" against the "broker." There isn't any market where you are trading with different sellers like in the stock market or the real choice market. In real choice trading, you are trading options agreements or concurrence with different market creators and options traders. This suggests you can buy and sell the options contract that you own at whatever point you wish before termination while in binary options trading, you will not have the choice to sell it once you "get" it and is resolved to hold it until one of the two likely outcomes. You're not for the most part purchasing anything in binary options trading as explained above, you are just putting down an electronic bet on an electronic game.

Differences Between Real Options Trading and Binary Options Trading—Real Underlying Asset vs. No Real Underlying Asset

Real options contracts permit you to purchase and sell the underlying asset that it addresses. For instance, an AAPL call option grants you to buy Apple Stocks at the strike cost at whatever point before termination should you choose to do in that capacity and AAPL put options licenses you to sell your present Apple stocks at the strike cost. This shows genuine options trading exchanges genuine options, and gets for that exchanges genuine securities in a genuine stock market. While Binary options can't be drilled to buy or sell anything.

A Binary Call Option can't be drilled to buy the underlying asset nor can a Binary put option be exercised to sell the underlying asset. Binary options simply exist in their electronic construction, which is the explanation they are otherwise called "Advanced Options," with no genuine assets behind it. Simply a bet on a lot of moving numbers deciding whether you win or lose. Again, no distinction from an online casino.

Differences Between Binary Options Trading and Real Options Trading—Unregulated Brokers vs. Regulated Brokers

Another huge distinction, and a genuinely significant differentiation, is that most (if not each and every) Binary Options Brokers are normally unregulated brokers while real options brokers are regulated, brokers. The guideline suggests that they are selected with the Securities and Exchange Commission (SEC) in the event that they are in the USA and is a piece of an investor assurance program, for example, the or FINRA or Investor Compensation Scheme in the USA. This ensures that your money will not be lost through extortion or insolvency by the broker and that the specialist is playing out a genuine insurances market administration in the genuine stock trade and not just an electronic game. Genuinely, in a real options trading account, you are guaranteed by the guideline and the assembly with the ultimate objective that if the broker closes down, you get back a couple, if not all, of your money. Be that as it may, when you "invest" in an unregulated broker, for instance, binary options brokers, your money is lost when and if the broker closes down.

This takes us to the following enormous difference between real options trading and binary options trading...

Differences Between Binary Options Trading and Real Options Trading—Ease of Depositing Money Vs. Difficulty in Depositing Money

It is in reality difficult to begin depositing cash to a real options trading account while it's very simple to deposit cash to a binary options account.

Why? Since real options trading involves working with a genuine monetary organization with genuine obligations just like opening a bank account. That is the reason you would not have the option to simply "transfer money" utilizing a charge card simply like you can with binary options accounts. Real financial organizations are not permitted by law to accept money from a credit card since that would not be your cash, see? Be that as it may, binary options brokers, being unregulated elements on the web, is much the same as any web-based business website, selling you web-based gaming credits, as such credit installments are accepted and why they are growing so rapidly because of the simplicity of payment.

Differences Between Binary Options Trading and Real Options Trading—Hard to Withdraw Money vs. Ease in Withdraw Money

Despite the above distinction, it is far simpler to move your cash from a real options trading account back to your bank than it is to move your cash from a binary options trading account back to your credit card or bank. Truly, in real options trading, it's difficult to deposit, however simple to pull back while in binary options trading, it's simple to deposit but difficult to withdraw.

In Binary Options Trading, normally when you endeavor to withdraw the cashback to your Visa or financial balance, you will get a call immediately, encouraging all of you sort of perks including additional credits if just you don't withdraw. Essentially all that they can guarantee you to persuade you out of withdrawing and to proceed "trading"—the very same thing on the online casino websites do. At that point, there are additionally numerous cases answered to the US Commodity Futures Trading Commission, CTFC of binary options brokers essentially declining to credit the cashback if you demand a withdrawal.

Chapter 26. The Final Step—Learning From the Pros

There is no doubt that options trading offers the most serious venture openings for speculators just as traders. The opportunity to acquire unfathomable benefits by investing a smallcapital is among the principal motivation behind why options trading is getting famous. All things considered, despite the fact that the expected risk exists for all, most speculators can't dependably book benefits and construct abundance utilizing options. As referenced over, some normal blunders and missteps add to the negative consequences of options dealers. Attempting to keep away from such errors can give the necessary edge to any options broker.

This part will talk about the most well-known slip-ups made by speculators during options trading and the tips from the stars to have the total information on being a fruitful broker when you wrap up perusing this book.

The Most Common Mistakes

It isn't surprising to feel baffled as a new options dealer. One of the upsides of trading options is the way it offers you various approaches to appreciate the advantages of the hidden security. An expanded possibility of making blunders is additionally among the compromises for the advantage of this reach. The reason for this part is to bring issues to light of the most widely recognized trading botches in options to help dealers settle on more instructed choices about options.

Contingent Only Upon the Market Timing

Numerous options brokers making perhaps the most widely recognized mistakes are to depend excessively emphatically on "available planning" to buy "put" or "call" options. Market clocks expect that to produce benefits in options trading, all it requires is to address market timing. Notwithstanding that, another basic misguided judgment that market clocks hold is that when the market timing is correct, purchasing any put or call option of the fundamental resource would bring in cash.

This isn't right and is one of the basic explanations for the drawn-out deficiency of cash by market clocks. In a couple of exchanges once in a while, contingent solely upon the market's planning will deliver great results. All things considered, the lacking component will be consistency, which would be the most basic component in isolating victors from disappointments over the long haul.

Each market clock understands that despite the fact that the call option is gained when the fundamental resource has wound up in a difficult situation, it doesn't guarantee better benefit or can deliver negative returns at focuses. Not to neglect that the business sectors don't have time in any event, for the most powerful market clocks precisely. It is difficult to effectively time the business sectors. We have been encountering an options trading situation that doesn't yield the ideal advantage despite the fact that the financial specialist got the market timing right. "Suggested vulnerability" must be the accentuation.

For any options merchant, the way to long haul achievement is to evaluate if the current degree of suggested unpredictability for the given fundamental resource is low or high. Try to buy a choice at whatever point the instability suggested is negligible and sell a choice at whatever point the unpredictability inferred is generous. It is discovered that the meaning of assessing suggested unpredictability is disregarded by a great part of options dealers who design and deal with their options exchanges exclusively on market timing, which is the thing that demonstrates deadly for the merchant over the long run.

Hopping in options trading without an exit plan you have presumably caught wind of this one ordinarily. It is fundamental to deal with your driving forces when trading options, similar to when you are trading stocks.

This doesn't mean basically that you should have ice going through your veins or that, powerfully, you need to overcome all your feelings of dread.

It is significantly simpler than that: you generally get a pledge to convey, and your technique consistently succeeds. Also, don't digress from your arrangement, regardless of what your emotions ask you to do. On the off chance that things begin to turn out badly, orchestrating your getaway isn't just about moderating misfortunes on the downtrend. Also, in any event, when a trade is playing your best, you shuould have a departure system period.

Your upward leave point and descending way out point should be picked early.

However, it is vital to remember that you would require positive and negative parts of assumptions for options. For each leave, you should set up the time span.

Regardless of what kind of procedure you are running, or whether it is a champ or a debacle, you shuould have the arrangement to escape an exchange. Try not to stay nearby on the grounds that you are voracious on rewarding exchanges or wait in washouts apparently perpetually on the grounds that you anticipate that the exchange should move in support of yourself in the long run.

Trading with a system permits you to assemble more powerful trading designs, what's more, keeps your issues more under wraps. Without a doubt, it very well may be energizing to exchange, yet it isn't just around one-time ponders. Also, it ought not to be tied in with considering creating hypertension, by the same token. In this way, make your technique early, and afterward, follow like super paste to it.

Trading Options That Are Illiquid

You will take note of a variety between the offer cost (what someone will pay) of a choice and its ask cost (what someone is set up to offer a possibility for) when you get a citation for any alternative on the commercial center.

The ask cost and the offer cost at times don't show what the choice is worth. The "valid" estimation of the choice would be someplace close to the focal point of the ask and offer. Also, precisely how much the ask and offer rates veer off from the choice's real worth depends generally on the choice's liquidity.

"Liquidity" implies that clients purchase the items and merchants being consistently on the lookout, with solid rivalry to fulfill exchanges. This activity pushes the offer and calls at stock and alternative costs very near one another.

Commonly, the securities exchange is considerably more fluid than its related options markets. This is on the grounds that stockbrokers are generally selling just one stock. Simultaneously, people trading options on even a particular portfolio have different options from which to pick, with various strike rates and shifting expiry dates.

Close-the-cash and at-the-cash options are commonly the most fluid having a close term expiry date. In this way, the hole between the ask and offer costs should be more limited than different options traded on exactly the same stock.

For the most part, options will be substantially less fluid as the cost moves dynamically away from the at-the-cash choice cost or the termination date gets more into what's to come. Therefore, the hole would normally be more extensive between the offers and ask rates.

At the point when you take part in illiquid stocks, an absence of liquidity all through the options market seems an undeniably more serious issue. All things considered, the options would potentially be substantially more latent if the stock is inaccessible, and the ask-offer spread would be considerably more far-reaching.

Bending Over Trying to Make Up for the Losses

We won't ever sell in-the-cash options or never purchase out-of-the-cash options; a few alternative dealers guarantee this. Except if you wind up in an exchange that has moved against you, these sureness's appeared to be senseless.

The entirety of the accomplished options merchants has been there when they were beginning as well. You are additionally enticed to disregard a wide range of individual guidelines notwithstanding the present circumstance.

As a stock merchant, you have likewise taken in an equivalent pardon for bending over to get ahead. On the off chance that you preferred the stock at 100 when you got it, for example, you must respect it at 70. This might be enticing to buy more and diminish the net expense balance on the exchange. Be wary, however: in the options universe, what sounds consistent for stocks doesn't work without fail. Typically, bending over as an options strategy doesn't bode well.

Purchasing OTM (Out-of-the-Money) Options

Most alternative brokers pick a choice instrument for strange profit.

Albeit the choice instrument is organized so that, with an insignificant measure of cash, colossal advantage or gain is conceivable, the issue starts when most theorists see options further in accordance with gambling club chips than speculation conspire. It is noticed that an enormous level of dealers of options intuitively decided to quit money options or those that have less length to the termination.

There isn't anything unseemly in buying an out of the cash alternative or maybe a choice that has a lesser termination time. In any case, it tends to be crushing in the more drawn-out term to do so routinely without investigating the probability of winning.

In the long run, this outlook is the thing that results in annihilations. Buying out of the cash (OTM) Call Option as an options dealer must be done when the broker accepts the stock costs to jump immediately and drastically upward. In the event that the broker envisions the fundamental resource for inch up step by step and marginally without any spikes, despite the fact that the basic stock cost is edging up, purchasing out the cash Call Option can prompt misfortunes. Merchants of options should compute the probability of the choice being in real money at the hour of expiry. The dealer would have to take a gander at the delta esteems suggested an instability and theta esteems top-to-bottom for that.

Utilizing Complex Trading Strategies

The tastefulness of the trading options encourages a wide range of merchants, contingent upon their speculation systems. There are opportunities for high-hazard speculators where dealers can sell exposed options or buy out of the cash put and call options. Interestingly, generally safe dealers regularly have possibilities where the broker can purchase simply those options that are well on the way to win, despite the fact that it implies that the rate returns are not remarkable but rather better than those on the money markets.

Merchants regularly lose all sense of direction in making "a definitive options trading procedure" and making it excessively hard for them to get a handle on the technique's result. When the speculator has not completely gotten a handle on the system and its "pay-off" accurately, does the procedure become muddled? Generally, the hazardous arrangement requires procuring two or much more options contracts.

Chapter 27. Time Management in Trading

There are numerous advantages to being a broker. One of the fundamental reasons we love being a broker is about adaptability. This implies we don't need to get up right on time to get down to business, we don't have a supervisor to instruct us, we can take get-away at whatever point we need and we can likewise control our very own time.

Numerous traders anyway have a test in dealing with their time, since they don't have the foggiest idea how to oversee it in a compelling way. In this chapter, we will feature a couple of approaches to deal with your time successfully as a broker.

1. A Decent Rest

A few people like to boast about sleeping for a few hours. "I will rest soundly when I bite the dust," they say.

Donald Trump, renowned businessman, multimillionaire and former United States president, has consistently boasted about how he sleeps for three hours consistently. He contends that it is hard for an individual that sleeps for 8 hours to rival one who rests for 3 hours.

About this, I have an alternate opinion.

I have faith in having a decent night's rest. Rest causes you to remain invigorated during the day. It additionally encourages you to maintain a strategic distance from the burnout that has affected such a large number of individuals. The ideal approach to deal with rest is to rest early and afterward get up right on time also.

2. Have Objectives

One of the fundamental reasons why a great many people don't accomplish their time management goals is that they don't have objectives. Having objectives implies having a lot of things that you need to accomplish inside a specific timeframe. Without objectives, you will have a test of time management.

For example, each morning, you need to have a list of things that you need to accomplish during the day. At the point when you have this arrangement of things, you will be in a decent position to accomplish most during a brief timeframe.

3. Organize

You should figure out how to organize your undertakings. This implies you must consistently attempt to do the most significant things first. For example, if your primary occupation is trading, have to do the best to attempt to do or plan your trading early in the morning. This is the place you shuould invest a ton of energy.

Set aside some effort to peruse, watch, and do your trading tasks first. By doing this, you will be in a decent position to make progress. You shuould abstain from trading when you are drained or when you have a great deal going on.

4. Go on Breaks

The issue with numerous individuals is that they need to seem occupied. In any event, when they do not have anything to do, you will see them attempt to accomplish something. The test with this is efficiency is exceptionally diminished.

As a broker, you should consistently concentrate on profitability. You must be content on each one hour spent well. Hence, on your trading day, you shuould have breaks.

5. Stay Away From Interruptions

Finally, you have to give a valiant effort to evade interruptions. This is a zone where numerous individuals have a significant issue. For instance, you may wind up caught up in social media networking. You may end up investing a great deal of energy talking with companions. You may likewise be disturbed by TV shows and even music.

To keep away from these interruptions, you must put forth a valiant effort to have a decent workspace that is liberated from disturbances. You have to likewise be sufficiently principled to diminish occasions of being stressed or distracted.

6 Must-Know Time Management Tips for Traders

Low maintenance dealers have it harsh. While we as a whole prefer to consider online markets trading nonstop as a colossal favorable position, it doesn't come without its obstructions. Because a market is open doesn't imply that the time you are available is a fitting time to trade. Nor does it constantly imply that one has sufficient opportunity to really break down the market in the way that it shuould be, and settle on proper choices dependent on the data consumed. The lucky opening for any low maintenance dealer is moderately little, and not many individuals adjust a trading reasoning around this while genuinely figuring out how to make it work.

Managing time is an enormous roadblock for some fire up dealers, as they are just not used to a fixed daily schedule, also experimentation/expectation to learn and adapt gets in the way of clean consistency.

Attached to risk, time is an issue that should take into account one's character type. Basically, if your character type searches for fast activity and for the most part comprises little patience at that point trading low maintenance will be such a lot harder thing to achieve.

Discovering transient opportunities consistently can be simple when you're spending the main part of the day on the investigation. That being said, extremely high-likelihood trading dependent on your individual speculation system is, in many cases, rare all through the session. In this manner endeavoring to pack in a full trading session where you end level in 60 minutes or 3 hours with interruptions is heading off to all that a lot harder to sharpen in and center on what you truly need to.

Terrible traders will, in general, be brimming with gaps. Be that as it may, very frequently, those gaps are just inadequacies in information, both present, and long haul. With an absence of time accessible, important data can without much of a stretch get skipped, putting the trader at an extreme hindrance.

Here are some quick tips that can conceivably guide you the correct way with regards to dealing with your time as a dealer:

1. Adjust Your Trading Theory With Your Character Type and the Time You Have Accessible

I can't reveal to you the number of traders I witness endeavoring to trade a specific program that conflicts with each embodiment of who they truly are.

Elements may meddle with their speculation on this issue, and time is surely one of them.

It is safe to say that you are the sort to show restraint? Is it safe to say that you are restless and can't keep still? If you will, in general, feel fidgety and are a part-time trader, at that point, you extremely just may have one alternative: adjust a transient technique that you can manage serenely in the time you have and compel yourself not to "try too hard." As such, take transient trades, however, don't over-strive regarding the number of sets you are exchanging. The appropriate examination requires some investment, and in the event that you are everywhere as far as what you can sensibly assimilate in during a solitary session, you are likely trying too hard.

In the event that youfit into the patient, orderly type, at that point, you are likely more qualified towards longer-term objectives. You may utilize cutoff orders for execution or basically float in the method for longer-term specialized or principal plays. Stops and go out on limb benefits are large and risk is ordinarily a lot lower. Individuals without a great deal of time on their plates may favor more extended term techniques as they're just not there to observe each tick, nor do they want to.

Full-time dealers that longer-term utilization procedures are generally contributed over a scope of monetary standards, adding more enhancement to the pot (also keeping them occupied all through some random day).

Regardless of whether your character type takes into account short, medium, or longer-term trading reasoning all depends. In any case, this should be stage one with stage two concentrating on fitting that way of thinking inside the limits of time that you have accessible.

2. Never Sacrifice Sound Investigation

If there is one territory that you never need to hold back on is sound examination. Traders that exclude pertinent pieces of data are truly doing simply aimlessly taking a look at an outline and making an uneducated supposition with respect to what will occur straightaway. Take the brief period that you have and assimilate yourself into the investigation. In the event that you don't have the opportunity to think about the setting of all sets accessible, at that point, don't anticipate exchanging them. The sound investigation is basic.

In the event that I glance back at any of my deplorable minutes as a trader, they, as a rule, happen essentially in light of the fact that I missed something little preceding execution. When I understand a slip-up was settled on, I would have no real option except to cut the string, a difficult exercise. Utilize your time carefully and possibly execute when your degree of certainty is exceptionally high.

3. Burrow Deep and Do It Quick—Maintain a Strategic Distance From the Interruptions

Telephone ringing free, TV blasting out of sight, taking a look at general news sites, or YouTube are basically horrendous for your trading. Likewise, with some other work, they represent an immense interruption and are the snappiest method to get prevented from acquiring essential data that will do just help you as far as execution. Take the brief period that you have and basically dispose of interruptions that represent a danger to perfect, succinct, and profound examination that is essentially required for your advancement.

Close the door, shut out the clamor, and pay attention.

4. Adjust to an Organized Method to Ingest Data

You should commonly utilize a straight approach with regards to investigation with a significant accentuation on the association. Traders that are disorderly in their investigation or just navigate starting with one theme then onto the next will in general, end up dispersed or confounded.

Start with explicit, respectable news destinations: those that generally give me an "enormous picture" sees on current happenings. These are all at the front of my bookmarks and effectively available. "Fun" bookmarks are sorted independently and avoid the ones that issue most.

For a point of interest, you should, at that point, drill down into your intraday news channel action. Go ahead and check relationships and different markets so as to build up a balanced and widely inclusive information bank of the present circumstance. When you make a general assurance that you are happy with your insight into the world of that specific trade, you can start boring into outlines. Do the same straightforward investigation you have been doing for a considerable length of time, looking over numerous time spans and separating everything into littler segments.

While it does not have to be carefully "top-down," it still has to be organized.

Start with a large-scale picture and make endeavors to separate things into littler parts. The conventional top-down investigation has its inadequacies: on the off chance that you are making conclusions dependent on a full-scale view alone and that view isn't right, everything that follows is a wash and you might be setting yourself up for calamity. Remember a worldwide approach and understand that market timing is similarly as critical as some other part.

5. Try Not to Drive a Window of Time

Risk management rule #1: don't do anything by any stretch of the imagination. Straightforward? Indeed. Easily done? No.

In the event that you happen to lean toward a short window of time as far as normal trade length, you need to comprehend the consequences that accompany it: you will have days where you are basically not happy with any trade, paying little mind to the time you put resources into the investigation.

Experts are like acrobats in the sense that they can bend over backward to drive action each possibility they get (also most are specialists— you exchange, it is beneficial for them). The reality, be that as it may, is if you can't profit from what you know, you shouldn't do anything. You should appreciate trading and everything that accompanies it, so don't attempt to constrain something that simply isn't right.

Throughout time, I have seen a huge scope of trading methodologies that incorporate various windows of time. However, a trader shouldn't pick this way of thinking dependent on this factor alone. Spare time is something that is valuable to every one of us, however, utilizing it admirably and positive P/L is about the main thing that will enable us to have a greater amount of it.

In a business where "timing is everything," dealing with your work process is similarly as essential as any arrangement of trade execution.

Chapter 28. Markets

Markets

A market is a place that buyers and sellers come together for the exchange of goods, information, and services. A market is not necessarily a physical situation, and it can be virtual too. When you get in a deal to sell a product, you will do that with one aim. The aim is to make a profit. You will not involve in any transaction if you are sure there is no profit you are going to make. It is necessary to know that you are not the only person who is out there in the market. There are numerous buyers as well as sellers who will do all they can to make sure that they have the monopoly. You have to get away and use a strategy that will make you win the buyers out there. You need to be unique so that you will thrive in the market. Markets differ in size and the products, services as well as the information it offers.

Financial Markets

It is a market where buyers and sellers transact things like foreign exchange, bonds, derivatives, and stock. Financial markets are also called capital markets. When you get into the financial market, you can do that to get money for growing your business and get some profit.

Different types of financial markets vary according to their size. Some of the markets are small, while others have stakeholders even internationally. They are known for transacting vast amounts of money in a day. Some of them include:

Stock Market

It is a market that trades shares, and each share has a price on it. When you decide to go this way, you will make a profit when you have determination. It will be easy for you to buy shares, but you need to be extra careful when choosing the stock. Some of the capital that is in the market will not give back profit, and so there is no worth buying them. You need to be up-to-date with the best approaches to use so that you get information about how the market is doing. To earn from the stock, you need to make sure that you sell at a higher price than the actual amount you bought. Adequate knowledge about the company that you want to buy stock from is vital so that you will not make a mistake. You need to reach a decision and know the action to take when it comes to the profitability of the institution being traded. The mutual fund will give you a chance to buy more stock at a go. Hence the best option to invest in when you compare with the individual stock. The mutual fund has a calming effect, and they are helping to reduce market volatility.

Bond Market

The bond market gives a chance to the government as well as the companies to secure funds for purposes of financing a project or an investment. As an investor, you will buy bonds, and they will give back the bond amount in the period that you agree with them. An organization will obtain a jumbo loan so that they can invest and pay with some interest after a given period. When the price of the stock increases, the price of the bonds is likely to go down. They are numerous types of relationships that you can invest in. They are municipal bonds, treasury bonds as well as corporate bonds. Bonds can also provide liquidity and help maintain the economy and make sure that it runs smoothly.

It is good you know the relationship that is there between the bonds and the yields it will make. When the value of the bond goes down, yields rise so that it can compensate. When the treasury yields go up, the mortgage interest rate goes up as well. If the treasury value will go down, that means everything else goes down as well.

Commodities Market

It is a market whereby traders and investors involve buying and selling natural resources and commodities. The price of these commodities is unpredictable, and the amount of some to be transacted in the future can be determined at the moment. That means that the cost can be underestimated, and that will lead to huge losses. When you get into the commodity market, it can be an excellent way for your future risks. The market will sell all kinds of natural resources. The price of some of these things can be volatile. The exchange is public, and your aim to trade in these commodities should be to make a profit. There are cases when the rise in prices of some commodities leads to an increase in the cost of other related products. It is possible that the number of specialties that we use daily can be put in control for future purposes. Futures will increase the leverage and allow you to borrow the money that you need to buy the commodity. If you can play relaxed, you will have significant gains. When you are not able to put the necessary strategies to make things work, you will suffer huge losses. That will even make the volatility increase. Some commodities will grow in their price, and that will make there be economic uncertainty. Gold is one of the products that will cause such ambiguity in a country's economy.

Derivatives Market

It is a market that involves contracts and derivatives whose value has a basis on the value of the item you are going to transact. Futures are one example of derivatives. They are known to be among the complicated financial products.

You can use this to increase your potential gains. They are known to be accessible, and they decrease the level of volatility in the market.

The Function of the Markets

All these financial markets have the roles that they play to make sure that the economy grows. They strengthen the economy and will as well make you achieve success. Some of the functions are:

Make Savings to Be Productive

When people deposit their money in a savings account, the money is put to other uses. The money is given to people in loans, which they later return with an extra amount with what they were given. The additional amount is the interest that is making sure that the money does not sleep in the account but is invested in a production deal. The financial markets give people as well as companies loans so that they can benefit themselves instead of letting the money remain in the account. That, too, will make people grow to another level, and their businesses also grow since they get more money than they had before to inject and boost their investment.

Functions as the Determinant of the Prices of Securities

The main aim that investors have in mind when they want to make any investment is to make some profit. The guards they have are what give them the benefit. That, too, should be your aim as an investor. To make a profit and leave alone anything that you think will make you suffer losses. The price of goods and services is known to be determined by the trend in supply and demand in the market out there. That is the same case when it comes to security. The prices of securities depend heavily on the financial markets.

Liquefies Financial Assets

When in trade, both the buyer as well as the seller has the freedom to decide when to trade. When the securities sell, they attract a buyer, and they, in turn, give liquid money to pay for the guards. If you have invested in securities, you can make use of the financial market to dispose of them and get liquid cash in return.

Brings Down the Transaction Cost

When you want to involve in any trade, you should have full information so that you will not get into a mess. You will never get any information for free since there is a particular cost that is involved. In any financial market, you are likely to acquire any information that you need at a relatively low price.

That makes it worthy of investing in financial markets since there are no many deductions when you realize your profit.

However, every kind of market has a structure depending on certain things.

The structures will give you a good understanding of the economic principles. The market structures are:

Perfect Competition

It is a market where numerous small firms are competing against one another so that they can make maximum profit out of their transactions. When one person is out there in the market, it will be no significant power, and the prices will have nothing to influence them. Some assumptions are made on this type of market structure. That all the firms out there will maximize the profit, and there are no limitations to the market entry. The market deals with similar products.

Monopolistic Competition

It is a market structure, whereas there are numerous small firms as well, and they all aim at making a profit. Each firm will try their level best to be the leading, and that will lead to stiff competition. They deal with almost similar products, but there are small distinguishing features. And for that, there is a specific market power that they will impact, giving them an advantage. The prices are likely to favor the market, and they go up to a particular range. The firms that are in the market will maximize profit, and there are no limits set to enter the market.

Oligopoly

An oligopoly is a market where just a few firms are dominant. There is not much competition when you compare with the rest market structures. The traders out there can agree to collaborate, or each does on their own and compete. They have more power in the market, and they can decide to hike the prices to a specific range and make some extra profit.

Monopoly

A monopoly is a market entity where only one firm is present. The firm has all the market power and can decide on what will happen and the price levels.

The consumers do not have a choice but to get the products in the market since there is no competitor. That will make the market have fewer products so that the prices can go up and the profit being made to go up as well. It will make the market manufacture products that are of low quality since there is no one else to compete with them. And for that, the government comes in to make sure that it regulates the activities that go on in such a market.

The financial markets are in one way or the other vital when it comes to particular things. They ensure smooth running and make things possible for the people who decide to invest in them. When you enter the financial market, whether you are an investor or a debtor, you will not be discriminated against. You will receive a fair as well as a proper treatment without them looking whether you are small or a big catch when you need some capital, whether as an individual, they will not deprive you. Make sure that you fulfill the requirements that they have set. The market also offers loans to companies and governments who meet their expectations, aiming for a return after the end of the loan period.

Chapter 29. Currency Option

What Is a Currency Option?

The currency option (also known as the Forex option) is a contract that gives the purchaser the right, but not the obligation to purchase or sell, at or before a given date, a certain currency at a specified exchange rate. A fee is charged to the seller for this right.

Currency options are one of the most common forms of avoiding adverse currency movement for businesses, individuals, or financial institutes.

Basics of Currency Options

By buying a currency put or call, investors may hedge from the risk of foreign currency. Currency options are derivatives dependent on the currency pairs underlying them. Trading options for currency include a range of strategies for use in forex markets. The strategy used by a trader depends in large part on the type of option and the broker or platform it is offered. In competitive forex markets, the characteristics of options differ much more widely than in more regulated stock and futures exchanges.

For several reasons, traders like to swap currency options. They can only lose the premium they pay to purchase the options, but they have infinite upside potential. Some traders use FX options to hedge open positions in the forex cash market. In contrast to the futures market, the cash market, also known as the physical market and the spot market, is the direct settlement of goods and securities transactions. Traders like the trading of options because this gives them the opportunity to trade and benefit from the forecast of the market direction on the basis of economic, political, or other news.

However, the premium on trading contracts for currency options can be quite high. The premium depends on the price and expiry date of the attack. They cannot be re-traded or sold once you purchase an options contract. The trading of forex options is complicated and has several moving components, making it difficult to assess their value. The risks include interest-rate differentials (IRDs), market volatility, the expiry time horizon, and the current currency pair prices.

Vanilla Options Basics

Two key options, calls and puts are open.

Call options give the holder the right (but not the obligation) to buy the asset for a certain length of time at a specified price (the strike price). If the stock does not meet the strike price before the expiry date, the option ends and is valuable. Investors buy telephone calls if they believe that the share price of the underlying security will increase or sell a call if they think it will fall. The selling of an option is also known as "writing" an option.

Put options allow the holder to sell an underlying asset at a specified price.

The seller (or author) of the put option, must purchase the shares at the strike price. You can exercise options at any time before the option expires.

Investors buy posts if they think the underlying stock's share price will fall, or if they think it will, though, they sell one. Put buyers—those with a "long" position—either are speculative purchasers looking for leverage or insurance purchasers, seeking to secure their long stock positions for an option-set period. Salespersons keep a 'short' in anticipation that the demand will go up (or remain stable at least) A worst-case scenario for a put vendor is a downward trend. The maximum profit will be proportional to the premium received and will be realized when the underlying price is at or above the strike price of the option at the expiry. The maximum loss for an exposed writer is indefinite.

Trade will still require a long currency and a short currency pair. In essence, the buyer must say how much they want to purchase, the price at which they want to buy, and the expiry date. A seller then addresses the trade with a quoted premium. Common choices may have expirations in American or European models. Traders are entitled to put-and-call options, but there is no responsibility. When the current exchange rate takes the money (OTM) options out, they will expire without interest.

SPOT Options

An exotic alternative used for trading currencies involves the trading of single payment options (SPOT). Spot options have higher premium costs than conventional options, but can be set and implemented easier. A currency trader buys a SPOT option when entering a scenario (for example, "I assume that EUR/USD will settle above 1.5205 15 days."), and an award is quoted.

If this option is bought by the buyer, the put immediately pays out if the situation happens. In essence, the option is transformed into cash automatically.

The SPOT is a financial product with a contract structure more flexible than conventional alternatives. This strategy is all or nothing and is also known as binary or digital options. The buyer will be selling a scenario like EUR/USD in 12 days, which will hit 1, 3000. We offer premium quotations, which are paid on the basis of the probability of the occurrence. If this event occurs, the buyer will benefit. If this does not happen, the purchaser will lose the premium paid. SPOT contracts require a higher premium than standard options. SPOT contracts can also be written to compensate whether they reach a particular point, a number of specific points, or do not meet a particular point. Naturally, the premium requirements for different choice arrangements will be higher.

Certain types of exotic options add more than the value of the underlying instrument maturity to the payoff, including but are not limited to features, such as a barrier option, a binary option, a digital option, or a lookback option.

Example of a Currency Option

Let's say an investor is bullish about the euro and believes that the US dollar will rise. The buyer acquires a currency call option for the euro at a hard price of $115 because currency premiums are

100 times the exchange rate. If the buyer buys the deal, the euro spot rate is $110. Assume that the spot price of the euro at the expiry date is $118. The currency option is then stated to have expired in the capital. Consequently, the investor's income is $300 or (100) × ($118–$115) less than the premium paid for the currency call.

Chapter 30. Trading With LEAPS

LEAPS

When you get involved with options trading, you may hear the phrase "LEAPS" mentioned. This means long-term Equity Anticipation Securities.

This refers to call and put options that have expiration dates ranging from 1-2 years into the future. Since these options have a very long time to expiration, they have a large amount of "time value" and so they are far more expensive.

They also lose little-value due to time decay. However, they are fairly sensitive to changes in the underlying stock price. LEAPS can represent an opportunity to make profits if you have the capital to invest in them. A call option on Apple that is slightly in the money expiring in 2 years costs about $4,000.

Other than expiring a long way in the future and having a little impact from time decay over the course of a few weeks, LEAPS are no different than any other option. However, there is one particular method that experienced traders use that you should be aware of. Some investors use a strategy called the poor man's covered call to leverage LEAPS to sell covered calls. This allows the trader to sell covered calls and earn income with a lower investment, since LEAPS, even though they are pricey compared to short-term options, offer a large discount as compared to actually buying the stock.

Consider that Apple is trading at $264 a share, which means 100 shares of Apple necessary to sell a covered call would require an investment of $26,400. That is far more than the $4,000 you'd have to invest in a LEAP that expires in two years.

The details of the poor man's covered call are as follows. First, you purchase an in-the-money LEAP call option. So, in this case, we will go with the $260 call at $4,000. Then you sell an out of the money call option that expires in the near term. We can sell a $270 call on Apple that expires in 30 days for $418.

Now we need to calculate the width of the call strike prices. This is: $270−$260 = $10

Next, calculate the net debit (per share) paid:

$40−$4.18 = $35.82

The intrinsic value of the LEAP is found by subtracting the strike price from the share price. That is:

$264−$260 = $4

Over the course of 30 days, if the stock price doesn't change, the LEAP will lose about $1.00 in value, or $100. So, the high strike price option we sold expires worthless, and we keep the $418 we earned. That gives a net profit of $318, and we still have the LEAP. We could sell it, or use it to sell a second call option.

Now let's look at what happens in the case that the stock rises. Suppose that the stock price rises $4 over the 30 days, to $268 a share. In that case, the $270 call we sold against the LEAP still expires worthless, so we earned $418. However, the LEAP actually gains in value in that scenario, probably by about $1.50 per share. We could sell the LEAP at this point for a $147 profit, for a total profit of about $565. Alternatively, you can hold onto the LEAP and then sell another out of the money call against it to earn even more income.

The process can be repeated for a time, but you need to be aware of the time decay that will start to impact the LEAP as the weeks go by.

One risk is that the stock price will rise to the point where the out of the money call goes in the money. Suppose that the share price of Apple rises to $271 by the end of the 30 days. That means we'd have to buy the option back or face assignment. If we buy it back, we will be able to buy it back at a reduced price. The reason is that since the option we sold is so close to expiration, it will lose a lot of value (extrinsic value or time decay) by the time it is 1-2 days from expiration.

However, the LEAP has risen in value by $3.35 at this point. So, we can buy the option we sold back, and we will still be in a position of net profit.

Conclusion

At the point when you are investigating turning into an options trader, much the same as with whatever else in your life, you will have things that you need to know, and this book has had the option to give you that data to ensure that you are an effective options trader. We have given you the best data and the most precise information with the goal that you can utilize this for your potential benefit. Through this book, you will have found out about the economy and have received the correct mentality, which is a significant perspective to option trading and throughout everyday life.

We have additionally helped you comprehend the significance of danger and the computations you need to know well in order to understand what it is that you are getting into. At the point when you can comprehend what you will get into, it will be simpler for you to see how you will have the option to settle on choices and stick with using sound judgment for yourself and you're trading. Numerous individuals bounce into something like this, however, they don't get familiar with the information that they need, and you need to ensure that you are getting this data since it will help you advance yourself appropriately.

Understanding your odds for benefit and misfortune is another enormous issue that numerous individuals don't comprehend with regards to option trading. We have clarified the two sides of it so you won't need to stress over having data that will lead you to settle on helpless choices. With this data, you have the best data that will allow you to settle on the best choices for your trading all things being equal.

You will comprehend the lots risks and benefits that you can make too. You should have the option to ensure that you have the right stuff to monitor your cash. Alongside cash the board, we give you the data you need to set up your assets and ensure that you are doing this appropriately. It very well might be astounding, however, such countless individuals have issues with cash the board and considerably more about ensuring the assets are being readied appropriately. Numerous individuals will, in general, get into a monetary field this way, and they consume their wallets quicker than they intend to, and this is something that you need to evade.

Two of the greatest snippets of data that you can get from this book are that you gain proficiency with the various kinds of options you can use for yourself and the various business sectors accessible to you. Understanding your options and the business sectors will give you an enormous edge over the opposition that is attempting to get into a similar field you are in, and it will help you advance. By perusing this book and learning the data and skills that you can use for yourself, you have guaranteed that you will be an extraordinary options trader.

www.ingramcontent.com/pod-product-compliance
Lightning Source LLC
Chambersburg PA
CBHW080453220526
45465CB00006B/2254